HARVARD DISSERTATIONS IN AMERICAN HISTORY AND POLITICAL SCIENCE

EDITED BY
FRANK FREIDEL
HARVARD UNIVERSITY
AND
ERNEST MAY
HARVARD UNIVERSITY

A GARLAND SERIES

BAPTIST COLLEGES IN THE DEVELOPMENT OF AMERICAN SOCIETY

1812-1861

DAVID B. POTTS

GARLAND PUBLISHING, INC.
NEW YORK & LONDON 1988

Library of Congress Cataloging-in-Publication Data

Baptist colleges in the development of American society,
1821–1861/ David B. Potts.
p. cm. — (Harvard dissertations in American history and political
science)
Thesis (Ph. D.) — Harvard University, 1967.
Bibliography: p.
ISBN 0–8240–5143–2 (alk. paper)
1. Baptist universities and colleges — United States — History —
19th century. 2. Baptists — United States — History — 19th
century. I. Title. II. Series.
LC562.P67 1988
377'.86'071173 — dc19 88–30104

Printed on acid-free, 250-year-life paper
Manufactured in the United States of America

PREFACE

Two decades after its completion, this dissertation may
still be useful for exploring the role of American colleges
in the early nineteenth century. The research reflects a
point in the development of scholarship about nineteenth-
century colleges when a close examination of major issues of
interpretation was just beginning. In subsequent years the
work of more than three dozen scholars has explored a variety
of questions about these institutions. A body of writings
that once consisted of little beyond several general surveys
and a host of institutional histories now includes a
substantial array of monographs, dissertations, and articles.
Where this scholarly literature intersects with topics
covered in my analysis of colleges affiliated with the
Baptists, it tends to extend the findings reported in 1967
rather than suggest a need for revision.

My work on this dissertation began in late 1963 with a
sense that there was much more to the story of antebellum

colleges than that found in the path-breaking studies
published during the prior decade by Richard Hofstatder,
Frederick Rudolph, and a few others. By the spring of 1964 I
formulated the central question to be pursued: To what extent
were antebellum colleges sectarian or denominational
ventures; to what extent were they more broadly conceived
local enterprises? My inquiry was directed to Baptist-
affiliated colleges for three reasons. They had not been
previously studied with such a question in mind, they had
connections with one of the two largest denominations, and
many of the basic sources related to their histories were
located in a well-administered repository.

With support from a federal research grant, I devoted an
extended summer in 1965 to collecting data from college,
local, denominational, and state archives in the South, the
Middle Atlantic states, and the Midwest. I returned with the
thesis of my dissertation clearly formulated: These colleges
were largely local enterprises and were much more secular in
origin than previously portrayed. Daniel Boorstin's <u>The
Americans: The National Experience</u> was published that fall.
More than a year later, when the writing of my dissertation
was well advanced, I encountered Boorstin's ten-page section
on "the booster college." By looking primarily at colleges
outside New England, we had developed similar perspectives on
higher education prior to the Civil War.

Major findings from my doctoral research were published in articles that placed them in some larger contexts.* I am pleased to have the full analysis of sixteen antebellum colleges now made readily available to all who join me in seeking to understand the ways in which a commitment to institutions of higher education became so deeply rooted in American cultural and economic life.

D.B.P.

Wesleyan University
May 1988

*See, for example, "American Colleges in the Nineteenth Century: From Localism to Denominationalism," History of Education Quarterly 11(Winter 1971):363-80; "'College Enthusiasm!' as Public Response, 1800-1860," Harvard Educational Review 47(February 1977):28-42.

TABLE OF CONTENTS

Page

ACKNOWLEDGEMENTS

In the course of our four-month, four-thousand-mile research trip during the summer and early fall of 1965 to twelve of the sixteen colleges in this study and numerous repositories en route, my wife, children, and I received many kindnesses from people too numerous to mention here but always to be gratefully remembered. A special word of appreciation must be extended to Edward C. Starr, Curator of the American Baptist Historical Society. His generous assistance and the collection which he has developed over the last thirty years have been invaluable to my exploration of Baptist history.

Research for this dissertation was financed with funds provided by a contract with the United States Department of Health, Education, and Welfare, Office of Education, under provisions of the Cooperative Research Program.

NOTE

Spelling errors in quotations have been corrected to facilitate reading. Punctuation and capital-
ization have not been altered.

Institutions are referred to in the text by
their current names, except for: Howard College,
which changed its name to Samford University in 1965;
Shurtleff College, which sold its facilities to Southern Illinois University in 1957; and Union University,
which had only an indirect connection with the present
institution of that name in Jackson, Tennessee.

INTRODUCTION

Historical viewpoints on early-nineteenth-century
colleges usually stress one or more of the criticisms expressed by Francis Wayland, a contemporary of those institutions. Wayland, president of Brown University (1827-55),
contributed two important documents to the history of American colleges. His Thoughts on the Present Collegiate System in the United States, published in 1842, contained a
detailed critique of antebellum colleges. Most of the
analyses and conclusions of this volume were repeated in
a condensed and more polemical form in his Report to the
Corporation of Brown University on Changes in the System
of Collegiate Education, Read March 28, 1850. Wayland
capped his argument in 1850 with proposals for extensive
reforms in the curriculum and system of teaching at Brown.
Since these documents have exerted an enduring influence
upon the ways in which historians approach American higher
education between 1800 and 1861, a brief examination of
Wayland's ideas provides important reference points for
exploring collegiate history during this period.

Wayland faced a financial crisis at Brown resulting
from steadily declining enrollments, but he viewed this

1

problem as stemming from certain serious defects common to
all American colleges. Unlike their British counterparts,
Wayland asserted, American colleges formed "no integral and
necessary part of the social system." Neither individual
success nor national economic growth was furthered by the
present collegiate system of the United States. "In no
other country," Wayland concluded after traveling abroad,
"is the whole plan for the instruction of the young so entirely dissevered from connection with the business of subsequent life."[1]

This isolation of colleges from American society was
attributed by Wayland to a few key institutional weaknesses.
Trustees and other visitorial boards empowered to govern
American colleges tended to stand "between the public and
the College." Usually self-perpetuating and elected for
life terms, such boards lacked even a small degree of public supervision. Rarely meeting more than once a year and
generally uninformed about the internal workings of the college, they were poorly equipped as well as inadequately
motivated to represent the public interest. College professors were also separated from public opinion, especially

---

[1]Francis Wayland, Report to the Corporation of Brown
University on Changes in the System of Collegiate Education,
Read March 28, 1850 (Providence, R.I., 1850), pp. 41, 47-48;
Francis Wayland, Thoughts on the Present Collegiate System
in the United States (Boston, 1842), pp. 40-41.

3

when compared with private school instructors. Although
teaching in institutions to which the public had given
special degree-granting privileges and generous contributions, professors were elected on a noncompetitive basis,
given virtual life tenure, and paid fixed salaries, irrespective of their merits in the public eye. Dormitories
also set the colleges apart from society and prevented
students from being "exposed individually to the salutary
restraints of public observation and public opinion." Endowments helped widen the gap by raising colleges still
further "above the control of enlightened public opinion."
Despite his position of leadership within the Baptist denomination, Wayland suggested that lack of contact between
the colleges and the public might even be partly due to the
fact that "almost every college in this country is either
originally, or by sliding from its primitive foundations,
under the control of some religious sect."[2]

Indicative of and helping to perpetuate the separate-
ness of American higher education was the traditional classical curriculum. "It seems to have been taken for granted,"
Wayland observed, "that our colleges were designed exclusively for professional men." Colleges provided the American
people with little more than an intermediary education

---

[2]Wayland, Thoughts, pp. 23-28, 51-62, 43-46, 62-75, 122-23; Wayland, Report, p. 37; Wayland, Thoughts, p. 55.

4

"between the elementary studies of the academy and the
immediate preparation for one of the three learned professions." The degree to which a curriculum so limited in
its content and functions was out of touch with the course
of American society was suggested by Wayland's query: "What
could Virgil and Horace and Homer and Demosthenes, with a
little mathematics and natural philosophy, do towards developing the untold resources of this continent?" Colleges
had lost contact with individual as well as social obligations by denying merchants, mechanics, and manufacturers
the opportunity of giving their sons a higher education
preparatory for something other than law, medicine or the
ministry.[3]

Wayland asserted that nonprofessional men desired a
different type of higher education and that American colleges were unresponsive to such public demands. Conceding
that previous efforts at collegiate reform had not been
sustained by the public and had revealed that "the public
does not always know what it wants, and that it is not always wise to take it at its word," Wayland nevertheless felt
that "the demand for something additional" to the present
college courses was, by 1850, "general and imperative."
When Wayland applied his classical economic theories to this

---

[3]Wayland, Report, p. 14; Wayland, Thoughts, pp. 28, 153;
Wayland, Report, pp. 12-13; Wayland, Thoughts, pp. 154-55.

situation, he found "an unnatural state of things." Colleges not only failed to supply a long-standing demand for more practical higher education, but they also continued to prepare professionals even when society was threatened by a glut of such men. Although he repeatedly noted the "demand for change," Wayland also suggested that perhaps educators and boards of visitors must stimulate and cultivate this demand. Needed changes would occur through initiatives taken by these small groups, and then the public could be "brought into harmony with their action." Once changes were made the large portion of the community which colleges were "excluding," would "willingly participate" and "cheerfully avail" itself of the new and more relevant knowledge offered.[4]

This reform strategy included several changes in the collegiate system, all designed to place "our institutions of higher learning...in harmony with the advanced and rapidly advancing condition of society." Wayland suggested that each professor be given a partial salary, and that the remainder depend upon the number of students attracted to his courses. An elective system would also place Latin and Greek "upon their own merits." The major feature of Wayland's reform

[4]Wayland, Report, p. 34; Wayland, Thoughts, p. 13; Wayland, Report, p. 13; Wayland, Thoughts, pp. 15, 46-47, 150, 112, 152, 104; Wayland, Report, pp. 50-51.

proposals was a vast expansion of course offerings in a
scientific and technological direction. Besides "being
a preparatory school to the professions," each college
should be "a Lowell Institute to the region in which it
is placed." For Wayland this analogy meant quality as
well as breadth, since "in order to secure...popularity,
we must strive to render education good."[5]

The indictment of contemporary colleges contained in
Wayland's critique and reform proposals was wide-ranging.
In addition to being "of no service" to the nonprofessional
classes in American society, colleges offered only a "superficial" education to their traditional clientele. And the
value of a narrow classical education was "not so universally
acknowledged as formerly, even by this class."[6] Colleges
were unresponsive to American economic and cultural needs.
Colleges were isolated from the development of American
society by outmoded forms and functions.

Evidence offered by Wayland to support these sweeping
charges, however, raises the question of their applicability
to antebellum colleges in general. Despite the scope of his
titles and conclusions, Wayland relies on data from New England colleges to support his analysis. The key to his

[5]Ibid., pp. 59, 62, 73-74, 52-53; Wayland, Thoughts,
pp. 156, 149.

[6]Ibid., pp. 143, 87; Wayland, Report, pp. 31-32, 34.

argument is declining college enrollments, and this trend is illustrated by figures from only a dozen New England colleges. Wayland's data on financial trends and curricula are similarly restricted to higher education in his own region.[7] Given these limitations, can Wayland be used as a reliable observer of the entire pre-Civil War collegiate scene?

It is important to ask this question because various elements in Wayland's analysis, and his generally critical attitude toward the colleges of his era, figure prominently in most interpretations of early-nineteenth-century higher education. Historians have been more concerned with the intellectual quality of antebellum colleges than with the impractical or undemocratic aspects of these institutions stressed by Wayland. But even roots of the quality-oriented viewpoint can be traced to Wayland. He pictured colleges during the colonial period as "eminently successful," but found that after the Revolution "the character of education deteriorated, and after some years had passed it had sunk lamentably low. It has since improved, but I doubt whether in many points it has yet surpassed its ante-revolutionary standing."[8] Whether they attribute this decline to

---

[7]Ibid., pp. 22-30; Wayland, Thoughts, pp. 34-35.

[8]Wayland, Report, p. 11; Wayland, Thoughts, p. 78.

sectarianism, local boosterism, or educational conservatism symbolized by the Yale Report of 1828, historians
ever since Wayland have usually agreed that higher education in this period failed to provide the quality and type
of education needed and demanded by American society.[9]
Since this viewpoint implies that colleges in the early
nineteenth century were generally insignificant classical
citadels with superficial functions, it has done little to
encourage serious research on the precise nature of these
institutions and their role in American cultural history.

Although the Wayland critique and subsequent historical
variations of it may be accurate in many respects, they may
also provide only a limited picture of antebellum colleges.
Perhaps historical understanding of these institutions and
their role in the development of American society can be
enlarged by new approaches and new questions. In addition
to viewing early-nineteenth-century higher education through
the eyes of critics and reformers, it may be useful to explore this topic by way of the denominational press, local

---

[9]For examples of this viewpoint among historians of
American higher education and their use of Wayland, see:
George P. Schmidt's The Old Time College President (New York,
1930), chaps. iii, v, "Intellectual Crosscurrents in Ameri-
can Colleges, 1825-1855," American Historical Review, XLII
(October 1936), 46-67, "Colleges in Ferment," ibid., LIX
(October 1953), 19-42, and The Liberal Arts College (New York,
1957), chap. iii; R. Freeman Butts, The College Charts Its
Course: Historical Conceptions and Current Proposals (New
York, 1939), chap. viii; Richard Hofstadter and C. De Witt

histories, and a variety of other primary sources. This material and that found in institutional histories might be approached with questions which will both test the validity of current historical assessments and significantly enlarge their scope. To what extent were pre-Civil War colleges sectarian or denominational and to what extent were they community enterprises? What was their relationship, if any, with the portion of society outside these two spheres? Did they exert any significant influence upon the development of American culture? Can they best be understood in terms of curriculum, quality, and number of students enrolled, or are other approaches better suited to this period in American cultural history?

The colleges of Wayland's own denomination are an appropriate and convenient starting point for developing

---

Hardy, The Development and Scope of Higher Education in the United States (New York, 1952), chap. i; Richard Hofstadter and Walter P. Metzger, The Development of Academic Freedom in the United States (New York, 1955), chap. v; Richard Hofstadter and Wilson Smith, American Higher Education: A Documentary History (Chicago, 1961), vol. I, part iv, vol. II, part vi; Richard Hofstadter, "The Revolution in Higher Education," Paths of American Thought, eds. Arthur M. Schlesinger, Jr. and Morton White (Boston, 1963); Frederick Rudolph, The American College and University (New York, 1962), chaps. iii-xii; Theodore R. Crane, The Colleges and the Public, 1787-1862 (New York, 1963). In chapter xx of The Americans: The National Experience (New York, 1965), Daniel Boorstin briefly develops a perspective on nineteenth-century colleges emphasizing the combination of denominational initiatives and local booster spirit in most of their origins. Schmidt also noted these two elements as early as 1930, but like Boorstin does not explore this relationship in depth or consider its implications for the subsequent development and cultural role of American colleges.

new perspectives on higher education in antebellum America.
A case study of Baptist colleges provides the material for
assessing the applicability of Wayland's observations to
those colleges outside his own region with which he was
probably most familiar. The denomination's decentralized
church polity facilitates access to relationships between
colleges and communities which have not been explored by
Wayland and subsequent historians. Baptist historical
materials are especially well-preserved and skillfully administered in a few large collections.

The sixteen colleges in this study represent all but a
few of the institutions of higher education affiliated with
the Baptists, founded after 1800, and in operation for at
least a decade prior to the Civil War. Considerations of
time, distance, and resources were mainly responsible for
the exclusion of Baylor University, Mississippi College,
William Jewell College, and Kalamazoo College. Almost all
known materials on the selected institutions were examined,
yet only certain aspects of the history of each are included.
By standing somewhere between general and institutional histories, it is hoped that this study will contribute questions, insights, and techniques of value to research and
interpretation in both of these more traditional forms.

CHAPTER I

MINISTERS AND CITIZENS

Baptist ministers interested in creating a better-educated ministry provided leadership in the founding of almost all pre-Civil War colleges affiliated with their denomination. Vital assistance in the creation of these colleges came from Baptist laymen and non-Baptists who resided in the college community. A mixture of motives and a variety of strategies, both denominational and secular, pervaded efforts to establish these institutions of higher education. Detailed examination of the ways in which these forces interacted provides a necessary foundation for understanding the nature and functions of Baptist colleges prior to 1861.

The first Baptist college of nineteenth-century origin to offer collegiate instruction was Colby College in Waterville, Maine. In its early years, Colby embodied a combination of denominational, educational, and local elements which was to recur, in varying proportions, in the founding of other early-nineteenth-century Baptist colleges. Non-Baptist elements in the origin of Colby were somewhat stronger than those found at most other Baptist schools, but the basic relationship between Waterville and its

11

college rendered Colby a prototype of Baptist beginnings
in education.

Examination in less detail of initiatives and alliances
in the founding of other Baptist colleges up through 1850
reveals six variations within the basic pattern established
by Colby. The key role in the origin of each institution
can be assigned to one of the following: Baptist laymen with
primarily religious objectives, individual Baptist ministers,
ministers and laymen organized into Baptist education societies, Baptists acting primarily as citizens, non-Baptists,
and Baptist state conventions. The common element in all
but a few of these origins is the alliance forged between
college and community. These alliances proved to be major
factors in the subsequent development of each institution.
The resulting picture is not one of an official denominational movement to found colleges, but a rather haphazard
series of essentially local enterprises with only a partially
religious character.

I

Jeremiah Chaplin, first president of Colby College,
arrived in Waterville, Maine, on June 25, 1818. He made
his five-day journey from Boston by coasting sloop as far

as Augusta and covered the final twenty miles on a long-
boat. Leaving the pastorate of the Baptist church in
Danvers, Massachusetts, to assume the task of building a
Baptist "literary and theological institution" on the banks
of the Kennebec River, Chaplin brought with him his wife
and five children, and the seven ministerial students he
had been tutoring for the Massachusetts Baptist Education
Society. A group of Waterville citizens met Chaplin and his
party at the landing and escorted them to the home of Timothy
Boutelle.[1]

Boutelle was not a Baptist, but he had played a key
role in securing the college for Waterville. After graduating from Harvard College in 1800, Boutelle taught for a
year at Leicester Academy and then studied law, first in his
home town, Leominster, and then at the office of Edward Gray
in Boston. Soon after his admission to the bar in 1804,
Boutelle set up practice in Waterville. He resided there
until his death in 1855.[2]

---

[1]Ernest C. Marriner, The History of Colby College
(Waterville, Me., 1963), pp. 27-28.

[2]Ibid., p. 141; Edwin C. Whittemore, Colby College,
1820-1925: An Account of Its Beginnings, Progress and Service
(Waterville, Me., 1927), p. 76. A sketch of Boutelle in
William Cathcart, The Baptist Encyclopaedia (Rev. ed.; Philadelphia, 1883) notes that he later became "an habitual wor-
shiper at the First Baptist Church in Waterville." For biographical data on Boutelle, see "Association of the Alumni
of Harvard College--Necrology of the Past Year," Boston Daily
Advertiser, July 16, 1856. This clipping can be found in
Sibley's "Collectanea Biographica Harvardiana," III, 23 in
the Harvard University Archives.

14

By the time of Chaplin's arrival and the beginning of instruction in 1818, Boutelle owned much of what was to become the business section of Waterville and important adjacent water rights in this promising young town. Four years earlier, Boutelle procured the charter for the Waterville Bank, and he was a member of its original board of directors. When the Maine legislature in 1821 incorporated the proprietors of the first bridge across the Kennebec River between Waterville and the neighboring town of Winslow, this enterprising lawyer in his early forties was one of the original shareholders. In the mid 1820's, Boutelle donated a valuable piece of land for the Baptist meetinghouse and another for the town academy. The crowning achievement in this career of public activity occurred in 1849 when, largely due to his efforts, the Androscoggin and Kennebec Railroad was extended to Waterville. At the public celebration honoring completion of the railroad, Boutelle delivered the opening speech. His welcome to the railroad was probably made in much the same spirit as his earlier greeting to Chaplin and the students for the new Baptist college.[3]

[3]Ernest C. Marriner, Kennebec Yesterdays (Waterville, Me., 1954), p. 40; Interview with Ernest C. Marriner, February 28, 1966; The Centennial History of Waterville, Kennebec County, Maine, ed. Edwin C. Whittemore (Waterville, Me., 1902), p. 135; Henry D. Kingsbury, "City of Waterville," Illustrated History of Kennebec County, Maine, eds. Henry D. Kingsbury and Simeon L. Deyo (New York, 1892), I, 582a; Clement M. Giveen, A Chronology of Municipal History and Election Statistics,

15

Alliances between non-Baptist and Baptist interests
appeared even earlier in the history of Colby. When Daniel Merrill, "father" of the movement to found a Baptist
school in the District of Maine, attempted to obtain a
charter for the institution from the Massachusetts legislature in 1811, he enlisted the assistance of a prominent
non-Baptist politician, William King. Merrill, a Dartmouth
graduate, was ordained as a Congregational minister in 1793.
By 1804 he became convinced of the lack of scriptural justification for infant baptism and the following year he persuaded most of his congregation to reconstitute the town
church of Sedgwick, Maine as a Baptist church and to reordain
him as its Baptist minister. He soon became known through
his publications as an active apologist for Baptist polity
and ordinances. By 1807 Merrill was calling for contributions to aid ministerial candidates "in gaining profitable
information and in rendering them more expert for the war."
Anticipating the warfare that would ensue from attempts to
institutionalize Baptist ministerial and higher education in
a territory already occupied by a Congregational college
(Bowdoin) and governed by the legislature of a state where

Waterville, Maine, 1771-1908 (Augusta, Me., 1908), p. 77;
Centennial History of Waterville, p. 61; Whittemore, Colby,
p. 44; Centennial History of Waterville, pp. 68-69;
Marriner, Kennebec, p. 84; Edward W. Hall, History of Higher
Education in Maine (Washington, 1903), p. 103.

Congregationalism was still the established church, Merrill
solicited General King's support in late 1811.[4]

King "generously volunteered" his services. He was an
Overseer of Bowdoin at the time, but he was also an aspiring
Democratic-Republican politician disturbed by the fact that
a majority of Bowdoin's trustees were Federalists. Baptist
leaders in Maine were generally associated with the prevailing
party in the District, the Democratic-Republicans, and considering the substantial number of Baptists in Maine, Merrill
was in a position to make an effective appeal to King's Jeffersonian sentiments. In late December of 1811, Merrill
wrote to King that the prime objective in founding the Baptist school was "the advancement of the Christian religion;
yet as that Religion is in its very essence favorable to
political freedom, such an Institution... cannot fail of
having a salutary influence in a political point of view."
King soon became a champion of the Baptist school, making
it a part of his larger campaigns for religious toleration
and for the elevation of Maine to the status of a separate
and sovereign state. When the separation of Maine from

---

[4]Marriner, History, pp. 4, 589; Samuel P. Merrill,
"Rev. Daniel Merrill, A.M.--An Appreciation," Centennial of
the First Baptist Church, Sedgwick, Maine (n.p., ca. 1905),
pp. 32, 41-52; Daniel Merrill to William King, December 23,
1811, Manuscripts Concerning the Early History of Colby College, Colby College Archives.

Massachusetts was effected in 1820, King was elected governor of the new state.[5]

King and Merrill failed to obtain a charter in 1812,
but successfully guided a noncollegiate charter through the
legislature in 1813. Later that year King became the first
non-Baptist trustee of Colby and played an active part in
translating the charter into an institutional reality. His
most important function was to serve as a contact between
the trustees and two enterprising citizens of Waterville.
One was Timothy Boutelle, and the other was Nathaniel Gilman,
a wealthy merchant and landowner. Like King and Boutelle,
Gilman was a non-Baptist and a Jeffersonian Republican who
advocated independence for Maine.[6]

Finding their original land grant from the Massachusetts legislature too isolated and otherwise unsuitable for
a college, the trustees spent the years immediately following
the Peace of Ghent sounding out several communities on the
prospects of locating the school. Although it had no Baptist church, Waterville made the most attractive financial

[5]Ibid.; Marriner, History, p. 11; Biographical Encyclopaedia of Maine in the Nineteenth Century (Boston, 1885),
pp. 78-79; Marriner, History, pp. 6, 603; Merrill to King,
December 23, 1811, Manuscripts Concerning Early History of
Colby; Robert E. Moody in DAB, s.v. "King, William."

[6]Marriner, History, pp. 6-7; J.T. Champlin, A Histori-
cal Discourse Delivered at the Fiftieth Anniversary of Colby
University, August 20, 1870 (Waterville, Me., 1870), p. 17;
Marriner, History, pp. 15, 61, 35, 590.

offer. Gilman and Boutelle persuaded the Waterville voters
to appropriate $3,000 as the town's bid. Then, along with
a few other citizens, they personally guaranteed a private
general subscription of an additional $2,000. On the basis
of these pledges the trustees voted in October, 1817, to
locate the college at Waterville. The town's pledge was
never fully paid, but that of the wealthy owners of Waterville real estate was soon used by the trustees in purchasing
the college site.[7]

A fourth non-Baptist substantially aided the college
before it closed its first decade. In early 1828, Sylvanus
Cobb, pastor of the Waterville Universalist Church, joined
his fellow legislator, Boutelle, in successfully arguing for
state aid to the college. Cobb contended in his speech before the House of Representatives that the state, by char-
tering and granting land to the college, had incurred a continuing financial obligation to those who invested money in
and attended the institution. By its original "solemn act"
of incorporating the college, Cobb asserted, the legislature
decided that "the public good would be served by the establishment of this Institution." Arguing that the college continued to serve the public good and therefore should not be

---

[7]Ibid., pp. 11, 16; Champlin, Historical Discourse,
pp. 4-5; Centennial History of Waterville, p. 59; Sylvanus
Boardman to Elijah T. Warren, March 8, 1818, Manuscripts
Concerning Early History of Colby.

shunned by the state in favor of aiding only the common
schools, Cobb concluded that both common schools and colleges are "designed for the good of all. All classes of
the community, rich and poor, are equally interested in
them; and they are as important to the good of the whole,
as are both the greater and the smaller arteries to the
life of the animal body."[8]

The motives of Colby's non-Baptist supporters, such as
Cobb, Boutelle, Gilman, and King, were various and sometimes
inscrutable. Yet these men argued with firm conviction that
the college, in addition to serving certain private interests,
made an important contribution to the commonweal. Both Cobb
and Boutelle thought Colby benefited the poorer as well as
the wealthier classes. Boutelle calculated the expenses of
attending Colby as one third those of Harvard, and he felt
that this made the institution accessible to most segments
of society. Beneficial effects of the college upon the common schools both in terms of supplying competent teachers
and in promoting a respect for learning were also cited by
Boutelle.[9]

Separation of private from public interests was uncon-
genial to the thinking of such men. Waterville's newspaper

---

[8]Marriner, Kennebec, pp. 217-18; "Waterville College,"
Waterville Intelligencer, February 21, 1828.

[9]Ibid.; "Waterville College," Waterville Intelligencer,
February 2, 1825.

exemplified this attitude in 1823 while reporting on "the
rapid growth of the village" and especially the construction
of the bridge across the Kennebec to join Waterville with
Winslow. "For this convenient work," the editor commented,
"we venture to say that the public feel greatly indebted to
the enterprising proprietors, and wish them ample remuneration for their expensive and perhaps hazardous undertaking.
It has apparently given...new life to...part of the town."
In a growing early-nineteenth-century town such as Waterville,
the private and public activities of a man like Timothy
Boutelle were virtually indistinguishable. By bringing a
college, a bridge, and railroad facilities to Waterville,
Boutelle improved not only the cultural and economic status
of himself and his family, but also the town and region to
which he committed his talents and fortunes for over fifty
years. His death in 1855 was fittingly described by the
Waterville Mail as a "public loss."[10]

While prevailing ideas of service to the general welfare
facilitated non-Baptist assistance to Colby, lack of general
Baptist support for the college made such seemingly strange
alliances imperative. Little support for the college of an

---

[10]"Waterville," Waterville Intelligencer, October 31,
1823; Frederic Allen, "The Early Lawyers of Lincoln and Kennebec Counties," Collections of the Maine Historical Society,
VI (1859), 69; Illustrated History, p. 309; "Death of Mr. Boutelle," copied from the Waterville Mail in an undated and un-
identified clipping in Sibley, "Collectanea," I, 124.

official denominational nature came from any of the three

major levels of Baptist church polity.[11] Waterville's Baptist

church was not founded until a few months after the arrival of

Chaplin and was essentially a "child of the College." Re-

sources of the small congregation of this church during the

first decade were primarily expended for the erection of a

church building. It was the college that sustained the church

in these years, largely through faculty members' filling the

pulpit without remuneration. On the association level, men-

tion of efforts to found a Baptist school in Maine appeared

as early as 1810, when the Bowdoinham Association appointed

a committee of five to "take into consideration the propriety

of petitioning the General Court for incorporation" of an

institution for "promoting literary and theological knowledge."

Yet other than resolutions in 1818 and 1819 urging Baptists

to contribute to the school at Waterville, no further mention

of the enterprise can be found in the minutes prior to 1830,

---

[11]The primary unit of Baptist polity is the autonomous
local church. Baptist associations are voluntary unions of
self-governing local churches, usually located in a particular
geographical area of a single state. State conventions operate in much the same fashion as associations, except with a
larger geographical base and with greater responsibilities for
directing the benevolent, educational, and missionary enterprises of the denomination. In the early nineteenth century,
churches were represented at the annual (or occasionally semi-
annual) association meetings by "messengers," who were "not
considered as delegates, since that term connoted a transfer
of power." Convention membership was diverse, but generally
consisted of messengers sent by individual churches, associations, and auxiliary societies. See Walter B. Posey, The
Baptist Church in the Lower Mississippi Valley, 1776-1845
(Lexington, Ky., 1957), pp. 117, 126.

when the Waterville church joined another association. The
Maine Baptist Convention was not organized until 1824, and
no reference to the college at Waterville appeared in its
minutes until 1832.[12]

Lack of verbal support for the college from association
and convention indicates the general disinterest if not hostility of most Maine Baptists toward such an institution.
Absence of financial support from these organizations could
be expected because Baptists usually raised money for benevolent enterprises by means of voluntary societies organized
for the purpose of aiding a specific cause such as missions
or ministerial education. These societies had no formal connection with the official levels of Baptist polity. In Maine,
however, the Education Society, like the Waterville church
and the State Convention, was organized after the founding of
the college. Chaplin founded the Maine Baptist Education
Society in 1819, and it was incorporated two years later.
Although the Society gave some help to the college during its
first few years, its resources, reflecting a lack of contributions from Maine Baptists, were "exceedingly limited" and
its appropriations for ministerial education proportionately

---

[12]Kennebec Association, Maine, Minutes, 1838, pp. 13-14;
Minnie S. Philbrick, Centennial History of the First Baptist
Church of Waterville, Maine (Waterville, Me., 1925), pp. 18,
26; Bowdoinham Association, Maine, Minutes, 1810, p. 5;
Maine Baptist Convention, Minutes, 1824-1831; Ibid., 1832,
p. 5.

small. The Massachusetts Baptist Education Society probably
sent some of its beneficiaries to Waterville for a few years,
but the attention of this society soon turned to the new
Baptist theological school founded at Newton, Massachusetts,
in 1825.[13]

Lacking substantial support even from the Education
Society, one of Chaplin's principal and continuing tasks was
to overcome "the apathy and prejudices of his own denomination."
Robert E. Pattison, a member of the faculty during part of
Chaplin's presidency, recalled that "the Baptists in Maine
were not prepared liberally to sustain a college. They needed
its influence for at least one generation upon themselves,
before they could justly appreciate the advantages of such
an institution, or their obligation to support it for the public good." About the only Baptist support Chaplin could count
on was that of a small body of laymen and ministers who favored ministerial education.[14]

Faced with the problem of Baptist support, this small
group of promoters turned from the beginning to non-Baptist
groups and individuals who would more quickly perceive and

[13]Henry S. Burrage, History of the Baptists in Maine
(Portland, Me., 1904), pp. 241-44,.

[14]Robert E. Pattison, Eulogy on Rev. Jeremiah Chaplin,
D.D., First President of Waterville College, Me., Delivered
in the Baptist Meeting House, Waterville, On the Evening Preceding Commencement, August 8, 1843 (Boston, 1843), p. 13.

appreciate the benefits of a college and who could therefore be more rapidly enlisted to support it. When Colby's trustees began to consider the financing of the proposed school, they first looked not to the denomination but to the neighborhood of the land grant which it was then thought would be the site of the school. In May, 1815, the trustees instructed a committee "to obtain such pecuniary aid by subscription from the people near Township No. 3 or elsewhere as can with conveniency be obtained." Legislative grants such as this township and local support such as that of Waterville citizens in return for location of the college in their town were necessary to sustain the college for the generation or so required to cultivate the more reluctant Baptist constituency.[15]

Simultaneous cultivation of non-Baptist and Baptist support often required certain considerations of strategy. Chaplin wrote to William King in the early spring of 1819: "Mr. Boutelle and I believe that little or no money can be obtained from the Baptist churches by addressing them through the medium of the newspapers. Besides, we fear that, to address them in that manner, would give a political character to our seminary, which we ought to avoid." This problem was solved by issuing a separate pamphlet for each audience.

---

[15]Marriner, History, p. 11.

An Address to the Public, published that May, assured prospective non-Baptist patrons that "the design of the Trustees
in founding this Seminary is not limited to such students as
have the gospel ministry in view, but extends to those who
are desirous of engaging in any of the learned professions."
A circular directed to the Maine Baptists a few months later
emphasized the denominational nature of the school. Esti-
mating that "there are in this District about 10,000 persons
who belong to Baptist churches /and/...probably double that
number who regularly attend Baptist worship, though not members," this circular stressed Baptist responsibility for the
institution.[16]

With institutional success--and probably even survival--
dependent upon legislative and local support, however, the
principal aim of Colby's promoters in the early years was to
solicit non-Baptist support, even at the risk of alienating
Baptists. A pamphlet of 1822, addressed to "the people of
Maine" and entertaining the "sanguine hope that the Legislature of Maine will shortly make an additional appropriation"
to the college, contains no mention of the word Baptist.
Such measures as this and the admitting of non-Baptists to
the Board of Trustees created tensions between the college

[16]Ibid., pp. 36, 40, 617, 41.

and some of its small Baptist constituency. Early atrophy
of the theological department and its abandonment in 1825
prompted a further withdrawal of Baptist support.[17]

II

Baptist laymen played particularly important roles in
the origins of Colgate University and Georgetown College.
Colgate's beginnings were closely tied to a circular letter
of the Boston Baptist Association written in 1816 by Jeremiah Chaplin. The proposal for regional Baptist seminaries
contained in this circular letter led Daniel Hascall, pastor
of the Baptist church in Hamilton, New York, to make plans
for such an institution. Although the initiative in this
case was ministerial, Baptist laymen in the Hamilton area
were almost immediately enlisted in the cause and provided
vital assistance in the founding of Colgate. Georgetown
College in Georgetown, Kentucky, owes its existence largely
to the bequest of a Baptist layman, Isaacher Pawling. Pawling's initiative and the efforts of some other Baptist lay-

---

[17]Waterville College: Origin, Progress, & Present State
of the College (Portland, Me., 1822), p. 8; Joshua Millet, A
History of the Baptists in Maine: Together With Brief Notices
of Societies and Institutions, And a Dictionary of the Labors
of Each Minister (Portland, Me., 1845), p. 431; Marriner,
History, pp. 21, 33, 69.

men under the guidance of a few Baptist ministers resulted in the founding of this institution in 1829.[18]

After a preliminary meeting of five or six ministers and brethren in May, 1817, the thirteen founders of Colgate met in Hamilton four months later and decided to found an institution devoted exclusively to ministerial training. Almost half of the original thirteen were Baptist laymen from Hamilton and the immediate vicinity. Hamilton had been settled by Baptists in the mid-1790's and was still a Baptist stronghold. One of the first settlers, Samuel Payne, substantially aided the Baptist school in 1826 by making available for a campus his large farm at half of its estimated value. The institution had outgrown its facilities in town when this moderately wealthy farmer and prominent member of the Baptist church came to the rescue.[19]

---

[18]Howard D. Williams, "The Origin of Colgate University," New York History, XIX (July 1938), 246-47; George W. Eaton, "Historical Discourse Delivered at the Semi-Centenary of Madison University, Wednesday, August 5th, 1869," The First Half Century of Madison University (1819-1869), or the Jubilee Volume (New York, 1872), p. 37; Leland W. Meyer, Georgetown College: Its Background and a Chapter in Its Early History (Louisville, Ky., 1929), pp. 35-37.

[19]Williams, "Origin," pp. 249-251; Eaton, "Historical," p. 35; Howard D. Williams, First Baptist Church, Hamilton, New York: Historical Sketch, 1796-1961 (n.p., n.d.), pp. 1, 7; Howard D. Williams, "The History of Colgate University to 1869," unpublished Ph.D. dissertation, Harvard University, 1949, pp. 56-59.

Other Baptist laymen of Hamilton had earlier assisted
in the establishment of Colgate by subscribing to the agreement which brought the school to their village. Several
other villages bid for the institution, but a promise of
facilities costing $3,500 and $2,500 worth of board over a
period of five years or more secured the school for Hamilton.
Baptist laymen were largely responsible for seeing that the
agreement was fulfilled. Additional assistance in the early
years came from wealthy Baptists outside the immediate vicinity. Nicholas Brown of Providence and William Colgate of
New York City both gave generously.[20]

Control of the school was vested in the Baptist Education Society of the State of New York, incorporated in 1819.[21]
This voluntary organization of ministers and laymen was a
convenient agency through which a few promoters of ministerial education could act in the name of the denomination
in New York without having to work through its official organizations. The Society enabled a small group of brethren,
despite widespread apathy and hostility toward ministerial
education within their denomination, to provide the Baptists
of New York and neighboring states with their first formal
institution for training ministers.

---

[20]Ibid., pp. 54-55; Williams, "Origin," pp. 252-53;
Williams, "History," pp. 61, 52.

[21]Williams, "Origin," pp. 251-52.

An impending bequest from a wealthy layman led to the founding of Georgetown College in 1829. Sometime during the previous year, Isaacher Pawling, "a pious and devoted" Baptist from Mercer County, communicated to Silas Noel, pastor of the Great Crossings Baptist Church, a desire to bequeath a portion of his estate for the education of Regular Baptist ministers. Both Pawling and Noel were concerned about the increasing influence of Alexander Campbell within the Baptist ranks and envisioned an educational institution to confront this challenge. Former Governor Gabriel Slaughter, a "near neighbor and personal friend" of Pawling probably also contributed to these plans. Slaughter was both a prominent Baptist and an outspoken supporter of education. Georgetown's trustees were incorporated in January, 1829, and the next month Pawling made his will, appointing the trustees as his executors and bequeathing them about $10,000 in addition to an estimated $17,000 he contributed at that same time. Pawling's will specified that his bequest was to be a perpetual fund and the interest "applied exclusively to the education of such Baptist preachers or candidates for the Baptist ministry, as adhere to the articles of the General Union of Baptists in Kentucky."[22]

---

[22] J.H. Spencer, A History of Kentucky Baptists. From 1769 to 1885, Including More Than 800 Biographical Sketches (Cincinnati, 1886), I, 601; J./onathan/ E.F./arnham/, "Georgetown College--No. 4: Its First Decade," Western Recorder, September 11, 1875; Cathcart, Baptist Encyclopaedia, p. 853;

With ambitious plans to found a college rather than
merely use the Pawling fund to support future preachers in
attending existing institutions such as Transylvania University, the trustees decided to receive bids for the location
of the institution and thus obtain funds for buildings and
equipment. Several towns in the Lexington vicinity submitted
bids ranging from $15,000 to $25,000. The latter sum made
Georgetown the highest bidder and secured for this community
the proposed Baptist college. The precise conditions of the
contract between the trustees and the citizens of Scott county
seem to have been that the college was permanently located
in Georgetown, the county seat, in return for a pledge of
$20,000 with interest payable semiannually and the principal
payable in five years. Also included in the agreement was the
building and other property (valued at $5,000-6,000) of Rit-
tenhouse Academy, a then defunct school in Georgetown which

Leland W. Meyer, The Life and Times of Colonel Richard M.
Johnson of Kentucky (New York, 1932), p. 388; Meyer, Georgetown, pp. 32-33; "Kentucky Baptist Education Society," Baptist Banner, March 19, 1836; Francis G. Davenport, Ante
Bellum Kentucky, A Social History, 1800-1860 (Oxford, Ohio,
1943), pp. 64-65; R.M. Dudley, "The Early History of Georgetown College," Georgetown College Magazine, II (January
1887), 125-26; Meyer, Georgetown, p. 37; "Kentucky Baptist
Education Society," Baptist Banner, March 19, 1836.

had been founded in 1798 as part of the state's county academy system.[23]

After negotiation of the agreement was completed in July,
1829, Noel wrote: "You would be utterly surprised to learn
the number of wealthy men, divided in politics and religion,
who have most cordially united in this College enterprise."
One witness of this mobilization of Scott County support
assigned a key role to Baptist lawyer-preacher, John Bryce.
More a Georgetown lawyer than a preacher at the time, Bryce
"was very active in representing to the people of the town
and county the advantages that would result to them both in
a literary and pecuniary point of view provided the Institution could be located in Georgetown." Although he was a
trustee of the college, Bryce "urged the subject as a citizen" and emphasized "the advantages that would result by the
location and the diffusion of knowledge and the influence of
those employed as instructors upon society." This message
was communicated both at town meetings called to consider
bidding for the college and through agents who carried

---

[23]O.R. Corey, "Historical Chronology, General College
History: 1775-1954," typescript in Georgetown College Li-
brary, pp. 10-11; Meyer, Life and Times, p. 389; Meyer,
Georgetown, pp. 38-39; J. William Black, "The History of
Georgetown College, Georgetown, Ky.," History of Higher
Education in Kentucky, ed. Alvin F. Lewis (Washington,
1899), p. 142; Orlando E. Huddle, "A History of Georgetown
College," unpublished M.A. thesis, University of Kentucky,
1930, p. 6.

subscription papers "to all or nearly all the inhabitants in the county."[24]

Scott County, like the area around Hamilton, New York, was a Baptist stronghold. Yet Georgetown College was planned primarily as a literary rather than a theological institution.[25] This was partly due to substantial opposition to specialized ministerial training within the denomination in Kentucky. A college, however, was probably also better suited to the non-denominational interests of Baptist laymen in Kentucky such as Gabriel Slaughter and John Bryce. They acted as citizens as well as members of a denomination in promoting their college.

III

Prime promoters in the beginnings of George Washington University and Shurtleff College were individual Baptist

[24]"Prospects of Education," Columbian Star and Christian Index, August 1, 1829; A History of Bourbon, Scott, Harrison and Nicholas Counties, Kentucky, ed. William H. Perrin (Chicago, 1882), p. 191; Cathcart, Baptist Encyclopaedia, p. 155; Ben F. Ford MS., quoted in part in Cory, "Historical Chronology," p. 10; Ford MS., quoted in part in Dudley, "Early History," p. 128.

[25]History of Bourbon, Scott, pp. 180-81, 192-98; "The Church at Georgetown," Baptist Chronicle and Literary Register, I (April 1831), 58-59; G.W. Samson, Memorial Discourse on the Life and Character of Joel Smith Bacon, D.D., Third President of the Columbian College, in the District of Columbia, Delivered at the E. Street Baptist Church, Washington, D.C., On Sunday, June 27, 1870 (Washington, 1870), p. 9.

ministers. George Washington University was described quite accurately in 1852 as "the child of Luther Rice." Although there were other forces at work, this enterprising young minister was by far the single most important factor in the creation and survival of the institution from the time of its founding in 1819 until at least 1826. Shurtleff first existed in the mind of John Mason Peck, a Baptist home missionary. The story is frequently told of how a Presbyterian minister named John Ellis, while riding through Rock Spring, Illinois, in 1827 came upon Peck, axe in hand, preparing the land and buildings for his school. Asked what he was doing, Peck replied, "I am building a theological seminary." "What, in these barrens?" said Ellis. "Yes," answered Peck, "I am planting the seed."[26] Legendary as this story may be, it accurately conveys the sense in which Rock Spring Seminary, a predecessor of Shurtleff, was quite literally the creation of John Mason Peck. Both Rice and Peck soon learned, however, that their schools could not prosper as one-man enterprises.

Convinced of the need for formal ministerial education and greater denominational unity, Luther Rice solicited subscriptions for a national Baptist theological school and

---

[26]"Columbian College," Biblical Recorder, May 21, 1852; Matthew Lawrence, John Mason Peck, The Pioneer Missionary: A Biographical Sketch (New York, 1940), p. 52.

college as early as 1818. On his own responsibility he raised
money, purchased land, and commenced the building of facilities for the institution. Having acquired the assistance of
only a few fellow Baptists up to this point, Rice next sought
the support of the national Baptist convention at its meeting
in 1820. Although they had been discussing plans for ministerial education for several years and were helping to support, through the efforts of their agent (the same Rice), a
small theological school in Philadelphia, convention delegates had not yet made a major commitment to education.
Rice's near *fait accompli* forced such a decision, and the
Convention voted to adopt his nascent institution.[27]

While thus lending its sanction to Rice's school, accep-
ting control of its property, and assuming general supervision
of its operations, the Convention refused to accept financial
responsibility for the institution. Rice was instructed to
contract no debts and was dependent for income primarily upon
his own efforts as agent.[28]   With only limited official

---

[27]Luther Rice to Adoniram Judson, January 6, 1823, in
Luther Rice Letter Book, January 6-June 2, 1823, Baptist His-
torical Collection, Wake Forest College Library; James B.
Taylor, Memoir of Rev. Luther Rice, One of the First American
Missionaries to the East (Baltimore, 1840), pp. 179, 181, 137-
38; Elmer L. Kayser, Luther Rice, Founder of Columbian College
(Washington, 1966), pp. 15-16; letter from Robert B. Semple
in Columbian Star and Christian Index, March 27, 1830; James
C. Welling, Brief Chronicles of the Columbian College From
1821 to 1873 and of the Columbian University from 1873 to 1889
(Washington, 1889), p. 2; "Fourth Annual Report of the Board,"
Latter Day Luminary, I (May 1818), 135; "Proceedings of the
General Convention at Their Second Triennial Meeting and the
Sixth Annual Report of the Board," ibid., (May 1820), 120, 128.

[28]Ibid.

support from his denomination, Rice's position was basically that of an educational entrepreneur governed primarily by expediency.

If he could obtain a Congressional charter this might serve as a justification for federal assistance. Scruples about separation of church and state in this situation resided more in the Congress than with Rice and his fellow Baptist promoters of the school. Congressional opposition based on the First Amendment thwarted attempts first to charter the Convention and then to charter just a Baptist literary society. Enlisting the aid of Burgess Allison, Chaplain of the House of Representatives, Richard M. Johnson, a prominent Baptist layman and senator from Kentucky, Henry Clay, and several other congressmen, Rice decided by the end of 1820 to secularize his requests to the point of asking only for a strictly collegiate charter. One further concession required by the Senate was a clause in the charter permitting persons of all religious denominations to be eligible for election as trustees and admittance as students.[29]

With a charter granted in early 1821 placing management of the institution in the hands of trustees elected triennially by contributors to the institution, relations between

---

[29]Meyer, Life and Times, pp. 380-82; /Andrew Rothwell/, History of the Baptist Institutions of Washington City (Washington, 1867), p. 32; "Seventh Annual Report of the Board," Latter Day Luminary, II (May 1821), 381; Meyer, Life and Times, pp. 382-83.

the school and the Convention were significantly changed.
Instead of the theological seminary envisioned by many Baptists, there was a college, which the Convention, as a contemporary observer recalled, "did not at that time, certainly,
mean to erect." Even the theological institution of Philadelphia, when moved to Washington the following September,
became a mere department of the college and was thus no
longer under the direct control of the Convention. The deed
conveying the college property originally purchased by Rice
and a few associates stipulated that at least two-thirds of
the trustees should be chosen from nominations submitted triennially to the trustees by the Convention or else the whole
property would pass over to the Convention. The Convention
also loaned $10,000 to George Washington University in 1821.
Yet the connection between college and Convention in the early
1820's was limited. The loan was made not so much out of concern for the college as for the purpose of freeing Rice, as
Convention agent, to do more collecting for missionary concerns. The Convention was not even legally liable for the
mounting debts of Rice's enterprise.[30]

---

[30]Ibid., p. 383; James D. Knowles, "History of the Colum-
bian College, District of Columbia," Christian Review, II
(March 1837), 120-21; "Report of the Trustees of the Columbian
College," Latter Day Luminary, IV (June 1823), 169; "Seventh
Annual Report of the Board," ibid., II (May 1821), 381, 363;
Knowles, "History," p. 122.

Left to his own devices, Rice resorted to a variety of expedients. He used his own funds, involved himself in a tangle of borrowing schemes, made exhausting trips to solicit donations from individual Baptists, and uttered an occasional "Brethren, help!" through the columns of his monthly journal, the Latter Day Luminary. He even made early plans for noninstructional medical and law departments which would examine candidates and confer degrees. Such departments would elevate "the reputation of the establishment." In soliciting funds for the original purchase of land, Rice had reached outside Baptist ranks to gather contributions from men such as President Monroe, many members of the cabinet, and dozens of members of Congress. In 1824 and 1825 loans totaling about $13,000 were obtained from John Quincy Adams.[31]

To tap such sources and eventually obtain a Congressional grant, Rice and his fellow trustees cultivated a "national feeling" for the public benefits of their college in the nation's capital. Placing themselves in the tradition of those advocating a national university, they made frequent references

---

[31]"Eighth Annual Report of the Board," Latter Day Luminary, III (June 1822), 178; Luther Rice to O.B. Brown, October 5, 1821, Luther Rice Letters, Office of the University Historian, George Washington University; "Columbian College," Columbian Star, March 5, 1825; Welling, Brief Chronicles, p. 2; Elon Galusha, The Crisis Is At Hand (Whitesborough, N.Y., 1826), p. 1; Samuel F. Bemis, John Quincy Adams and the Union (New York, 1956), p. 197.

to the connection between their institution and the national
university idea supported by "the illustrious Washington and
his successors." By 1822 the Boston Patriot was predicting
in regard to George Washington University that "bringing together young men from the various quarters of our extended
country, to meet as it were on neutral ground, removed from
all their sectional feelings and prejudices, and placed within the immediate sphere of operations of our national government...will have a highly important and beneficial effect
upon the stability of our Union." George Washington University's request in 1824 that Congress provide relief from
debts to the government of about $30,000, however, was not
granted until 1828.[32] Meanwhile, Luther Rice was left to
juggle debts and solicit individual support on a day-to-day
basis.

John Mason Peck, in founding Rock Spring Seminary,
predecessor of Shurtleff College, did not even have a legally responsible board of trustees for his school. Although he began in December, 1826, to cultivate extensive
support within the Illinois Legislature, "from the Governor
down to the doorkeeper," Peck was unable to obtain a charter
for the school he founded the following year. Since the

[32]"Columbian College in the District of Columbia,"
Latter Day Luminary, III (January 1822), 14; "Columbian
College in the District of Columbia," Columbian Star, Feb-
ruary 2, 1822, copied from the Boston Patriot; "Columbian
College," Columbian Star, April 24, 1824; Meyer, Life and
Times, p. 385.

Baptist Convention of Illinois was not organized until 1834
and there was no education society in the state until 1836,
Peck's major source of Baptist support consisted of the few
wealthy individuals he could successfully solicit during his
trips to the East. Like Rice, Peck also made personal financial sacrifices to sustain his educational enterprise. Having
conceived of the school, organized its small body of local
supporters, given the land on which it was located, and la-
bored with his own hands to build it, Peck also made a larger
financial investment in the school than that of any other
individual supporter.[33]

Lack of substantial local support was the ultimate reason why so much of the burden of sustaining the Rock Spring
Seminary fell upon Peck's shoulders. Had his school been
located in a larger and more prosperous community, the defi-
ciencies in legislative and denominational assistance might
not have been so damaging. Rock Spring, however, was just a
small settlement offering "no claim to the rank of a village
or town." Peck chose this location in the midst of a tract
of barrens (second-quality land combining the features of

---

[33]John M. Peck, "New Seminary in the West," Evangelical
Inquirer, I (April 1827), 213; "Record Book of the Rock Springs
Theological and High School, Rock Springs, Illinois, 1824-1831,"
typescript in the Dargan-Carver Library, Nashville, Tennessee,
pp. 70-72; Austen K. deBlois, The Pioneer School: A History
of Shurtleff College, Oldest Educational Institution in the
West (New York, 1900), pp. 179, 79, 26-29; Rufus Babcock,
Forty Years of Pioneer Life: Memoir of John Mason Peck, D.D.
(Philadelphia, 1864), pp. 228-29; Lawrence, John Mason Peck,
p. 53.

timber and prairie) for his permanent home and settled there
in 1822. About seventeen miles from St. Louis on the principal stage route from that city to Vincennes, Rock Spring
possessed for Peck "the advantages of being removed from the
contaminating influence of a village." The settlement was
remote enough to permit Peck to purchase a half-section of
government land, and small enough for him to appropriate
quickly the position of postmaster and thus be able to frank
his voluminous correspondence for a period of about twenty
years. Only a few years after the opening of the Seminary
in November, 1827, however, it became apparent that Rock
Spring's remoteness was a liability so far as sustaining a
school was concerned. Dwindling enrollments and Peck's ill
health forced the closing of the Seminary in the spring of
1831.[34]

Alton Literary and Theological Seminary, successor to
Rock Spring Seminary and progenitor of Shurtleff College,
opened in the fall of 1832. Reconstituting the school in
Alton, a promising young river port, provided many new

[34]J.M. Peck, A Guide For Emigrants, Containing Sketches
of Illinois, Missouri, and the Adjacent Parts (Boston, 1831),
pp. 291, 118; Babcock, Forty Years, p. 172; Peck, Guide,
pp. 246, 291; Babcock, Forty Years, p. 172; Helene L. Jennings, "John Mason Peck and the Impact of New England On the
Old Northwest," unpublished Ph.D. dissertation, University
of Southern California, 1961, p. 82; Peck, Guide, p. 248;
Babcock, Forty Years, p. 250; David Wright, Memoir of Alvan
Stone of Goshen, Mass. (Boston, 1837), p. 164; Daniel H.
Brush, Growing Up With Southern Illinois, 1820-1861 (Chicago,
1944), p. 64; Jennings, "John Mason Peck," p. 117; J.M.
Peck, Alton Seminary and College (n.p., ca. 1835), p. 1.

opportunities to cultivate substantial local support. Jonathan Going, a visiting home missionary who was chief advocate of the Alton site, quickly struck a bargain with the
citizens of the town and vicinity. An agreement was made
that if the local people would raise $800-$1,000 for a
building, aid to the amount of $20,000 would be solicited
in the East. Prominent men in this booming community were
soon enlisted in the cause of higher education for Alton.
Enoch Long, a well-known Presbyterian was a member of the
new board of trustees. Another member was Benjamin F.
Edwards, a Baptist physician in nearby Edwardsville. Cyrus
Edwards, a successful lawyer and politician in the area, contributed not only land and money but also the political
skills and influence necessary to obtain a charter from the
Illinois General Assembly in 1835. Edwards did not become
a member of the Baptist Church until well after the Civil
War.[35]

With a promising base of local support and a collegiate
charter, Peck's attempts to raise funds in the East were
probably greatly facilitated. About nine months after the

[35]Peck, Guide, p. 293; Centennial History of Madison
County, Illinois, and Its People, 1812 to 1912, ed. Wilbur T.
Norton (Chicago, 1912), I, 472; Hubbel Loomis, A Documen-
tary History of Alton Seminary to March 7, 1835... (Alton,
Ill., 1854), p. 12; deBlois, Pioneer, p. 49; Justus Bulkley,
Historical Sketch of Shurtleff College, Upper Alton, Illinois
(Upper Alton, Ill., 1865), p. 2; Cathcart, Baptist Encyclo-
paedia, p. 361; Bulkley, Historical Sketch, p. 3.

42

charter was granted, Peck was able to secure from Dr. Benjamin Shurtleff of Boston a pledge of $10,000 for the college. A Brown graduate, Shurtleff did not become a member of the Baptist church until 1841. Since he owned a considerable amount of land in the Alton-Edwardsville vicinity, even this major Eastern contribution may be due in large part to a "local" interest.[36]

Although Peck prepared himself for the founding of Rock Spring Seminary by a visit in 1826 to the existing Baptist institutions in the East,[37] it appears that he learned little from the difficulties Luther Rice was at that time having in sustaining George Washington. One important reason why Rice's one-man enterprise was in trouble was that it had failed to cultivate significant support from either local or official denominational sources. Located on the outskirts of the city, Rice's college was in many ways on the periphery of Washington life. The school was cast off by the Convention at the 1826 meeting which Peck attended and although one final attempt was immediately made through trustee elections to create more

---

[36]Babcock, Forty Years, p. 266; Hiram S. Shurtleff, "Benjamin Shurtleff, M.D.," Memorial Biographies of the New England Historic Genealogical Society, I (Boston, 1880), 32-36; Baptismal Certificate, September 1, 1841, Benjamin Shurtleff Papers, Massachusetts Historical Society; A.T. Strange, "John Tillson," Journal of the Illinois State Historical Society, XVII (January 1925), 716.

[37]Babcock, Forty Years, p. 221.

local interest, the college ultimately had no base of local support to fall back on. Having observed Rice's plight, it would seem that Peck, without any hope of official denominational support, would have been more skillful in choosing the original location of his seminary. Perhaps he felt he could rely on Eastern support or was just too enamoured of rural virtues. A few years of experience in educational entrepreneurship, however, soon demonstrated the crucial importance of location.

IV

Small groups of Baptists organized into education societies provided the initiatives in the founding of Denison University, Franklin College, and Union University. Anyone who made an annual contribution of a dollar or more to these single-purpose organizations became a voting member. Ministers provided much of the leadership. These voluntary groups were less local in character than the Baptist Education Society of the state of New York, but they found the support of a specific community essential to the success of their enterprises.

There were stirrings over the issue of ministerial education in several Ohio Baptist associations just prior to 1820, but even a decade later those within the denomination

44

who were interested in or sympathetic to this issue were a
very small minority. Stimulated in part by the cerebral
challenge of Campbellism around 1830, some of this minority
felt the time had come to launch a full-scale educational
movement. After the adjournment of the Ohio Baptist Convention in May, 1830, "a little band of brethren" remained for
the rest of that day and organized themselves into the Ohio
Baptist Education Society. At this initial gathering they
resolved to establish a literary and theological seminary
in Ohio, and in this meeting lay the origins of Denison University.[38]

About six months later a few Baptists in the Granville
vicinity made plans for bringing the proposed institution
to their community. They obtained an option on a two-hundred-
acre farm for sale about one mile from the village and soon
afterwards began to solicit subscriptions toward the $3,300
purchase price. Although only about half of the amount was
subscribed in time for the annual meeting of the Education
Society in May, 1831, two local Baptists, one an evangelist
and the other a merchant, personally guaranteed the unsub-
scribed portion, submitted the farm as Granville's bid, and

[38]Francis W. Shepardson, Denison University, 1831-1931,
A Centennial History (Granville, Ohio, 1931), pp. 1-2; Memorial Volume of Denison University, 1831-1906 (Columbus, Ohio,
1907), pp. 51, 3; G. Wallace Chessman, Denison: The Story of
an Ohio College (Granville, Ohio, 1957), pp. 4, 7-8; Memorial
Volume, p. 15; "Minutes of the Ohio Baptist Education Society," Western Miscellany, I (June 1830), 140.

secured the location of the school for their town. Upon informing the townspeople of these actions, the two men found their fellow citizens of all faiths willing to complete the subscription.[39]

Facilitating this rapid procurement of a site for Denison was the decision of the Education Society at the same meeting to de-emphasize the ministerial aspect of the school and allow non-Baptists to be trustees. The importance of acquiring a community for the institution can be quickly seen in the fact that the Society provided only $43 for ministerial education that year while the town supplied property worth more than $3,000. A liberal stance also allowed the Society to appeal to "the friends of education generally in our State" at a time when the importance of an institution was "not duly appreciated by our brethren generally."[40]

Support of ministerial education was such a potentially divisive issue among Indiana Baptists that the question was rarely raised within churches and associations. No mention of the school which became Franklin College appears in the minutes of the local association to which the Franklin Baptist church belonged. Minutes of the state convention contain

---

[39]Chessman, Denison, p. 19; Memorial Volume, pp. 52, 103, 16; Chessman, Denison, p. 20.

[40]Chessman, Denison, pp. 11-14; Memorial Volume, p. 63; "Circular Address," Baptist Weekly Journal of the Mississippi Valley, October 19, 1832; "Granville Institution," ibid., November 23, 1832.

only a few sporadic endorsements of the efforts to found and support the institution. Confronted by this official indifference, the Indiana Baptist Education Society originated from informal correspondence among a small group of interested ministers and laymen. Only thirteen men attended the first meeting of the Society, in June, 1834. Undaunted by their small numbers, members of the Society adopted a constitution in January, 1835, calling for the establishment of one or more seminaries.[41]

There were four locations competing to be the site of the proposed seminary. Should the school be located on his farm and he be designated as a teacher, one J.M. Robinson offered $1,400 in subscriptions. The town of Franklin probably topped this bid. Largely through the efforts of the local Baptist minister and those of a colleague in a neighboring county, an eighty-acre farm near Franklin was selected as the college site. Having obtained a charter in January, 1836, the Indiana Manual Labor Institute opened in Franklin in August, 1837.[42]

---

[41]John F. Cady, The Centennial History of Franklin College (n.p., 1934), p. 17; Flat Rock Baptist Association, Indiana, Minutes, 1833-1855; Cady, Centennial History, p. 90; Indiana Baptist General Association, Minutes, 1833-1860; Cady, Centennial History, pp. 23-25, 27.

[42]Ibid., p. 28; William T. Stott, History of Franklin College: A Brief Sketch (Indianapolis, 1874), p. 4; W.C. Thompson, "The Board of Directors," First Half Century of Franklin College, Jubilee Exercises (Cincinnati, 1884), p. 30; Cady, Centennial History, pp. 20, 28, 32.

Well-informed of the work of the education society in
Ohio and probably aware of contemporary efforts by brethren
in Indiana, a group of Baptists led by R.B.C. Howell, a
Nashville minister, organized the Tennessee Baptist Education Society in October, 1836. Initial plans were limited
to the support of beneficiaries at existing institutions.
Finding these institutions unwilling to reduce their tuition
charges for preministerial students, the Society was, by
1839, making plans for its own school. After discarding
Nashville as a location and while entertaining plans for a
separate school in each of the three natural divisions of the
state, the Society opened the preparatory department of Union
University in temporary quarters in Murfreesboro.[43]

Facilities in Murfreesboro were loaned to the Education Society by the trustees of Bradley Academy, a school
founded in 1806 as part of the state's county academy system. Local support for Union was built up at a meeting of
interested citizens of Rutherford County about one month
prior to the opening of the school in May, 1841. The citizens were assured by Howell, the Society president, that

---

[43]"Granville Institution," Baptist, I (October 1835),
154-55; /R.B.C. Howell/, "A Memorial of the First Baptist
Church, Nashville, Tennessee, From 1820 to 1863," typescript
in the Dargan-Carver Library, Nashville, Tennessee, pp. 250-
54; R.B.C. Howell to Samuel Wait, February 18, 1840, Samuel
Wait Correspondence, Baptist Historical Collection, Wake
Forest College Library; "Union University," Baptist Banner
and Western Pioneer, October 29, 1840.

48

Union would "be in no sense whatever either sectarian or
political." After four years of academy-level instruction,
another mass meeting called by the Education Society was
held in Rutherford County. The purpose of this meeting was
to elevate the school to a level worthy of the collegiate
charter which had been obtained in February, 1842. The
assembled brethren and citizens resolved to raise $50,000
within one year to endow Union. They then agreed to rec-
ommend to the trustees that the University be located in
Murfreesboro "on condition that the citizens of that place
will give the sum of ten thousand dollars for erecting
buildings." With the endowment fully subscribed and transferred from the Education Society to the trustees of the
University, college classes began at Murfreesboro in January, 1848.[44]

Once a community was found to help sustain the schools,
education societies did not relinquish all control of their
progeny. Trustees of the institutions were sometimes directly
elected by members of the education societies. Societies
also continued as important sources of income for the young
schools through the collections of society agents and the

---

[44]"Union University," *Tennessee Telegraph* (Murfreesboro),
October 23, 1841; Frank E. Bass, "Education in Rutherford
County," *A History of Rutherford County*, ed. Carlton C. Sims
(n.p. ca. 1947), p. 147; "The College Meeting," *Baptist Ban-
ner and Western Pioneer*, April 1, 1841; "Education Society,"
Baptist, May 17, 1845; "Union University," *Tennessee Baptist*,
December 18, 1847; *Ibid.*, May 3, 1851.

tuition fees paid for beneficiaries attending the schools.
In negotiating with legislatures for a charter and with communities for a site, however, the concession was usually
made that at least some of the trustees were to be non-
Baptists. And since many of the Baptist trustees were also
citizens of the college community, there could be no assurance that the governing boards of these schools would always
be sympathetic to the statewide interests of the Baptist
education societies.

V

Examples of Baptists promoting educational enterprises
as citizens and parents can be found in the beginnings of
Bucknell University and Howard College. The origins of
these colleges resided in the local and educational interests
of influential men who also happened to be Baptists. In
both cases a previous attempt to found a school had been
made by official denominational organizations and had lasted
only a few years. Motivated as much by civic pride and parental concerns as by denominational loyalty, a few men were
able to succeed where the denomination had failed.

In the course of a casual conversation one day in early
1841, General E.D. King is reported to have looked out the
window toward a particular lot in Marion, Alabama, and

remarked to two friends, "There is the very place for a male college." King's vantage point was inside the building recently constructed for the Judson Female Institute, and one of his listeners was Milo P. Jewett, Principal of this Baptist school. The third man in the party was the local Baptist pastor, James H. DeVotie.[45] With a strong Baptist church and a flourishing female seminary, these three men had begun to build Marion into a center for the interests of Alabama Baptists. Within two years a state Baptist newspaper would be founded and begin publication in Marion. From the casual remark of E.D. King in 1841 would grow their crowning achievement, Howard College.

General King, a prominent Perry County planter, had the resources to make his suggestion more than just wishful thinking. One of the wealthiest men in Alabama, King was a Baptist and a frequent contributor to "the cause of learning and piety." Indicative of the fact that King was probably more pious than learned is his frequently employed assertion, "Money are power and I are got it." DeVotie, a shoe salesman before becoming a preacher, was not much more of a scholar than King, but he was a skillful fund raiser. Probably starting with a substantial contribution from King, DeVotie was soon able to raise enough money among the Baptists of

[45]Mitchell B. Garrett, Sixty Years of Howard College, 1842-1902, Howard College Bulletin, LXXV, No. 4 (Birmingham, Ala., 1927), p. 18.

Marion to purchase the property. At the Alabama Baptist
State Convention meeting in November, 1841, the Marion Baptists offered the property to the Convention on condition
that it be used as the site for a male college under Convention patronage. The offer was accepted.[46]

Almost a decade earlier the Convention had laid plans
for a literary and theological school. Marion bid for the
institution, but, because the Presbyterians had recently
established a potentially competitive manual labor school
there, Greensboro was chosen. The Baptist school opened in
January, 1836, and closed the following year because of faculty dissension and the financial panic. The Convention
sold the property and returned to an apprenticeship form of
ministerial training. Even with the assurance of strong
local support for a school in Marion, the Convention's return in the early 1840's to the area of institutional education was a cautious one. Convention support focused on
the endowment of a theological professorship, and liability

---

[46]Memorial Record of Alabama (Madison, Wisc., 1893),
II, 788; S.A. Townes, The History of Marion, Sketches of Life
in Perry County, Alabama (Marion, Ala., 1844), reprinted in
Alabama Historical Quarterly, XIV, Nos. 3 and 4 (1952), 203;
W.C. Ward, "Historical Summary," Fiftieth Annual Catalogue
and Register of Howard College, East Lake, Alabama, For the
Academic Year 1891-92 (Birmingham, Ala., 1892). p. 66; E.B.
Teague, "An Outline Picture of the Baptist Denomination in
Alabama in Former Times," ca. 1880, typescript in Special
Collections of the Howard College Library, pp. 17-18; Cath-
cart, Baptist Encyclopaedia, p. 331; Garrett, Sixty Years,
pp. 18-19.

for any debts of the school was vested in an incorporated
board of trustees.[47]

To encourage maximum local support, and thus insure the
"future prosperity" of the school, Howard's supporters began
assuring the citizens of Marion less than a month after endorsement by the Convention that the classical department
would "not partake in any degree whatever, of sectarianism."
With a collegiate charter dated December 29, 1841, some
pupils and apparatus obtained from the now defunct Presbyterian manual labor school, and the name of a famous British
Baptist leader in prison reform, Howard opened in January,
1842. Functioning primarily as a town academy, the school
was soon regarded by many Marion residents as "a cherished
local enterprise." Substantial proof of the successful cultivation of widespread local support came in 1844 when a
fire destroyed Howard's building. The day following the
fire a public meeting was called at the court house. After
several speeches urging "the claims of Education on the patriot, the philanthropist, and the Christian," the "citizens
and the strangers present at Court, without distinction of
party, sect, or class," subscribed $4,000 for new facilities.
Although "the denomination did not respond to the ardor of
the citizens of Marion and vicinity and appeals for help were

---

[47]Ibid., pp. 7-8, 9, 11, 15-16, 19-20; "Howard College,"
South Western Baptist, October 28, 1853.

unheeded," local supporters soon raised the subscription total to over $8,000, thus insuring the survival of Marion's school.[48]

Bucknell University owes its origins to the desire of a small group of Baptists in central Pennsylvania to improve the educational opportunities of their children.[49] The leader of this group was James Moore, Jr., a wealthy farmer and railroad builder who resided near Milton, Pennsylvania, in the mid eighteen thirties. With a growing family which eventually numbered six sons, Moore began to concern himself with the education of his offspring. Soon after his plans for "an academy of high grade" in Milton were destroyed by the panic of 1837, Moore moved to a large farm outside Lewisburg. Deciding this was the town for his school, Moore

---

[48]"The Baptist College Again," Marion Herald, December 1, 1841; Garrett, Sixty Years, pp. 20, 23, 22; Benjamin F. Riley, A Memorial History of the Baptists of Alabama (Philadelphia, 1923), p. 77; "Howard College," Alabama Baptist, May 18, 1844; Samuel S. Sherman, Autobiography of Samuel Sterling Sherman (Chicago, 1910), p. 59; "Howard College," South Western Baptist, October 28, 1853.

[49]cf. J. Orin Oliphant's studies, which place the origins of Bucknell within the context of the "movement of Christian benevolence" which swept through the United States in the early nineteenth century. Oliphant locates the "immediate impetus" for the founding of the University in the "urgent demand for educated ministers to serve the needs of an enlarging population." See his The Beginnings of Bucknell University: A Sampling of the Documents (Lewisburg, Pa., 1954), pp. 1-4, and The Rise of Bucknell University (New York, 1965), pp. 1-8.

raised the issue once again within a little circle of friends and relatives who also had children.[50]

The nucleus of this coterie was formed by the marriage of one of Moore's sisters to a Lewisburg physician, William H. Ludwig, and that of another sister to Joseph Meixell, a Lewisburg businessman and farm owner. Ludwig, whose sister had married Moore, was a Christian willing to unite with the Baptists and would later become first chairman of Bucknell's board of trustees. Meixell, already a Baptist, was also named to the original board of trustees. Other brethren and friends of education in the vicinity joined the small kinship group in perceiving "the need of a school conveniently near where their sons and daughters might receive an education superior to what the public system (especially in that day) could afford." Samuel Wolfe and Levi B. Christ,

---

[50]James Moore, "The Original Manuscript Concerning the Founding of the University at Lewisburg by One of the Founders," Bucknell Mirror, December 10, 1896, p. 52; Lewis E. Theiss, Centennial History of Bucknell University, 1846-1946 (Williamsport, Pa., 1946), p. 24; George R. Bliss, "Incidents in the Early History of Bucknell University," University Mirror, XII (January 1893), 45; Moore, "Original Manuscript," pp. 49, 53; Theiss, Centennial History, pp. 25-27; Moore, "Original Manuscript," p. 49; Lewis E. Theiss, "The Beginning of Bucknell University and Early Lewisburg," Northumberland County Historical Society, Proceedings and Addresses, XIV (1944), 150-152.

prominent Lewisburg merchants, were among those early enlisted in the cause.[51]

Even though Moore soon had the local support for a liber-
ally-conceived Baptist college in Lewisburg, he was concerned
about the propriety of founding such an institution in a town
lacking a Baptist church. Due to the evangelical interests
of another of Moore's brother-in-laws, Collins A. Hewett,
pastor of the Milton Baptist Church, a New York revivalist
happened to be in the area while Moore was projecting plans
for a college. Unable to finance a revival in Milton, Hewett
brought this evangelist, William Grant, to Moore. Moore
quickly seized the opportunity by hiring Grant to hold a
series of protracted meetings in Lewisburg during the fall
and winter of 1843. Grant's meetings lasted seven weeks and
among his converts were William Ludwig, Samuel Wolfe, and
Levi Christ. On January 3, 1844, the recent converts joined

---

[51]Theiss, Centennial History, p. 25; Theiss, "Beginning,"
pp. 151-53; Theiss, Centennial History, p. 40; Stephen W.
Taylor, "A Brief History of the Origin of the University at
Lewisburg," manuscript dated April 18, 1850, in the Bucknell
University Archives, p. 1; Bliss, "Incidents," p. 45; "Report of the Curators of the University at Lewisburg," Lewisburg Chronicle, September 11, 1850; Moore, "Original Manuscript," p.50; Eric G. Stewart, "Living in Lewisburg in the
1840's and Early 1850's," term paper written for History 221,
1934, Bucknell University Archives, p. 11; Theiss, Centennial
History, p. 30. An examination of the catalogues of the University and the affiliated Female Institute indicates that
more than fifteen children of the Moore, Ludwig, Meixell,
Wolfe, and Christ families attended these institution prior
to 1861.

with James Moore and some other Milton Baptists to form the
Lewisburg Baptist Church.[52]

The next problem for Moore and his group was to obtain
for their school the sanction and support of the Baptists of
Pennsylvania. Represented by Ludwig, they began with the
nearest Baptist organization, the Northumberland Association.
This Association considered establishing a manual labor academy as early as 1832, but soon afterward threw its support
to Haddington Institution, the short-lived Baptist venture
near Philadelphia. By the early 1840's, interest in ministerial education among the churches of the Association had
greatly diminished and threatened to vanish entirely. Then
suddenly at the annual meeting of 1845 Joel E. Bradley, pastor of the Baptist churches in Milton and Lewisburg and
probably speaking for the Moore group, proposed the "establishment of an Institution in our midst." A committee of
five, chaired by Dr. Ludwig and including Bradley and James
Moore's father, was appointed to report in the afternoon of
that day "on the propriety of forming a Literary and Theological Seminary in central Pennsylvania." The committee
reported favorably and recommended enlisting the support of

---

[52]Moore, "Original Manuscript," p. 49; Theiss, Centennial History, pp. 24, 31, 33-34.

the Pennsylvania Baptist Education Society and the Pennsylvania Baptist Convention.[53]

Moore's group thus obtained the Association's sanction but placed little faith in the special committee or its time-consuming recommendations. Soon after the Association meeting, the "friends of /the/ enterprise at Lewisburg" formed an unauthorized, self-styled "State Association." Although Bradley and Moore also worked their way into the Pennsylvania Baptist Education Society, it was their own "State Association" which took the initiatives necessary for the speedy founding of a college in Lewisburg.[54]

The first step taken by the "State Association" was to recruit the services of Stephen W. Taylor who had just resigned his professorship at Colgate. Taylor was an experienced Baptist educator, well-qualified to advise the Lewisburg group on all the details of establishing a Baptist college. Another important action taken was the purchase of the college site by Moore, Ludwig, and Wolfe. Once a charter was prepared, this same group financed Taylor's trip to

[53]Ibid., p. 36; Frank G. Lewis, A Sketch of the History of Baptist Education in Pennsylvania (Chester, Pa., 1919), pp. 20-21, 23; Northumberland Baptist Association, Pennsylvania, Minutes, 1844, p. 7, and 1845, pp. 8, 11.

[54]Stephen W. Taylor, "University at Lewisburg," Christian Chronicle, September 2, 1846; Taylor, "Brief History," pp. 2-3; Oliphant, Beginnings, p. 11; Pennsylvania Baptist Education Society, Reports and Minutes, 1844, p. 50, and 1845, p. 9.

Harrisburg and his work there in obtaining the charter
granted on February 5, 1846.[55]

The charter stipulated that the trustees of the new
university could not fully exercise their corporate powers
until $100,000 in subscriptions for the school was obtained.
The State Association turned first to Lewisburg which they
in 1845 had selected as site for the university. At a mass
meeting of the town citizens, Taylor proposed that $20,000
of the $100,000 be raised within a twenty-mile radius of the
school. More than 100 Lewisburg residents became subscribers,
and Taylor later recalled that "citizens other than Baptists
imbibed the spirit of the enterprise and cheerfully added
their names to the subscription list." Taylor then presented the Philadelphia brethren with these results of up-
country enterprise and secured their pledge to match whatever was raised within the confines of the Northumberland
Association. By January, 1849, the $100,000 was subscribed
and the trustees assumed their full corporate authority.
With secondary instruction having begun in October, 1846,
and a freshman class formed the following fall, seven

[55]Oliphant, Rise, p. 24; Cathcart, Baptist Encyclopaedia, p. 1136; Moore, "Original Manuscript," p. 50;
Oliphant, Rise, p. 26.

students were prepared to receive degrees in August, 1851, at the University's first commencement.[56]

VI

As in the origins of Colby, non-Baptists were deeply involved in the establishment of the University of Rochester, Hillsdale College, and Mississippi College. Rochester, New York, although it had several well-established Baptist churches in the late 1840's, was a community in which Presbyterians were predominant. There were few if any Free Will Baptists living in Hillsdale, Michigan, until the college of that denomination arrived in 1853.[57] Mississippi College, although not included as a full-fledged member of this study, is briefly examined at this point as the epitome of a community enterprise.

[56]Oliphant, Rise, pp. 28, 26; Stephen W. Taylor, "University at Lewisburg," Christian Chronicle, November 18, 1846; "Stephen William Taylor," Bucknell Mirror, XXV (May 1906), 5; Taylor, "Brief History," pp. 5-6; Moore, "Original Manuscript," p. 51; Stephen W. Taylor, "University at Lewisburg," Christian Chronicle, November 18, 1846; Oliphant, Rise, p. 31; "Stephen W. Taylor," p. 9; Oliphant, Rise, pp. 51-52.

[57]Blake McKelvey, Rochester, the Water-Power City, 1812-1854 (Cambridge, Mass., 1945), pp. 279-80; Jesse L. Rosenberger, Rochester and Colgate: Historical Backgrounds of the Two Universities (Chicago, 1925), p. 8; Centennial History of Rochester, New York, ed. Edward R. Foreman (Rochester, 1933), III, 247, 255; Compendium of History and Biography of Hillsdale County, ed. Elon G. Reynolds (Chicago, 1903), pp. 56-57; Ransom Dunn, "The Story of the Planting: A Reminiscence of the Founding and Early History of Hillsdale College," Reunion, May 6, 1885.

Although the University of Rochester was in part the
product of a split in the ranks of Colgate supporters, its
location was determined and its success insured by an in-
digenous movement for a college in western New York. Presbyterian efforts to found a university in Rochester in the
mid-1840's helped prepare the way for the primarily Baptist
institution founded in 1850. Baptist promoters of the removal of Colgate to Rochester (and when that failed the establishment of a separate school in Rochester) had widespread
community backing from the beginning. By 1848, an offer of
$100,000 was made to Colgate if it would remove to Rochester.
When most of the faculty and many of the students moved from
Hamilton to Rochester in 1850, it was understood that community support of an equal magnitude would be made available
to them in establishing the University of Rochester. In
recognition of this initial non-Baptist support the first
board of trustees contained two Episcopalians and a Presbyterian. A Congregationalist was on the original faculty.[58]

This liberally conceived institution was so successful
in cultivating community support that its Baptist promoters
were somewhat defensive in their appeals to the denomination.
Articles in the denominational newspaper promoting the new

[58]Rosenberger, Rochester, pp. 13-15; Augustus H. Strong,
"Historical Discourse," Rochester Theological Seminary Gen-
eral Catalogue, 1850 to 1900 (Rochester, N.Y., 1900), p. 314;
Rosenberger, Rochester, p. 60; Williams, "History," p. 229;
Rosenberger, Rochester, pp. 157, 118.

university in 1850-1851 went to unusual lengths to assure the
Baptists of New York that "tender solicitude" would be extended to young men preparing for the ministry and that "our
enterprise /is/ denominational" and "not local in...design."
The citizens of Rochester meanwhile continued to be the major
source of support for the University so long as it provided
their children with an education of superior quality in a
religious but not sectarian context.[59]

Between sessions of the 1844 Michigan Yearly Meeting of
the Free Will Baptists, a group of ministers and laymen "ardent for a proper fitting of ministers and higher intelligence of the laity," held an informal conference which led
to the founding of Hillsdale College. Official mention and
endorsement of their activities did not come until the Yearly
Meeting of 1847, when $500 was appropriated to purchase appa-
ratus for the school these men had founded in Spring Arbor.
Located in a small deserted wooden store, Michigan Central
College held its first classes in December, 1844, and received
a noncollegiate charter in 1845. Spring Arbor originally
made the successful bid for the college and provided important non-Free Will Baptist leadership in organizing and
opening the school, but by the early 1850's Michigan Central

---

[59]"Circular," Annunciator, April 4, 1850; Ibid., October
6, 1851; "Rochester Subscription," ibid., April 4, 1850;
Rosenberger, Rochester, p. 122.

had outgrown the meagre resources of this country village
and was looking for a new location.[60]

One day in January, 1853, Professor Ransom Dunn of
Michigan Central rode into Hillsdale to explore the town as
a possible site for his college. Registering at the local
hotel, he asked the names of local leaders who were most
interested in education. Soon he was introduced to a physician who assembled a few leading citizens to consult with
Dunn. At a well-attended meeting of Hillsdale residents
called that same evening, Dunn assured the people that the
college, although denominational, would not be narrowly sectarian. After hearing Dunn, the citizens voted to bid for
the Free Will Baptist school, even though none of them was a
member of that denomination. One month later, the school's
trustees found Hillsdale's bid the most attractive and offi-
cially designated the town as the new site for their college.[61]

One important source of support which Hillsdale's promoters quickly tapped was of an only partially local nature.

[60]Vivian L. Moore, The First Hundred Years of Hillsdale
College (Ann Arbor, Mich., 1944), pp. 3, 13-14; John C. Patterson, "History of Hillsdale College," Collections and Researches Made By the Michigan Pioneer and Historical Society,
VI (1883), 145; Moore, First Hundred, pp. 6, 11; Willis F.
Dunbar, The Michigan Record in Higher Education (Detroit,
1963), p. 120; Patterson, "History," p. 147; letter from E.D.
Stewart, Morning Star, July 7, 1852; Patterson, "History,"
p. 148.

[61]Ibid., pp. 148-49; Dunn, "Story," Patterson,
"History," p. 150.

Esbon Blackmar, a prosperous Episcopalian merchant in
Newark, New York, owned 1,000 acres of land adjoining the
village of Hillsdale. Soon after the meeting between Dunn
and Hillsdale residents, Blackmar's local agent, Daniel
Beebe, was sent to solicit a contribution from his employer.
Blackmar was understandably interested in the proposed college and "generously" gave twenty-five acres of his land for
the campus and subscribed $500 toward the enterprise. To
protect his investment against further removals, Blackmar
stipulated that the land always be used for educational purposes and that a majority of the trustees be residents of
Hillsdale County.[62]

At their first meeting Dunn told the people of Hillsdale that since the Free Will Baptists could not provide
both buildings and endowment, "the locality must bear one,
the denomination the other." The agreement was then reached
that in return for locating the college in Hillsdale the
citizens would raise $15,000 for buildings within the town-
ship and $15,000 more in the remainder of the county. By
September, 1854, property owners in the county had contributed $35,000, but the estimated cost of the buildings now
stood at $50,000. H.E. Whipple, agent for the college,

---

[62]History of Wayne County, New York (Philadelphia, 1877),
p. 72; Landmarks of Wayne County, New York, ed. George. W.
Coles (Syracuse, N.Y., 1895), pp. 311-12; Patterson, "History,"
p. 151; Compendium, p. 70; Moore, First Hundred, p. 23.

wrote in the Hillsdale Gazette that the trustees were de-
pending on "the generous, but, we think, far from disinter-
ested liberality of the citizens of the village and county"
to make up the difference. Meanwhile the Free Will Baptists
"from Maine to Wisconsin" would be solicited for endowment
funds.[63]

Efforts were also made to bring denominational support
a little closer to the college. A few weeks after the opening of the college at Hillsdale in November, 1855, a Free
Will Baptist Church was organized in town. Emigration of
Free Will Baptists to Hillsdale County was promoted by Whipple
in the national newspaper of the denomination. "One of our
wants," he wrote, "and one of our greatest, is a girdle of
whole hearted, devotedly pious brethren and sisters around
the college. To attempt to sustain a denominational school
isolated from the denomination is folly."[64] With a campus
and a huge college building supplied by non-Free Will Baptists, however, Hillsdale College was prospering without
much denominational support.

---

[63]Dunn, "Story"; S.W. Norton, "Hillsdale College,
Hillsdale, Michigan," Collections and Researches Made By the
Michigan Pioneer and Historical Society, XXXII (1903), 454;
"Our College," Morning Star, September 20, 1854, copied from
the Hillsdale Gazette.

[64]Windsor H. Roberts, A History of the College Baptist
Church, 1855-1955 (n.p., n.d.), p. 5; "Michigan Central Col-
lege at Hillsdale--Its Prospects and Wants," Morning Star,
April 26, 1854.

Mississippi College had its start in a meeting in early
1826 at the Mt. Salus land office attended by nine men living
near Jackson. At least one and probably most of them were
extensive land owners since at that same meeting they laid
off the town of Clinton, selected the town as site for their
academy, and put up town lots for sale. These men, who had
themselves incorporated as trustees of the Hampstead Academy
in January, 1826, had no connection with any single religious
denomination.[65]

Renamed Mississippi Academy in 1827 and rechartered as
Mississippi College in 1830, this institution received various
forms of state aid and aspired to be the state university.
When state aid was terminated in the mid-1830's and Oxford
selected as site for the state university in 1841, the trustees decided to solicit the support of one of the major religious denominations in Mississippi. In 1841 the college was
offered to the Methodists. They accepted it, but soon reversed this decision and decided to found Centenary College
at Brandon Springs. The following year the Clinton Presbytery of the Mississippi Synod agreed to back the school, and
the local board of trustees transferred control to this

---

[65]Read and Preserve (n.p., ca. 1893), pamphlet containing the opinion of D. Shelton on the proposition to remove
Mississippi College from Clinton to Meridian, Harvard University Library (EducU 5865.50), p. 1; W.H. Weathersby, "A
History of Mississippi College," Publications of the Mississippi Historical Society, V (1925), 184.

denomination by electing as their successors men nominated
by the Clinton Presbytery. By the late 1840's the Old
School-New School split in the Presbyterian ranks caused
so much trouble in financing the school that the Presbyterian trustees offered it to the state for a normal school.
The state refused the offer. The financial burden finally
became so great that the Clinton Presbytery voted in July,
1850, to sever its connection with the college. They transferred control back to the community by a new set of trustee
elections. In August the local trustees offered the college
to the Mississippi Baptist Convention. Although the Convention had decided in 1845 that the establishment of Baptist
schools "should be entrusted to local associations or private enterprises," this body voted in November, 1850, to
adopt the institution. Still another round of trustee elections finally settled the college into its permanent religious
home.[66]

VII

Unlike the large majority of pre-Civil War Baptist colleges, three institutions, Wake Forest College, Mercer

[66]A.V. Rowe, History of Mississippi College (Jackson,
Miss., 1881), p. 7; Weathersby, "History," pp. 184-94; "Education," Baptist, August 2, 1845; Weathersby, "History,"
pp. 193-194.

University, and Furman University, were directly and exclusively initiated by their respective Baptist state conventions. A fourth, the University of Richmond, was the
product of the Virginia Baptist Education Society, but the
Society had very close ties with the Virginia Baptist Convention. With the exception of Mississippi and Howard,
Baptist colleges in the South resulted from official denominational actions. Such purely denominational beginnings,
however, did not eliminate but just briefly postponed for
these institutions the problems of establishment and support encountered by other early-nineteenth-century Baptist
colleges.

Organized by some of the delegates attending the Baptist General Association of Virginia in 1830, the Virginia
Baptist Education Society soon began making regular reports
to this state convention. After two years of placing beneficiaries with two established ministers, the Society felt
the number of ministerial candidates desiring instruction
merited establishing a school with full-time teachers. First
classes in the Virginia Baptist Seminary were held in July,
1832. A collegiate charter was granted to the institution
in March, 1840, and soon afterward the school's property was
transferred from the Education Society to the newly elected
trustees of the college. Too little information is available
to determine the nature of the relationship between the

University of Richmond and the city of Richmond, but one
step the Education Society was forced to take soon after
the school opened was to offer classical instruction to nonministerial students. The number of ministerial students,
although too large for apprenticeship training with the few
well-educated Baptist ministers, was not sufficient and self-
supporting enough to meet operating expenses. In promoting
ministerial education, the convention soon needed help from
the community in the form of tuition-paying nonministerial
students.[67]

The origins of Wake Forest College can be traced to the
desire on the part of Samuel Wait and a few other ministers
to improve the quality of the Baptist ministry in North
Carolina. Since Wait and his friends were also the founders
of the North Carolina Baptist State Convention in 1830, ministerial education immediately became one of the chief interests of the Convention. Assured that the institution "would
probably from the beginning support itself without being any
expense to the Convention," the Convention in 1832 authorized
the founding of a school to train ministers and one year

[67]F.W. Boatwright, "The Beginnings of Higher Education
Among Virginia Baptists," Religious Herald, August 13,
1931, Virginia Baptist Education Society (n.p., 1833), p. 3;
R.E. Gaines, "The Beginnings: The Seminary, the College,
1832-1866," The First Hundred Years: Brief Sketches of the
History of the University of Richmond (Richmond, Va., 1932),
pp. 20, 25; Garnett Ryland, The Baptists of Virginia, 1699-
1926 (Richmond, Va., 1955), p. 269; Virginia Baptist Education Society, p. 4.

later appointed a board of trustees to supervise the school.
The trustees made annual reports to the Convention. An independent North Carolina Baptist Education Society was not
organized until 1844.[68]

As in the case of Richmond, accommodations to the hard
facts of supporting a school soon became necessary. Original plans for merely providing "a plain English education"
for ministerial students were enlarged by 1834 to include
classical instruction and "to admit, as students, any young
gentlemen of good character, whether professors of religion
or not." There was also need for a sympathetic local community. Although located within fifteen miles of Raleigh and
in the center of North Carolina's Baptist population, the
school's site was an old plantation, "far removed from the
distracting influences of Towns and Villages." What was to
become the town of Wake Forest was little more than a post
office in Wake County operated by a local landowner. Indi-
cating that little local support for the school could be
generated even on the county level, Wait wrote, in regard
to problems of constructing facilities for the school, that

[68]Samuel Wait, "The Origin and Early History of Wake
Forest College," Wake Forest Student, II (October 1882),
49; George W. Paschal, History of Wake Forest College, 1
(Wake Forest, N.C., 1935), 29; North Carolina Baptist Convention, Minutes, 1832, p. 16; Paschal, History, I, 45,
306.

"the Baptists in Wake, with a few, and a very few honorable exceptions, are fast asleep."[69]

The advent of the Raleigh and Gaston Railroad, which ran within a few hundred yards of the college buildings, and the financial pressures of the panic of 1837 led Wait and his small band of supporters to promote a town at Wake Forest. The trustees in 1838 appointed a committee "to enquire into the expediency of laying off a town." Sale of college lands at Wake Forest was announced early the following year "with a view to erecting a village, on the grounds now belonging to the institution." By the mid-1840's most of the 615-acre plantation purchased as the college site in 1832 was sold, yet most of the purchases were probably made by faculty members and a few Baptists in the vicinity. Wake Forest did not become a station on the Raleigh and Gaston until 1874 and prior to the Civil War this "country village" had scarcely a dozen dwellings independent of the college. As a college without a town, Wake Forest College had to limit itself to the cultivation of almost exclusively denominational support.[70]

---

[69]Wait, "Origin," p. 49; Paschal, History, I, 45, 47; "Wake F. Institute. No. 2," Biblical Recorder, January 27, 1838; Wake Forest College, Catalogue, 1836, p. 3; Paschal, History, I, 48-52; Samuel Wait to John Armstrong, March 4, 1834, Wait Correspondence.

[70]"Wake F. Institute. No. 3," Biblical Recorder, February 3, 1838; Paschal, History, I, 115; J.H. Gorrell, "A Short Story of Wake Forest, Town and College," Wake Forest Student, XXXIX (January 1920), 165; advertisement in Biblical Recorder and Southern Watchman, January 5, 1839; Paschal, History, I, 190-93, 197-98, 52, 455.

In June, 1838, President Billington M. Sanders of
Mercer University in Georgia informed Wake Forest's President, Samuel Wait, that "we have determined to build up a
village to give stability to our institution." This quest
for the support of a college town is highly interesting in
light of the fact that Mercer was not only the most purely
denominational but also the wealthiest of the early-nineteenth-
century Baptist colleges. The roots of Mercer stretched back
through various educational efforts by Georgia Baptists in
the 1820's to at least the short-lived Mt. Enon Academy
founded in 1807. As with the founding of Georgetown, however, the immediate impetus for founding a school came from
the bequest of a wealthy Baptist layman. Josiah Penfield,
a Savannah jeweler well-acquainted with the educational efforts of the Georgia Baptist Convention, bequeathed $2,500
in 1829 as a permanent fund for Baptist education. Unlike
Georgetown's patron, however, Penfield left his money to the
Convention rather than college trustees and stipulated that
the Convention match his sum. This was promptly accomplished
and foundations of Mercer's munificent pre-Civil War endowment fund were laid. The Convention in 1831 voted to raise
still more money and to found a classical and theological
school. This school opened in January, 1833, and remained
under the direct supervision of the Executive Committee of
the Convention until 1838, when a separate board of trustees

was appointed. These trustees were elected triennially by
the Convention and reported annually to the parent organization. Despite firm convention support and an endowment
fund only one year away from topping $100,000, however,
Sanders and his trustees sought the supporting influences
of a college town.[71]

Having acquired considerable land near the site of its
school, the Convention had the town of Penfield laid out in
October, 1837, and soon realized over $10,000 through the
sale of lots. The college and a projected female seminary
were stressed as the chief advantages of residence in Penfield. One advertisement reasoned that "parents, by removing
to this spot, will have an opportunity of completing the education both of their sons and daughters. These advantages
will no doubt soon build up the town." Settlers, most of
them Baptists, soon began moving in. By 1839 there was a
sufficient number to merit some revealing advice from re-
tiring President Sanders. Having helped build both the college and the town, Sanders, in his valedictory address,

[71]B.M. Sanders to Samuel Wait, June 13, 1838, Wait Correspondence; Christian Index, History of the Baptist Denomination in Georgia: With Biographical Compendium and Portrait
Gallery of Baptist Ministers and Other Georgia Baptists (At-
lanta, 1881), pp. 139, 136, 138; B.D. Ragsdale, Story of
Georgia Baptists, I (Atlanta, 1932), 5-7;   Spright Dowell,
A History of Mercer University, 1833-1953 (Macon, Ga., 1958),
p. 40; Ragsdale, Story, I, 13; Christian Index, History,
p. 143; Georgia Baptist Convention, Minutes, 1831, p. 5;
Dowell, History, p. 42; Ragsdale, Story, I, 25; Christian
Index, History, pp. 151-52; Georgia Baptist Convention,
Minutes, 1839, pp. 7-8.

frankly acknowledged the relationship between the two in
a "word of counsel" to the citizens of Penfield: "Your
interests my friends, are intimately connected with the
interests of this Institution. Upon its success depends
the prosperity of your village in every branch of business,
as well as the education of your children. Let your un-
divided support be therefore given to it."[72]

In South Carolina, as in North Carolina, the founders
of the state convention had a Baptist school as one of their
major objectives. Building on a tradition of ministerial
education reaching back in the Charleston Association to the
mid-18th century, the South Carolina Baptist Convention at
its meeting in 1825 selected Edgefield as the site for a
permanent school. Furman Academy and Theological Institution
began instruction in January, 1827. The Convention drew up
the rules for this school, which lasted less than two years
in Edgefield. The school was subsequently operated at the
High Hills of Santee, from 1829 through 1834, suspended
during 1835-1836, and resumed at Winnsboro from 1837-1850

---

[72]Jesse H. Campbell, Georgia Baptists: Historical and
Biographical (Macon, Ga., 1874), p. 353; Adiel Sherwood, A
Gazetteer of the State of Georgia (Washington, D.C., 1837),
p. 347; "Mercer University," Christian Index, February 11,
1847; B.M. Sanders, Valedictory Address, Delivered Before
the Trustees, Faculty, Students, and Friends of the Mercer
University, Greene County, Ga. Dec. 12, 1839 (Washington,
Ga., 1840), p. 15.

under a board of trustees appointed by the Convention.[73]

During most of its weak and migratory existence prior
to 1850, Furman University functioned exclusively as a theological seminary. By 1849 sentiment was building among its
small body of supporters for a more broadly conceived and
better-located school. Thomas P. Lide voiced the sentiments
of several trustees in writing to Board President William B.
Johnson that the North Carolina Baptists were "not yet prepared to sustain" a "purely Theological Institution." Lide
could see "no practicable expedient to keep the Institution
alive, and to render it popular, with our own people, but to
afford facilities for the classical education of the sons of
Baptists and make it, by the revenue which will thus accrue,
to some extent, a self-sustaining establishment." Johnson
agreed with this strategy, and advocated removing the school
from its rural site three miles southwest of Winnsboro to a
town or city of substantial size, such as Columbia or Charleston. With Convention approval, both plans were implemented.
Nonministerial students were admitted in 1850 and that same
year the Convention selected Greenville as the new site for
the school. By 1853 all property held by the Convention for

---

[73]William J. McGlothlin, Baptist Beginnings in Education:
A History of Furman University (Nashville, Tenn., 1926),
pp. 26-98.

its predecessors was transferred to the trustees of Furman
University, incorporated in December, 1850.[74]

Although Furman had received financial inducements from
two out of its three previous sites, none of them could approach the amount of potential support residing in Greenville. Assessing the advantages of this site in 1851,
James C. Furman found its streams not only beautiful and
healthful, but also able to "afford the impelling power for
machinery enough to occupy thousands upon thousands of human
beings." Another resource of Greenville was wealthy and
willing non-Baptist patrons of religion and education such
as Vardry McBee. A merchant and farmer who at one time owned
most of the land comprising Greenville, McBee sold rather
than donated the campus of Furman to the trustees, but he
made a subscription to the college equal to over one-quarter
of the purchase price of the land. In a style reminiscent
of Maine's Timothy Boutelle, McBee contributed land for the
first five churches in the city and the male and female academies. About the same time he was helping to attract Furman to Greenville, McBee was financing much of the Greenville and Columbus Railroad, which was completed in 1853.

[74]Ibid., pp. 65, 67, 83-86; Thomas P. Lide to William
B. Johnson, October 19, 1849, William B. Johnson to J.S.
Mims, October 8, 1849, William B. Johnson Correspondence
South Carolina Baptist Historical Collection, Furman Uni-
versity Library; "To the Baptists in South Carolina,"
Southern Baptist, April 24, 1850; McGlothlin, Baptist Be-
ginnings, pp. 101, 105-106.

Leading the school named for his father out of the valleys
of almost nonexistent local support and into contact with
the great advantages of Greenville, James C. Furman was perhaps entitled to designate this new site as "the promised
land."[75]

Rather than resulting from an organized movement within
the denomination, early-nineteenth-century Baptist colleges
were primarily the products of local forces and circumstances.
Even when a state convention was the founder, as in the cases
of Wake Forest, Mercer, and Furman, local ties were sought
out and became important in the establishment of a viable
educational enterprise. With Bucknell, Rochester, and Mississippi, it was the community which took the initiative and
then went seeking denominational support for their planned
or existing school. The most common agency in Baptist college-founding was an individual minister or a small group of

[75]Ibid., p. 59; "For the Southern Baptist," Southern
Baptist and General Intelligencer, July 29, 1836; James C.
Furman, An Historical Discourse, Delivered Before the
Charleston Baptist Association, At Its Hundredth Anniver-
sary, Held in Charleston in November, 1851 (Charleston,
S.C., 1852), pp. 20-21; Laura S. Ebaugh, "A Social History,"
The Arts in Greenville, 1800-1960, ed. Alfred S. Reid (Green-
ville, S.C., 1960), p. 10; Marion M. Hewell, "Vardry McBee
of South Carolina," Proceedings and Papers of the Greenville
County Historical Society, 1962-1964 (Greenville, S.C.,
1965), pp. 41, 39; McGlothlin, Baptist Beginnings, p. 104;
Hewell, "Vardry McBee," pp. 46-47; Ebaugh, "Social History,"
p. 10; Hewell, "Vardry McBee," p. 46; Furman, Historical
Discourse, p. 20.

Baptists including both laymen and ministers and often with important assistance from non-Baptist citizens. Maneuvering skillfully between community and denomination, these men were able to tap both sources in establishing their schools.

The most important single element in this strategy of Baptist college-founding was the relationship between college and community. With the exception of two of the three most urban schools, George Washington and Richmond, a bargain was struck between the institution and the town or county. Usually this agreement involved the location of the school and ranged in formality from the "solemn compact" between Hamilton, New York, and the New York Baptist Education Society, to the verbal understanding between Bucknell and the citizens of Lewisburg, Pennsylvania, and vicinity who contributed to it. Financially the terms of these contracts ranged from the less than $2,000 bid by Franklin, Indiana, to the $100,000 offered by Rochester, New York, little more than a decade later.

Whereas communities supplied the small groups of educational promoters with substantial assistance in founding Baptist colleges, the official organizations of the denomination were able to give little more than their sanction and verbal encouragement. Even in the few cases where the conventions were founders of the colleges, these organizations represented only a small portion of the Baptists in their respective states. Thus once the colleges were under way, their promoters faced the twofold task of sustaining and enlarging local support while attempting to create a demand for ministerial and collegiate education within their own denomination.

CHAPTER II

DENOMINATION

When the handful of Baptist educational leaders turned
to their denomination at large for assistance in sustaining
colleges founded by small groups of ministers and citizens,
the prospects were far from encouraging. Although the denomination was numerically large, it was widely scattered
and adhered to a decentralized church polity. Important
minority groups within the denomination held conflicting
theological views, and most Baptists showed little interest
in either theology or the preparation of ministers to properly
expound it. Through the denominational press, traveling
agencies, pulpit, and platform, Baptist educators promoted
their institutions in the face of widespread apathy and occasional hostility. As educational persuaders, these men
constructed an elaborate rationale for increased knowledge
within Baptist ranks, allied themselves with contemporary
evangelical currents, and employed a variety of institutional
strategies in attempting to upgrade their denomination. Their
attempts to create both a demand for and supply of educated
Baptist ministers met with only limited success.

79

I

In 1812, when the founders of Colby College first peti-
tioned the Massachusetts General Court for a collegiate
charter, the Baptist denomination was the largest single religious group in the United States. Baptists had been first
in size since the turn of the century, and it was not until
around 1820 that their total membership was surpassed by that
of the Methodists. Statistics collected by Baptist historian
David Benedict place total Baptist membership in 1812 at
204,185, gathered in 2,633 churches with 2,142 ordained ministers. Prior to the Great Awakening there were only about
60 Baptist churches in the colonies, but by 1776 the number
of Baptist churches had increased almost tenfold and membership totaled about 10,000. Baptist support for the Revolutionary cause, a strong stand on the issue of religious
liberty, and a form of piety and polity attractive to converts of the Second Great Awakening stimulated still more
rapid membership growth during the three decades following
the War. Even with membership limited to baptized adult be-
lievers, the denomination comprised about 2.5 per cent of
the total population of the United States in 1812. Inclusion
of those who were Baptists in sentiment and attendants at
their worship services although not official members of the

denomination would at least double this percentage.[1]

From 1814 through 1844 Baptist membership increased 360 per cent while the United States population increased 140 per cent. By 1860 there were more than 1,000,000 Baptists, about 3.5 per cent of the population. Nonchurch members who supported Baptist worship would probably raise the figure close to 10 per cent. Much of this growth occurred along the southern and western frontiers. Yet in 1852 as in 1812, Virginia and New York were among the three states with the most Baptists. By 1812 over one-third of the denomination resided in Virginia, the Carolinas, and Georgia. About one-fourth of the Baptists could be found in New York and the New England States. Most of the remainder was located in Kentucky and Tennessee. While growth throughout the early nineteenth century was greatest in the South, the denomination continued to be dispersed in significant numbers throughout the country.[2]

---

[1]Edwin S. Gausted, Historical Atlas of Religion in America (New York, 1962), p. 52; David Benedict, A General History of the Baptist Denomination in America and Other Parts of the World (Boston, 1813), II, 553; Robert G. Torbet, A History of the Baptists (New rev. ed.; Valley Forge, Pa., 1963), p. 243; Jesse L. Boyd, A History of Baptists in America Prior to 1845 (New York, 1957), p. 189; Torbet, History, pp. 243-44; Robert B. Semple, "Address," Latter Day Luminary, 11 (May 1820), 114.

[2]Torbet, History, p. 253; Gausted, Historical Atlas, p. 52; American Baptist Register for 1852, ed. J. Lansing Burrows (Philadelphia, 1853), p. 407.

Little in the way of national church organization
united this widely-scattered denomination. Baptist churches
in America by 1812 had formed 111 local associations, but
movement toward any more centralized forms of church government up to that time had been slow and uncertain. In England
the General Baptists organized a General Assembly in 1660,
and Particular Baptists first held a national meeting in 1689.
Four General Baptist churches in Rhode Island formed the
first American Baptist association in 1670. Next came the
Philadelphia Association, organized in 1707 by five churches.
In the last half of the eighteenth century many more associations were organized from Charleston, South Carolina (1751),
to Bowdoinham, Maine (1787). Despite this proliferation of
regional organizations a national Baptist association, called
for as early as 1770, was never fully realized.[3]

In some respects the Philadelphia Association functioned
as a national Baptist organization during much of the eighteenth century. By 1760 its affiliates included churches from
Connecticut to Virginia. The Association's Confession of
Faith was widely influential and its missionaries operated
along most of the Atlantic coast. By midcentury the Association was exercising considerable influence upon its member

[3]Benedict, General History, p. 553; Torbet, History,
pp. 45, 68; Winthrop S. Hudson, "By Way of Perspective,"
Baptist Concepts of the Church, ed. Winthrop S. Hudson
(Philadelphia, 1957), pp. 18, 20; Torbet, History, p. 233.

churches in the areas of faith and practice, ministerial certification and supply, and missionary support.[4]

Yet the very principle of associational organization upon which the limited national efforts of the Philadelphia Association were based was soon subjected to challenges both within and outside the Association's boundaries. Some churches of the Middle Atlantic Colonies demonstrated their opposition by withholding financial support from the Association. A much greater threat to Baptist connectionalism developed among the Separate Baptist churches organized in New England in the wake of the Great Awakening and soon spreading into the South. Holding an essentially "atomistic doctrine of the church" which stressed the independence of the local church, Separates were highly suspicious of any attempts at regional or national organization.[5]

During the first few decades of the Separatist movement, its leaders generally supported the Philadelphia pattern of church organization, but the Separatist influence

---

[4]Winthrop S. Hudson, "The Associational Principle Among Baptists," Foundations, I (January 1958), 23; Winthrop S. Hudson, "Stumbling into Disorder," ibid. (April 1958), 45; Robert T. Handy, "The Philadelphia Tradition," Baptist Concepts, pp. 50-51, 31; Hudson, "By Way of Perspective," p. 20; Hudson, "Associational Principle," pp. 15-17.

[5]Torbet, History, p. 214; C.C. Goen, Revivalism and Separatism in New England, 1740-1800 (New Haven, Conn., 1962), pp. 258, 290, 298-99; Robert G. Torbet, "Bases of Baptist Convention Membership: An Historical Survey," Foundations, VI (January 1963), 27.

on Baptist polity was ultimately a divisive rather than centralizing one. Isaac Backus, finding the Connecticut establishment too presbyterianized, sought genuine congregationalism within the Baptist ranks in the early 1750's. Less than two decades later, however, Backus's church and seven others of the Separatist variety were persuaded by Philadelphia-oriented promoters to form the nucleus of the Warren Association. This seemingly radical shift in sentiment did not herald a permanent victory for greater Baptist connectionalism. Backus and his fellow Separates joined the Association primarily for reasons of expediency; they saw the organization as a useful device to promote greater religious freedom for their dissenting churches. They joined only after the Association's powers were carefully delimited. After the Revolution, when the Association was no longer needed in the service of religious liberty, the New England Separates generally reverted to their original advocacy of local church autonomy. In the South, John Leland did not speak out against the formation of Virginia Baptist associations in the 1780's but soon afterward became a strong opponent of national Baptist organizations. He was too much of a Jeffersonian and Separatist to endorse any potentially oppressive national organization. Shubael Stearns, another New England Separate who went South, supported the Philadelphia tradition but with little success.

The Southern Separates he gathered into the Sandy Creek
Association (1758) soon found the organization assuming too
much centralized power. Two major groups split off from the
Association little more than a decade after it was established, and those who remained soon restored the independence
of each member church.[6]

Challenged in both the North and the South by Separate
Baptists during the closing decades of the eighteenth century, the Philadelphia tradition of church government soon
encountered competition from an auxilliary method of Baptist
organization. In 1802, with the founding of the Massachusetts Domestic Missionary Society, the era of the voluntary
society dawned among Baptists. Plans to bring associations
of churches together in state conventions and then have these
conventions represented in a national convention were thus
confronted with an initially unrecognized but ultimately
conquering rival. Unlike the association, the society was
a single-purpose organization and was based not on the churches
but on interested, contributing individuals. During the
decade following 1802 about sixty new associations were
founded, but the number of societies organized during roughly

[6]Edwin S. Gausted, "The Backus-Leland Tradition," Bap-
tist Concepts, pp. 122, 107; Goen, Revivalism, pp. 279, 290;
Gausted, "Backus-Leland Tradition," p. 125; Goen, Revivalism,
p. 299, n. 9; George W. Paschal, History of North Carolina
Baptists, I (Raleigh, N.C., 1930), 404-06; cf. William L.
Lumpkin, Baptist Foundations in the South; Tracing Through
the Separates the Influence of the Great Awakening, 1754-1787
(Nashville, Tenn., 1961), pp. 159-61.

the same period in the region north of Philadelphia alone equaled this number.[7] By 1812 the continued predominance of the Philadelphia concept of church polity was far from assured.

After the Triennial Convention of 1826, the society method became the predominant type of Baptist organization. Many new associations and a dozen state conventions were organized in the decade prior to this turning point in Baptist history. Associations and state conventions continued to come into existence throughout the remainder of the antebellum period. Yet the major denominational activities were financed and controlled by societies. With voting privileges based on contributions, the society method proved to be an effective means of raising funds. Despite this advantage, however, and although there was a considerable overlapping of members and officers, Baptist societies tended to divide the denomination into competing interest groups.

Even the Baptist Triennial Convention was founded in 1814 as a national foreign mission society rather than a representative denominational assembly. Membership consisted of delegates from churches, associations, societies,

---

[7]Robert A. Baker, Relations Between Northern and Southern Baptists (Fort Worth, Texas, 1948), p. 11; Handy, "Philadelphia Tradition," p. 52; Hudson, "Stumbling," p. 46; Torbet, History, p. 232; Benedict, General History, II, 553; Robert A. Baker, "Organizational Differences Between Northern and Southern Baptists in the Nineteenth Century," Chronicle, XV (April 1952), 70.

87

and any other Baptist bodies which contributed at least $100
annually to the Convention. The first $100 enfranchised two
delegates and, after amendment of the constitution in 1820,
each additional $200 conferred the right to send one more
voting representative. At its first meeting President
Richard Furman envisioned an expansion of the Convention's
functions to include home missions and especially ministerial education. In 1817 the constitution was amended to
permit this expansion, and in 1820 the official name of the
Convention was lengthened so as to include, in addition to
foreign missions, "other important objects relating to the
Redeemer's kingdom." The basis of membership, however, did
not change, and after 1826 the Convention reverted to its
original role as a society existing for the sole purpose of
promoting missions abroad and among American Indians. Publications, education, and home missions were left to other
societies.[8]

Defeat of the eighteenth-century-based movement toward
a representative and multipurpose national Baptist convention

<hr>

[8] Proceedings of the Baptist Convention For Missionary
Purposes; Held in Philadelphia, in May, 1814 (Philadelphia,
1814), p. 3; "Proceedings of the General Convention at Their
Second Triennial Meeting and the Sixth Annual Report of the
Board," Latter Day Luminary II (May 1820), 123; Proceedings...
1814, p. 42; Proceedings of the General Convention...May, 1817
...(Philadelphia, 1817), pp. 131-32; "Proceedings...Second
Triennial," p. 123; Proceedings of the Fifth Triennial Meet-
ing of the Baptist General Convention, Held in New York,
April, 1826 (Boston, 1826), pp. 7, 20.

freed the society-minded Baptists to develop a new tradition
of church organization more in tune with the individualism,
voluntaryism, and provincialism of early-nineteenth-century
America. The man who both led the movement to "dismember"
the Triennial Convention in 1826 and publicized the new
rationale for decentralization two decades later was Francis
Wayland. More a man of his times than a lineal descendant
of the Separatist tradition of Isaac Backus and John Leland,
Wayland not only confirmed the course of Baptist history
since the turn of the century but rewrote Baptist history
prior to that date. In complete disregard of the Philadelphia tradition, Wayland began arguing in 1846 that the autonomy of the local church would be compromised by membership
in anything more co-operative than a voluntary society and
that this radical notion of church autonomy was a historic
Baptist principle.[9]

---

[9]Hudson, "Stumbling," pp. 55-58, 60-71; Norman H. Maring,
"The Individualism of Francis Wayland," Baptist Concepts,
pp. 146-57, 167-69. Wayland's role as the villain of the
piece seems to be somewhat exaggerated by these Baptist historians, who find his influence to have "tragic effects,"
especially in the light of present-day ecumenical sentiments. Maring finds that Wayland thwarted "normal denominational development in 1826" with "pietistic," "irrational,"
"illogical," and "naive" views on church order. Hudson identifies Wayland as the man most responsible for the "strange
turn of events" which prevented the movement toward a representative national convention from proceeding to its logical
conclusion. It appears that these historians hold unreason-
ably high expectations for the survival of an already-
challenged, eighteenth-century tradition in the peculiar
environment of the nineteenth century.

Baptist educational leaders in 1812 stood at the beginning of the era of decentralized Baptist polity advocated by Wayland. If they happened to be promoters of the three institutions founded between 1812 and 1826, they probably were acutely conscious of the challenges to closer Baptist organization. For those founding colleges after 1826, Baptist localism and the society method were hard facts. These hard facts were dramatized by omission in the widely adopted New Hampshire Confession of Faith (1833) of any references to the Church Universal or any church order beyond the local unit. Even the Southern Baptist Convention, formed in 1845, adopted the society criterion for membership and limited itself for many years to missionary work. While Old Landmarkism in the 1850's initially retarded the movement toward greater centralization in the South,[10] Francis Wayland in the North emphasized how little even voluntary societies could be considered denominational:

> In point of numbers, the members of our Societies, meeting at any one time, are a very inconsiderable fragment of the denomination. Or take the whole membership of these Societies together--and they are, in fact, generally the same persons over again--and they would amount not to a twentieth, probably not to a fiftieth of our whole number. But

---

[10]Hudson, "By Way of Perspective," p. 27; William W. Barnes, The Southern Baptist Convention, 1845-1953 (Nashville, Tenn., 1954), pp. 33-34, cf. Baker, "Organizational," p. 71; Barnes, Southern Baptist Convention, pp. 103-13; Baker, "Organizational," p. 150.

whether many or few, they come not as representatives of churches, for the churches have never sent them or commissioned them...and /they/ have no more right...to act <u>for the denomination</u>, than they would have if by chance they happened, each one in the pursuit of his own business, to meet at the central terminus of several railroads. They are members of these societies, and nothing more, and directly, or indirectly, to assume to be anything else, is by just so much to violate the principle of the independence of the churches.[11]

Lacking a unified denomination structure through which to promote and sustain their institutions, Baptist educational leaders also were handicapped by the absence of a common theological tradition for Baptist higher education to perpetuate. In theological as well as organizational terms it was difficult to rally support for an educational institution on the grounds that it would serve as an agency for the whole denomination. Although the theology of most Baptists in 1812 was a moderate Calvinism, a look both backward and forward from that date in Baptist history reveals this to be only a brief interlude in a long tradition of theological diversity.

British Baptist ministers in London in 1731 included seven antinomians or hyper-Calvinists, seven Calvinists,

[11]Francis Wayland, <u>Notes on the Principles and Practices of Baptist Churches</u> (New York, 1857), pp. 188-89.

six Arminians, three Unitarians, and two of Seventh-Day
persuasion. Both the Calvinist and the Arminian traditions were transported to the colonies, where the former,
as embodied in the Philadelphia Association, generally
prevailed throughout the eighteenth century. Arminianism
persisted, however, especially in New England, and found
new strength in the Free Will Baptist movement begun in
the 1780's.[12]

A third strand of Baptist theology was produced by
the Great Awakening, which split the denomination into
Regulars and Separates. Too evangelical for the Calvinistic Regulars and too Calvinistic for the Arminians, the
Separates were eventually to draw most of both camps onto
their middle ground of evangelical Calvinism. Their re-
vivalistic emphasis was a particularly effective healing
force in the South and on the early frontier. By the turn
of the century revivalism had effaced earlier distinctions
between Regular and Separate Baptists and the two groups
in these regions united on the basis of a compromise between their theological views and a common concern for
evangelizing the frontier.[13]

---

[12]Torbet, History, p. 63; Handy, "Philadelphia Tradition," pp. 30, 52; Torbet, History, pp. 213, 231, 256-57.

[13]Ibid., p. 223; James D. Mosteller, "The Separate Bap-
tists in the South," Chronicle, XVII (July 1954), 148; Goen,
Revivalism, pp. 275, 285; Torbet, History, pp. 220, 225;
William W. Sweet, Religion on the American Frontier, 1, The
Baptists, 1783-1830 (New York, 1931), pp. 23, 27.

The resulting mild form of Calvinism prevalent in 1812 was soon shattered by a resurgence of both Arminianism and antinomianism. Benjamin Randall organized the first Free Will Baptist church in 1780, and by 1812 the total membership, most of it located in New England, numbered about 4,000. Membership more than doubled during each of the next two decades, however, and after 1830 a period of even more rapid growth brought the total to over 60,000 by 1844. Free Will Baptists at this point comprised about ten per cent of the total Baptists in the United States, and their churches stretched across the Northern states from Maine to Illinois.[14]

Anti-mission sentiments were expressed within the Baptist ranks as early as 1818 and were articulated in pamphlet form the following year with the publication of John Taylor's Thoughts on Missions. In 1826 Daniel Parker set forth his Two-Seed-in-the-Spirit version of predestination and by the end of the decade anti-mission Baptists were multiplying in frontier states such as Kentucky and Tennessee and in the South. Although attitudes toward the urban and urbane east, a suspicion of all organizations, and economic factors

---

[14]Ibid., pp. 44-45; Torbet, History, p. 267; Norman A. Baxter, History of the Freewill Baptists: A Study in New England Separatism (Rochester, N.Y., 1957), pp. 23-25, 31; The Centennial Record of Freewill Baptists: 1780-1880 (Dover, N.H., 1881), p. 239; Free Will Baptist Register for 1844 (Dover, N.H., 1844), p. 69.

entered into the movement, at its roots was a sincerely
held hyper-Calvinism that split a great many associations,
churches, and even families. Resulting from these divisions
by the mid-1840's was a group of close to 70,000. This was
more than ten per cent of the denomination.[15]

Alexander Campbell, an Arminian opponent of the missionary movement, was baptized by immersion in 1812. His
Brush Run Baptist Church joined the Redstone Baptist Association in Western Pennsylvania the following year. As their
opposition to missions and other "unscriptural" practices
within the denomination were increasingly pressed by Campbell and his Reformers, their churches were excluded from
Baptist associations. This process began as early as 1825,
and the final break occurred in the years 1830-1832. Campbell's movement inherited over 10,000 members from Barton
Stone's Christian movement when the two groups merged in
1832, but the majority of the resulting Disciples of Christ
were drawn from Baptist ranks. The number of members which
Campbell led out of the Baptist denomination in 1832 has

---

[15]Ira D. Hudgins, "The Anti-missionary Controversy
Among Baptists," Chronicle, XIV (October 1951), 155; B.H.
Carroll, Jr., The Genesis of American Anti-Missionism
(Louisville, Ky., 1902), p. 88; Sweet, Religion, p. 69;
Hudgins, "Anti-missionary Controversy," p. 152; Byron C.
Lambert, "The Rise of the Anti-Mission Baptists: Sources
and Leaders, 1800-1840," unpublished Ph.D. dissertation,
University of Chicago, 1957, p. 412; Hudgins, "Anti-mis-
sionary Controversy," p. 156; Lambert, "Rise," pp. xi, 402-
403; Almanac and Baptist Register, 1846 (Philadelphia, 1846),
p. 25.

been estimated at 20,000 - 30,000. Even from outside the
denomination, Campbell and his Disciples, numbering over
300,000 by 1860, continued to engage in theological competition with the Baptists.[16]

In the era of theological conflict and splintering
characterized by the Free Will, anti-mission and Campbell-
ite movements, Baptist educational leaders also had to contend with theological indifference. Single-minded concern
with evangelism which permeated much of the denomination
bred a general disinterest in theology. Revivals brought
into the denomination great numbers who had little acquaint-
ance with and little concern for the details of Baptist theology. The few Baptists who were interested in perpetuating
the intellectual aspects of Baptist tradition could be recruited to form education societies, the first of which was
founded in Philadelphia in 1812.[17] But these societies and
the educational leaders who formed them were a tiny minority
with very dim prospects of exciting unified denominational
action or sympathy for their cause.

---

[16]Carroll, Genesis, p. 95; Winfred E. Garrison and Alfred
T. DeGroot, The Disciples of Christ: A History (St. Louis,
1948), pp. 160-62, 193, 115, 212; Errett Gates, The Early Relation and Separation of Baptists and Disciples (Chicago,
1904), p. 100; Walter W. Jennings, Origin and Early History
of the Disciples of Christ (Cincinnati, 1919), p. 190; Gausted,
Historical Atlas, p. 52.

[17]Hudson, "By Way of Perspective," p. 28; Maring, "Individualism," pp. 135-36; Torbet, History, p. 309.

Baptists in 1812 were not totally lacking an educational tradition. Bristol Baptist College was founded in England in 1720 by Particular Baptists. Just two years later the Philadelphia Association requested that its churches nominate prospective ministers who might benefit from an academy education paid for out of a fund set up by Thomas Hollis, a British merchant. In 1756 the Association helped establish a Baptist academy at Hopewell, New Jersey. Six years later, when the Baptists in the colonies numbered only about 5,000, the Association entertained a proposal to found a Baptist college. This idea was realized in 1765 when the charter granted by the Rhode Island Legislature the previous year to Brown University was signed into law. At the suggestion of President James Manning of Brown, the General Committee of Virginia Baptists appointed a committee in 1788 "to forward the business respecting a seminary of learning" for their state.[18]

Hopewell Academy lasted only eleven years. Plans for a Virginia seminary were abandoned in 1793 and not revived

---

[18]William Cathcart, Baptist Encyclopaedia (Rev.ed.; Philadelphia, 1883), p. 377; Robert G. Torbet, A Social History of the Philadelphia Baptist Association, 1707-1940 (Philadelphia, 1944), pp. 67-68; Reuben A. Guild, Early History of Brown University, Including the Life, Times, and Correspondence of President Manning, 1756-1791 (Providence, R.I., 1897), pp. 18-20, cf. Walter C. Bronson, The History of Brown University, 1764-1914 (Providence, R.I., 1914), p. 8; Ibid., p. 9; Robert B. Semple, A History of the Rise and Progress of the Baptists in Virginia, revised and extended by G.W. Beale (Richmond, Va., 1894), p. 104.

until almost forty years later. Even Brown, by 1818, had
many Baptists worried. In addition to being charged with
having "long been a nursery for Congregationalists rather
than Baptists," the University had a president suspected of
Unitarian leanings. And since the school's charter limited
the curriculum to nonsectarian studies, theological training,
for the few Baptists who sought it, still had to be obtained
by the tutorial method.[19]

One reason why theological education was sought by only
a few was that too much learning proved to be a liability
rather than an asset for many early-nineteenth-century Baptist ministers. In churches of the Lower Mississippi Valley,
anything more than the most rudimentary vocabulary inhibited
communication between a pastor and his congregation. Lack
of education did not disturb most Baptists or their preachers
because they deemed personal piety, feeling a call to the
ministry, and the leading of the Spirit in preaching as
sufficient for an effective pulpit performance. The President of the Board of Trustees of Georgetown College advised
a young ministerial aspirant in 1830 not to attend the new

[19]Dean Ashton, "Isaac Eaton, Neglected Baptist Educator," Chronicle, XX (April 1957), 68; Semple, History,
p. 106; William Staughton to Peter P. Roots, April 16, 1818,
quoted in Howard D. Williams, "The History of Colgate University to 1869," unpublished Ph.D. dissertation, Harvard
University, 1949, p. 15; Bronson, History, pp. 186-88;
Irah Chase, "The Theological Institution," Baptist Memorial
and Monthly Chronicle, I (April 1842), 102.

97

institution. His "principal argument was that Jeremiah
Vardeman, without a collegiate education, had been one of
the most useful preachers in the State."[20]

Attempts to build on the fragile Baptist educational
tradition were impeded not only by disinterest in educated
ministers but also by the fact that access to the ministry
was controlled on the local level, where this attitude was
strongest. Each Baptist church had the power to license
and ordain ministers according to its own standards. Intellectual standards were usually almost nonexistent, and
little care was taken in applying any criteria at all.
Feeling the call and an adequate trial sermon before a local
congregation were all that was usually needed to obtain a
license to preach.[21] With a constant shortage of full-time
ministers and few churches able or willing to offer an adequate salary, the standards for ordination were probably
equally low.

[20]Walter B. Posey, The Baptist Church in the Lower Mississippi Valley, 1776-1845 (Lexington, Ky., 1957), pp. 21-22;
Torbet, History, p. 305; James M. Pendleton, "The Condition
of the Baptist Cause in Kentucky in 1837," Memorial Volume...
of the General Association of Baptists in Kentucky (Louisville, Ky., 1888), p. 8.

[21]Posey, Baptist Church, pp. 22-23.

II

The very fact of a large, decentralized, and theo-
logically diverse denomination generally unsympathetic to
trained ministers was used as an imperative to act rather
than a justification for despair. Samuel Baker, drawing
on traditional Baptist political views and articulating
sentiments which had been held by Baptist educators for
many decades, wrote in 1853: "Every Baptist church is a
democracy, and an ignorant democracy, in Church or State,
may become the most oppressive and odious of all tyrannies
....Our form of church government imperiously demands an
intelligent church membership."[22] The primary means selected by most educational leaders to achieve this grass-
roots reform was a better-educated ministry which could in
turn educate and upgrade the denomination. A key problem
in initiating this strategy was to convince a significant
portion of the denomination that ministerial training was
both necessary and useful.

Arguments for ministerial education developed during
the years from 1812 to the Civil War usually took as their
starting point the axiom that knowledge was an indispensable
source of power at that point in human history. "The mind
of man," asserted George W. Eaton, in 1842, "never acted on

---

[22] "The Advantages of Education," Christian Repository,
III (November 1853), 289.

so great a scale, never was swelled with such grand conceptions, never gave birth to such magnificent designs,
and never prosecuted its enterprises, with such an array
of powerful and well adapted means as at present." A Kentucky Baptist journal echoed this intellectual optimism
and suggested its technological roots: "Knowledge is power.
It is the philosopher's stone; the true alchemy that turns
every thing it touches into Gold. It is the sceptre that
gives us our dominion over nature; the key that unlocks the
storehouse of creation, and opens to us the treasures of
the universe." Far from being limited to the material
sphere, however, knowledge was regarded by Eaton and others
as a source of power which enabled man to influence the
course of political and social development.[23]

Despite their great optimism, these men would not go
so far as the "visionary theorists.../who/ overlook the
capital circumstance that men are corrupt; and attribute
all their errors to a defect of education, to a mere ob-
liquity of understanding." Otherwise it would be difficult
to justify increased ministerial learning to the denomination
in light of the fact that "some of our greatest mathematicians

[23]George W. Eaton, Address, and Poem, Delivered Before
the Beta of the Sigma Phi, At Its Anniversary Meeting, Clinton, July 26th, 1842 (Utica, N.Y., 1843), pp. 11, 13; "Knowledge," Baptist Chronicle and Georgetown Literary Register,
II (February 1830), 30; Eaton, Address, p. 34; "Ministerial
Improvement," Baptist, I (October 1835), 151.

and philosophers are infidels."[24] After admitting this

troublesome fact, Stephen W. Taylor of Bucknell University

stated the middle ground position between piety and intel-

lect occupied by most educational leaders:

> The fact that some astronomers are not
> pious, proves not that they are corrupted by
> their astronomy, but, that the depravity of
> the human heart is next to indomitable, since
> it renders it possible for a rational being
> to study such a work as the material universe,
> without having his heart filled with supreme
> love towards its Divine Author.[25]

Reason without moral principle, Edward Baptist said in an

address at Howard College, "will prove but sounding brass,

or a tinkling symbol." At a meeting of potential supporters

of Union University, Joseph Eaton warned that "the human

mind is an instrument of far more power than a steam engine,

and if misguided and suffered to run off the track, the re-

sults are far more disastrous." President William Staughton

of George Washington University expressed the same sentiments

---

[24]James D. Knowles, Oration Delivered at the Columbian
College in the District of Columbia, July 4, 1823 (Washington, 1823), p. 11; Stephen W. Taylor, Inaugural Address
Delivered at the Commencement of the University at Lewisburg, Pennsylvania, On Wednesday, August 28, 1850 (n.p.,
n.d.), p. 14.

[25]Ibid., p. 15.

more succinctly: "Learning, without virtue, is a torch in
the hand of a lunatic."[26]

Noting recent statistics showing that in France "crime
is most prevalent in the most educated districts," President Howard Malcom of Georgetown stated the final point in
this line of reasoning about the relationship between piety
and intellect. "The grand desideratum," said Malcom, "is
moral influence, and when this is lacking there is no substitute." At properly designed educational institutions
knowledge could be "sanctified" and its power harnessed to
serve the good. Colleges could be "a means of grace."
One important way in which colleges controlled human de-
pravity and thus insured the proper use of intellectual power
was through the mental discipline resulting from studies
such as pure mathematics. These disciplinary studies served
to "strengthen, invigorate and sharpen the intellect, and
measurably redeem the judgment from vagaries and spectres
of a disordered imagination, and many of the unreasonable
prejudices and partialities of a depraved heart." But the
moral imperative undergirded a much more comprehensive def-
inition of education, one summarized by President Stephen

---

[26]Edward Baptist, _Address Delivered Before the Trustees,
Faculty and Students of Howard College, Marion, Perry County,
November 16, 1846_ (Tuskaloosa, Ala., 1846), p. 13; Joseph H.
Eaton, "Introductory Address, Delivered at the Educational
Meeting at Enon," _Baptist_, June 14, 1845; William Staughton,
_Address Delivered at the Opening of the Columbian College in
the District of Columbia, January 9, 1822_ (Washington, 1822),
p. 11.

Chapin in his inaugural address at George Washington in
1829. Education, said Chapin, is "the right application
of that whole combination of means, which are appointed to
be employed upon man, to give health and vigor to his constitution, dignity and grace to his manners; to develop
and mature his intellectual powers; to subdue his evil
propensities; and to train him up in the habits of morality
and religion."[27]

When intellect was properly controlled and placed within this broad concept of education, it could be safely argued
that "Learning and Religion are natural allies." Support
for this position was drawn from several sources. Throughout most of the course of human history, it was argued,
learning and religion had enjoyed a close and mutually
beneficial relationship. "Near the close of the eighteenth
century," however, "the unhallowed attempt was made to divorce Learning from Religion and wed her to infidelity."
Religion found science and literature at least temporarily
"seduced from her side." Although they differed as to
whether or not a reunion had ever been effected in the

[27]Howard Malcom, "Baccalaureate Address: Delivered by
the President to the Graduating Class in Georgetown College,
June 29, 1848," Georgetown Herald, July 19, 1848, clipping in
"Howard Malcom Memorial Scrapbook," American Baptist His-
torical Society, Rochester, New York, p. 73; George W. Eaton,
An Inaugural Address, Delivered in the Chapel of the Hamil-
ton Literary & Theological Seminary, June 4, 1834 (Utica,
N.Y., 1835), p. 28; Baker, "Advantages of Education," p. 284;

early nineteenth century, Baptist leaders agreed that the
divorce was a historical anomaly. The current challenge
of Catholicism (and the aspects of its history not used in
the previous argument) provided another reason for the propriety of and alliance between education and true religion.
Speaking at Bethel College in Kentucky, J.M. Pendleton contended: "That 'ignorance is the mother of devotion' is a
maxim which stands conspicuous among the many absurdities
and falsehoods of Romanism."[28]

The most important argument offered was that learning
and religion could be "mutually subservient to each other's
advantage." Learning could aid knowledge by providing historical facts and geological findings to "corroborate the
truths of the Bible" and "uphold /its/ chronology." Another
area of assistance resided in the educational process itself, for "intellectual culture naturally tends to the improvement of moral character." The properly cultivated or
disciplined mind would be able to make the proper distinctions, and acquire the knowledge necessary for "correct

"Colleges as a Means of Grace," Baptist Educational Reporter, I
(June, 1867), 25; Taylor, Inaugural Address, p. 6; Stephen
Chapin, An Inaugural Address Delivered in the City of Wash-
ington, March 11, 1829 (Washington, 1829), pp. 3-4.

[28]Jonathan Going, Inaugural Address at the Anniversary
of the Granville Literary and Theological Institution,
August 8, 1838 (Columbus, Ohio, 1839), pp. 4, 11; George W.
Eaton, Inaugural Address, p. 28; Going, Inaugural Address,
p. 12; J.M. Pendleton, Education (Nashville, Tenn., 1854),
p. 5.

deportment." With these abilities, the "Truth attained
will likely induce Virtue, her twin sister, to bear her
company." Religion, on the other hand, could make important contributions to learning. The founding and support of
educational institutions was an obvious one. In the area of
intellectual motivation, a "pious spirit" was "friendly to
scientific research" because the desire to obtain knowledge
of the divine architect provided "the strongest and most
noble incentives" for scientists. Although a revival drew
some students away from their studies at Denison University,
reported Jonathan Stevens, "there is no doubt that the amount
of study has been increased by it. It has not only strengthened the motives to diligence for the time being, but in
many minds at least it has magnified the importance of
thorough mental cultivation."[29]

While calling for an "intelligent piety" and a church
which would be "the intellectual as well as the moral light
of the world," Baptist educators always made it clear that
the alliance between religion and learning was not a union

[29]Going, Inaugural Address, pp. 4-7; "The Influence of
Intellectual Culture on Moral Character," Monthly Miscellany, I (April 16, 1849), 109; George B. Taylor, The Thinker:
An Address Delivered in Richmond, Va., Monday, June 30, 1856,
Before the Society of Alumni of Richmond College, At Their
First Annual Meeting (Richmond, Va., 1856), p. 17; Going, Inaugural Address, p. 8; George B. Taylor, Thinker, pp. 15-16;
"Religion Not a Hindrance to the Student," Latter Day Luminary, I (February 1819), 276; "Revival in Granville College,"
Cross and Journal, February 26, 1841.

of equals.[30] Jonathan Going, in his inaugural address as

president of Denison, expressed this position in 1838:

> With all my friendship for education and
> all my zeal for its promotion, give me sound
> morality though coupled with ignorance in
> preference to immorality connected with the
> highest intellectual attainments. Put down
> Learning, demolish the school-houses and col-
> leges, and dismiss all the teachers--let some
> modern Omar burn every library and every book
> in Christendom: let all this be done in prefer-
> ence to having an infidel literature.[31]

Science and Literature were held in high esteem only when

they served as "handmaids to religion." Learning was pro-

moted "simply as a means... of rendering the minister's

piety more conspicuous and efficient." Intellectual facul-

ties were viewed as "instruments" for building moral charac-

ter. The "learning we contend for," said Robert B. Semple

in 1820, "inculcates solid, useful knowledge; which is either

comprehended in true religion, or intimately connected with

it, and subservient to its purposes."[32]

---

[30]Basil Manly, Jr., _A Plea for Colleges_ (Philadelphia,
1854), p. 28; J.L. Reynolds, _Inaugural Discourse Delivered
Before the Board of Trustees of the Furman Institution at
Their Annual Meeting, Dec. 11, 1841_ (Columbia, S.C., 1842),
p. 20.

[31]Going, _Inaugural Address_, p. 13.

[32]George W. Eaton, _Inaugural Address_, pp. 27-28; "Influence of Intellectual Culture," p. 110; "Address," _Latter
Day Luminary_, II (May 1820), 109.

From this point of view the quest for knowledge might
be restricted in its aim but not, as Semple went on to
suggest, in its range. Faith in the unity of all knowledge, the key point in this approach, was well expressed
and explained by another writer three decades later:

> All truth is one. There is a glorious unity
> about it. Different parts of the great whole
> throw light upon each other and indeed no one
> portion can be comprehended alone. Hence that
> portion of truth which the Bible reveals stands
> connected with, illustrates and is illustrated
> by other portions existing elsewhere. Science,
> history, biography, astronomy, geology, mental
> and moral philosophy, and other branches of
> knowledge which we need not mention, and what
> in its limited form is termed literature, each
> and all throw light upon the inspired volume.[33]

With nature viewed as "a benign and faithful instructress,"
natural science could give a particularly powerful testimony to "God's wisdom, power, and goodness" and "His pres-
ence and control at every point in the universe." Study of
almost any field of human knowledge would thus improve man's
understanding of "the truth of God as displayed in his works
of nature and grace."[34]

While relevant to denominational education in general,
most of these arguments were made to demonstrate that

---

[33]"Importance of Secular Studies to the Minister," Baptist Messenger, December 20, 1850.

[34]Stephen Taylor, Inaugural Address, pp. 6-7; Jesse
Mercer, Knowledge Indispensable to a Minister of God (Washington, Ga., 1834), pp. 16-17.

ministerial education in particular was not only "eminently useful" but "in the present state of the world indispensable." A great many Baptists still believed a preacher must only open his mouth and God would "fill it" and that men who felt the call could "as by miraculous touch become qualified at once for standing up as teachers of congregations." Always conceding that the individual churches were the "legitimate judges" of which men were called of God to preach, Baptist educational leaders reasoned from their approach to knowledge that those who were called could also be improved by human means. Given the beneficial effects of science and literature upon religious understanding and belief, it seemed "manifestly the intention of our Creator, that the mind shall be improved and enriched by the employment of appropriate means." Baptists should thus recognize "the instrumentality of the schools."[35]

Each of the major subject areas in the curricula of denominational schools was justified in terms of its contribution to "ministerial efficiency." Natural sciences

[35]George W. Eaton, Inaugural Address, p. 28; David Benedict, Fifty Years Among the Baptists (New York, 1860), p. 298; Annual Report of the Baptist Education Society of the United States, Philadelphia, July 13th and 14th (Philadelphia, 1814), p. 24; "Ministerial Improvement," p. 135; Stephen Chapin, Triumphs of Intellect, A Lecture Delivered October, 1824, In the Chapel of Waterville College (Waterville, Me., 1824), p. 4; Stephen Taylor, "U. at Louisburg," Christian Chronicle, November 25, 1846.

put the minister "in possession of a vast store-house of
illustrations, which in this scientific age he will find
available and serviceable in the elucidation and enforce-
ment of divine truth." Classical studies served several
purposes. Facility in ancient languages gave ministers
access to "the fountain of divine truth" and thus freed
them from dependence on "fallible translators." The history contained in classical literature provided illustrations of "the dealings of God with his church" and "the
consequences of departure from the path of obedience and
the simplicity of the gospel" which "vindicate the justice
of God and inspire confidence in his providence." Classics,
along with mathematics, provided ministers with the mental
discipline necessary to develop fully their "reasoning
powers" and make them effective persuaders.[36]

Ministerial efficiency was developed not only by these
intellectual skills but also by the respectability they be-
stowed upon the minister who acquired them. Treating the
lack of respect for an educated ministry in some regions as
a passing phenomenon, advocates of an educated Baptist ministry argued that society "is rapidly advancing, and our

[36]George W. Eaton, Inaugural Address, p. 16; J.B. Jeter,
Importance of an Enlightened Ministry, A Sermon Delivered at
the Annual Meeting of the Virginia Baptist Education Society,
Saturday, June 7th, 1834 (Richmond, Va., 1834), p. 5; Joseph
H. Eaton, "Introductory Address," p. 679; Stephen W. Taylor,
Inaugural Address, p. 6.

ministry must keep pace with that improvement, or we will
inevitably lose our congregations, and consequently in the
same ratio, our usefulness." Especially damaging would
be the loss of present or potential members from a particular segment of society, and this was feared as early
as 1812: "There are some men in the higher circles of
society, who can be prevailed on to attend only a ministry
where evangelic truth is united with classic learning; but
their souls are as precious as are the souls of the poor."
Their pocketbooks were also precious. Loss of "all the influential and wealthy of the rising generation," would
greatly diminish the finances needed by the denomination
for the purpose of Christian benevolence. R.B.C. Howell,
minister of the First Baptist Church in Nashville, Tennessee,
was "painfully impressed with these facts" in the 1830's
and 1840's when he observed the second generation of ministers in his state. Less talented than their predecessors,
this group was "uncultivated and coarse." "The educated
sons and daughters of the wealthy members of their flocks,"
Howell later recalled, "nearly all joined other denominations. Thus were the Baptist churches drained effectively
of their wealth and social influence, elements of strength
...which no denomination can afford to lose." A circular
letter urging support for Franklin College in 1839 warned
that without a better-educated ministry "our gospel

operations will be more and more confined to the less
informed part of the community."[37] Ministerial respectability was crucial to the financial and evangelical future
of the denomination, according to Baptist educational
leaders, and education was the path to respectability.

Learning was useful not only in the internal improvement of the denomination but also in the relations between
Baptists and other groups in American society. Only with "a
much larger number of...ministers...able to wield at will
all the powers of the most profound and mature learning"
could the errors of infidels, Catholics, and other "sects"
be combatted. Education provided the denomination with
"armour intended for her defence." Knowledge also supplied
indispensable "weapons" for competition. A supporter of
Howard argued: "That denomination of Christians which will
not study the will of God in his providence as well as his
written word, and adapt its agencies for good accordingly,

[37] /R.B.C. Howell/, "Ministerial Improvement," Baptist
Advocate, I (October 1835), 235; "Address," Massachusetts
Baptist Missionary Magazine, III (September 1812), 211;
First Annual Meeting of the Baptist Education Society of
the North-Western States, Held at Beloit, Wis., Nov. 5th &
6th, 1852, With the Constitution of the Society and the
Address of the Board (Racine, Wis., 1852), p. 12; Baker,
"Advantages of Education," p. 286; /R.B.C. Howell/, "A
Memorial of the First Baptist Church, Nashville, Tennessee,
From 1820 to 1863," typescript in the Dargan-Carver Library,
Nashville, Tennessee, pp. 248-49; Indiana Baptist General
Association, Minutes, 1839, quoted in John F. Cady, The Cen-
tennial History of Franklin College (n.p., 1934), p. 34.

will be superceded by others more willing to be taught."[38]

Philosophical atheists and "men of powerful and cultivated but skeptical minds" were pictured as serious threats
to the Christian community. "By reason of their superior
intelligence," it was observed, "they have a commanding
influence in a community rapidly advancing in science and
general information. An illiterate or incompetent ministry
could stand no chance with such men in a contest for moral
influence over the minds of thinking people." Natural
science should be studied by ministers so they might "refute the opinions, falsify the assertions, and counteract
the influence" of these "infidel philosophers, who have represented it as an ally of infidelity." The "exigencies of
the times" also demanded classical and mathematical education, for "without intellectual culture, the undisciplined
mind of the minister is soon lost in the mazes of infidel
reasoning."[39]

Infidelity was "closely allied to a more imposing and
formidable enemy," popery. Jesuit priests, because of their

[38]R.B.C. Howell, "A Great Southern Theological School,"
Monthly Miscellany, I (March 15, 1849), 82; Reynolds, Inaugural Discourse, p. 17; S.W. Lynd, Address Delivered Before the Ohio Baptist Education Society, at the Annual Meeting Held in Granville, October 6, 1832 (Cincinnati, 1832),
p. 10;"Howard College," South Western Baptist, May 11, 1854.

[39]George W. Eaton, Inaugural Address, pp. 6, 8, 16;
"Ministerial Improvement," p. 150.

learning, might easily persuade infidels to support their schools. Many present members of the Christian churches probably would transfer their allegiances to either infidelity or Catholicism if all they could get from denominations such as the Baptist were "ministrations of mental imbecility and proudly conceited ignorance." The threat of Catholicism was largely intellectual and must be met on those grounds.[40]

Challenges of infidelity and Catholicism apparently provided sufficient evidence for advocacy of ministerial education as a defensive weapon. Detailed references to other Protestant groups are rarely found in antebellum Baptists rhetoric. One Protestant rival, however, certainly helped convince many Baptists of the need for an educated ministry. Alexander Campbell, with his quick wit, aggressive mind, and extensive learning, severely challenged many Baptist doctrines and practices. Few Baptist ministers were able to cope with him in public debate. In at least one case he was able to win over an entire Baptist church.[41]

---

[40]J. M. Peck, Alton Seminary and College (n.p., ca. 1835), p. 4; Rufus Babcock, Jr., The Claims of Education Societies: Especially on the Young Men of Our Country (Boston, 1829), p. 21; Joseph H. Eaton, "Introductory Address," p. 679.

[41]Benjamin F. Riley, A Memorial History of the Baptists of Alabama (Philadelphia, 1923), pp. 56-57; Albert H. Newman, "Baptist Ministerial Education Seventy-Five Years ago," Rochester Theological Seminary Bulletin (June 1925), p. 358.

Foreign missions as well as domestic respectability
and competition required well-educated ministers. "Such
men only," argued Rufus Babcock in 1829, "are fitted to go
forth to the heathen, to learn their languages, furnish
them with the scriptures, superintend their schools, and
train up from among native converts, those who should be
qualified to preach the gospel to their countrymen."[42]
Linguistic skills were particularly important if young
missionaries were to translate scripture into native tongues.
Adoniram Judson, a graduate of Brown and Andover Theological
Seminary before his conversion to Baptist beliefs, completed
his translation of the Bible into Burmese in 1834. This
widely-publicized project by the most prominent Baptist
missionary of the early nineteenth century provided a dra-
matic example of the utility of thorough training in languages.

Missionaries like Judson were salaried, well-trained
professionals. While urging the preparation of many more
like them for the mission field, Baptist educators attempted
to elevate pulpit ministers at home to a comparably high
status. Many articles in the denominational press offered
advice on preaching and pastoral techniques. Congregations
were advised to treat their ministers with more kindness
and greater respect. Pleas were made for higher ministerial

[42]Babcock, _Claims_, pp. 9-10.

114

qualifications and corresponding improvements in ministerial
support.

A majority of Baptist ministers in the early nineteenth
century received little or no pay for their services, and
few expected it. They supported themselves by other pursuits
such as farming, teaching, retailing, and occasionally even
by operating a distillery. In calling for a well-trained,
salaried, and full-time ministry, great care was taken not
to alienate this generation of self-made men who might sus-
pect that education "is a cunning artifice of the younger and
more literary, to cast further into the shade the older and
less privileged of our brethren in the Ministry."[43]

The new generation of professional ministers should be
able to "write a good essay" as well as preach a good sermon.
Jeremiah B. Jeter, a prominent supporter of the University
of Richmond, asserted that the minister must have "the ability to teach" as well as preach. "The minds of sinners must
be enlightened," Jeter contended; "their objections answered;
their sophisms dissipated; their prejudices subdued; their
slumbering consciences aroused; and their affections won.
The citadel, in which they are defended, must be stormed by

[43]J.S. Hougham, "Teachers in Franklin College," First
Half Century of Franklin College, Jubilee Exercises (Cincinnati, 1884), p. 57; Joseph H. Eaton, "Introductory Address," p. 678; Hosea Holcombe, A History of the Rise and
Progress of the Baptists in Alabama (Philadelphia, 1840),
p. 79; Hudgins, "Anti-missionary Controversy," p. 158;
Babcock, Claims, p. 3.

the resistless weapons of truth and reason." Rather than
merely "introducing all the doctrines of the gospel into
one sermon, let the text be what it may," S.W. Lynd told
the Ohio Baptist Education Society, the minister must "lead
the hearers to think."[44]

The primary qualification for the efficient minister
of this period, however, was that he "possess the power of
persuasion."[45] The need for this talent was perceived by
William Colgate, a wealthy Baptist soap manufacturer in New
York City who contributed liberally to several of the denomination's colleges:

> On one occasion, walking leisurely along
> Nassau Street with his pastor, a crowd was
> seen around a vendor of razor-strops. Deacon
> Colgate paused, and called the pastor's atten-
> tion to the street merchant's tact, in tones
> of voice and skillful appeal of wit and sen-
> tentious remark, in securing the attention of
> the crowd. He remarked, 'What a talent for
> a preacher this man has! How he manages to
> get and hold the attention of the passing
> multitude to so trivial a matter! Preachers
> have an infinitely more important appeal to
> make. They should try to succeed as he does,
> in commending the truth.'[46]

---

[44]George W. Eaton, Inaugural Address, p. 11; William
Hooper, Inaugural Discourse Delivered Before the Board of
Trustees of the Furman Institution at Their Meeting, May
20, 1838 (Charleston, S.C., 1838), p. 17; Jeter, Importance,
p. 7; Lynd, Address, p. 11.

[45]"Ministerial Improvement," p. 134.

[46]William W. Everts, William Colgate: The Christian
Layman (Philadelphia, 1881), p. 185.

Most Baptist educational leaders would have heartily agreed
with Colgate. Since the vendor probably lacked much formal
schooling, they also would have quickly pointed out that the
power of ministerial persuasion could be greatly enhanced by
collegiate and theological study.

III

More than just elaborate arguments were needed if
educational leaders were themselves to be effective persuaders. Facing great obstacles in the areas of Baptist
church polity, theology, and ministerial qualifications,
it was advantageous for this small group to ally itself
with the contemporary forces of revivalism. The alliance
was based more on natural affinities, however, than on cal-
culations of expediency. In many ways it was natural that
assistance should be accepted from revivalists, since they
were eminently successful persuaders and were rapidly at-
taining the professional status which it was hoped would
soon characterize the entire Baptist ministry.

Ties between revivalism and education[47] were numerous.
The denomination's two leading revivalists, Jabez Swan and

---

[47]A close relationship between revivalism and education
has been identified by historians, but never explained or explored in depth. William W. Sweet, in Revivalism in America,
Its Origin, Growth, and Decline (New York, 1944), pp. 147-51,

Jacob Knapp, both graduated from Colgate University. Swan

later became a trustee of this institution and supported

education as a helpful means toward the greater goal of

saving souls. Even a Methodist evangelist, Peter Cart-

wright, assisted the cause of Baptist education by piloting

the ill-fated bill to incorporate John Mason Peck's Rock

Spring Theological and High School through the Illinois

House of Representatives. Several professors, presidents,

and benefactors of Baptist colleges were successful evan-

gelists before turning their attention to education. Cam-

pus revivals such as those at Wake Forest College in the

1830's were started by students who had attended nearby

camp meetings. Howard Malcom, a leading Baptist scholar

and President of Bucknell whose administration was perme-

ated with college revivals, had to be restrained by the

---

views educational institutions such as denominational colleges as the "by-products" of revivalism, but does not
clearly define or convincingly establish any causal links
between education and evangelism. Jerry Breazeale's "Some
Contributions of the Second Great Awakening to Baptist
Higher Education in Kentucky and Tennessee, 1800-1860,"
unpublished Th.M. essay, New Orleans Baptist Theological
Seminary, 1959, pp. 22, 56, notes some "indirect relations"
between the revivals and colleges, but does not add much
to Sweet's generalization. For similarly limited observations on this point, see G. Adolph Koch, "The Growth of
Denominational Colleges in the United States, 1820-1850,"
an essay submitted for the Chandler Historical Prizes,
Columbia University, 1927, pp. i-iii, and Frank D. McCloy,
"The Founding of Protestant Theological Seminaries in the
United States of America, 1784-1840," unpublished Ph.D.
dissertation, Harvard University, 1959, p. 336.

University's trustees from permitting excessive off-campus
evangelism on weekends by ministerial students.[48]

Revivalism played a role in the founding and financing
of some Baptist colleges. In the late 1820's a major revival in Kentucky helped convince leading Baptists that the
time was ripe to found Georgetown. A few years later revivals in New York considerably increased the enrollment at
Colgate. A protracted meeting in Franklin, Indiana, in
1841 was primarily designed to rally support among Indiana
Baptists for Franklin College. Agents for colleges such as
Wake Forest and Richmond successfully combined evangelism
with collection of funds for their schools. Jeremiah B.
Jeter, in asking Samuel Wait to serve as an agent for the
latter institution, observed: "In prosecuting this work
you will enjoy an excellent opportunity of laboring as an
evangelist. Indeed, you could not more efficiently prose-
cute your agency than by aiding in protracted meetings."[49]

[48]Byron A. Woods, "In Memoriam, Elder Jabez S. Swan,"
Special Memorial Services at Hamilton, New York, June 17,
1885 (Utica, N.Y., 1885), pp. 9-10; Helen L. Jennings,
"John Mason Peck and the Impact of New England on the Old
Northwest," unpublished Ph.D. dissertation, University of
Southern California, 1961, pp. 115-16; Spright Dowell, A
History of Mercer University, 1833-1953 (Macon, Ga., 1953),
pp. 32, 35; "Lives of the Founders and Builders of Hills-
dale College," Advance, December 6, 1885; George W. Paschal,
History of Wake Forest College, I (Wake Forest, N.C., 1935),
159-61; J. Orin Oliphant, The Rise of Bucknell University
(New York, 1965), p. 64.

[49]O.R. Corey, "Historical Chronology, General College
History: 1775-1954," typescript in Georgetown College Library, p. 8; Williams, "History," p. 91; "Our Institute at

Objections by educators to the methods and doctrines
of evangelists were infrequent and generally very mild in
tone. Occasionally a college revival would become too
emotional for faculty sensibilities and they would exert
their influence in order "to prevent passion /from/
gaining the ascendency over judgment." Although they were
promoting "an intelligent piety" and a fear of God based
on a rational and careful "investigation of this subject,"
educational leaders such as John Mason Peck "tolerated"
the excesses of camp-meeting revivalists because they might
"do some good reaching those not otherwise accessible."
Duncan R. Campbell, President of Georgetown, was disturbed
by the "measures" or style of modern evangelism, but did
not oppose itinerant revivalists or protracted meetings per
se.[50]

What is probably the only straightforward public
challenge to revivalism by an antebellum Baptist educator
appeared in an address given in 1839 by John S. Maginnis,

Franklin," Baptist Banner and Western Pioneer, November 4,
1841; Paschal, History, I, 232-33; Robert Ryland, The Virginia Baptist Education Society. The Society, the Seminary,
the College (Richmond, Va., 1891), p. 18; J.B. Jeter to
Samuel Wait, August 6, 1845, Samuel Wait Correspondence,
Baptist Historical Collection, Wake Forest College Library.

[50]"Wake Forest Institute," Biblical Recorder, September
23, 1835; Rufus Babcock, Forty Years of Pioneer Life: Memoir
of John Mason Peck, D.D. (Philadelphia, 1864), pp. 200-201;
D.R. Campbell, "The Anti-Scriptural Character of Modern Evangelism," Christian Repository, VI (May 1856), 273-83.

Professor of Biblical Theology at Colgate. Speaking to an
audience in Hamilton just a few years after Jacob Knapp
held a protracted meeting there, Maginnis made a long di-
gression from his chosen topic (the utility of studying the
Bible) to urge the churches to "beware how they multiply
their numbers while they disregard the proper instruction
of those whom they receive." The problem was not that revivalists were anti-intellectual, however, but that the
"new measures" and "new doctrines" used "to hasten members
into the church" placed too much emphasis on human ability.
A genuine revival was promoted "not by awakening in the
bosom of the sinner a sense of his ability," said Maginnis,
"but by making him feel his utter helplessness and dependence, that he can be induced to cry to God for mercy."
Maginnis considered reason subordinate to personal piety,
but also felt that "neither noise nor excitement, the
thronged assembly nor the crowded anxious seat, can be
relied upon as an evidence of a work of grace." The best
means of evangelism was for every pulpit minister "to preach
the gospel in all its length and breadth—in all its doctrines and duties."[51]

Spoken in the town where Jacob Knapp resided and based
his campaigns, these words must be considered a direct

---

[51]John S. Maginnis, _An Inaugural Address, Delivered at
the Chapel of the Hamilton Literary and Theological Institution, August 21, 1839_ (Utica, N.Y., 1840), pp. 12-24.

challenge to this revivalist. In 1843 Maginnis led a group
which unsuccessfully tried to prevent the Hamilton Baptist
Church from giving its endorsement to Knapp. Four years
later, Knapp made an abortive attempt to have Maginnis removed from the Colgate faculty.[52] The common bonds between
education and revivalism were too great for personal differences of two men to provoke a split.

Maginnis's Calvinistic critique of revivalism suggests
that the intellectual foundation of the alliance between
educators and evangelists resided in their mutual high regard for the human will. Arminianism was an outstanding
characteristic of early-nineteenth-century revivalism.[53]
Thoroughgoing Calvinists such as Maginnis were rarities
among Baptist educators of this period. The faculty psychology which permeated Baptist educational thought placed
heavy emphasis on proper cultivation of the will:

> The will, as all know, is the commanding
> faculty or power of our nature: it was ordained
> as master, or king, to rule in the senate-
> chamber of the soul, controlling and directing
> every other power. But, like every other
> faculty, it needs to be educated: indeed, on
> account of its character and office, it re-
> quires the most special and careful culture.[54]

---

[52]Williams, "History," pp. 136, 204-205.

[53]William G. McLoughlin, Jr., Modern Revivalism: Charles
Grandison Finney to Billy Graham (New York, 1959), pp. 9, 12.

[54]"Culture of the Will," Mothers' Journal and Family
Visitant, XX (July 1855), 216.

122

In a defense of the collegiate system of the United States,
President Justin R. Loomis of Bucknell emphasized that "it
is exertion alone that will convert students into men.
This is a prominent aim of our system of culture." The
mental discipline characterizing this system was designed
so that the "other powers of the mind learn subjection and
become the efficient instruments of a vigorous will." Justification of ministerial education also leaned heavily on
human effort. A common approach argued that if those called
to preach fail to cultivate their talents and "leave all the
work to God, they can no more expect to produce edifying
sermons than a farmer can expect to secure a rich harvest
without labor on his part." Voluntary religious and reform
societies were also considered by contemporaries to be "a
peculiar and very striking feature of the age."[55] In such
an era, educators and evangelists could consider themselves
partners in the cultivation and mobilization of human will-
power.

The nature and strength of this alliance was perceived
by anti-mission Baptists. They often attacked Baptist colleges and theological schools in the same breath with

[55]J.R. Loomis, An Inaugural Address, Delivered July 27,
1859 (Philadelphia, 1860), pp. 21-22; "Ministers. Should They
Be Educated?" Baptist Messenger, September 5, 1849; George
W. Eaton, Address, p. 15.

attacks on revivalism. Revivalists were denounced by this group as "carnal priests, who...urge that a mere volition of the mind of man...can at any time in one moment cause his salvation." Proponents of theological schools were rebuked because they "profess to disbelieve, and to reject the doctrine generally termed Arminianism, notwithstanding the institutions /they support/ are perfectly Arminian in their character."[56]

Attacks such as these led John Mason Peck to term antinomianism "a heresy of the most pernicious tendency." With Arminianism currently considered the characteristic error of Methodism, the anti-mission charges clearly hit a sensitive spot. Arguing that he followed "the medium line of scripture truth," Peck took great care to disassociate himself from the excesses of Wesley and others who "in avoiding the errors of Antinomianism...verged into Arminianism."[57]

But the anti-mission Baptists could not be easily dismissed. In some states they were a powerful minority within the denomination, and it was important at least to quiet their opposition if not win their support. One opportunity

[56]Lambert, "Rise," p. 368; Breazeale, "Some Contributions," p. 45; C.B. Hassell, untitled article, Primitive Baptist, July 9, 1836; see also, "Revivals," Baptist Correspondent, II (September 1839), 75-76; Mark Bennett, "Comment," Primitive Baptist, March 12, 1836.

[57]"Antinomianism," Baptist Advocate, II (April 1836), 87-88.

for reconciliation was provided by the anti-mission distinction between types of educational institutions. Gilbert Beebe, editor of the anti-mission journal, Signs of the Times, conceded that "we do not object to learn our children the necessary branches of Education...but we do consider that a Theological Seminary, for the preparation of young men for the Ministry, is a work-shop of the Devil, and the hotbed of all kinds of delusion." This distinction was expanded to the point where it might sanction collegiate studies by Mark Bennett, editor of the Primitive Baptist: "We have no objection to education as such, and of the right kind--say of all the useful Arts and of the Sciences. But when education is sought for the purpose either of adorning the ministry, or of promoting its usefulness, there is evidently, in our opinion, something wrong."[58]

This anti-mission Baptist position suggests one important reason for the institutional strategies of Baptist educational leaders in states such as Tennessee and Alabama. Support was sought for a college rather than a theological school. Anti-mission Baptists by the mid-1840's comprised about thirty per cent of the denomination in Tennessee and over twenty-five per cent of the Baptists in Alabama.[59]

---

[58]"Popular Institutions," Signs of the Times, February 13, 1833; untitled editorial, Primitive Baptist, November 26, 18[

[59]Rufus Babcock, "Sketches of a Southwestern Tour," Baptist, January 18, 1845; Baptist Almanac and Annual Register, 1847 (Philadelphia, 1847), pp. 25-26.

Potential opposition from this growing minority probably influenced the plans of P.S. Gayle, agent for the West Tennessee Baptist Education Society a decade earlier:

> Our object is a Literary College, not a
> Theological Seminary. The time has not yet
> arrived for a theological school in this division
> of the State, nor will not for some years to come;
> when it does, then let that department be added,
> by erecting other and separate buildings for that
> purpose.[60]

Daniel P. Bestor, a founder of the Greensboro predecessor of
Howard, also found it expedient in the late 1830's to defer
plans for ministerial training. The "first object" of the
Alabama Baptist Convention in supporting this school was ministerial improvement, but, largely through the influence of
Bestor, a literary institution was organized and the addition
of a theological department left to some future date.[61]

Anti-mission opposition was only one of many factors
influencing the development of Baptist education in Tennessee and Alabama. Lack of enough ministerial students prepared to begin theological studies was another. A close
look at the course of events in these and other states reveals that although Baptist educational leaders were anxious
to promote ministerial education, considerations of strategy
and hard economic facts often dictated a somewhat devious
course to this goal.

---

[60]"Address," Baptist, II (October 1836), 342.

[61]Holcombe, History, p. 74; Mitchell B. Garrett, Sixty
Years of Howard College, 1842-1902, Howard College Bulletin,
LXXXV, No. 4 (Birmingham, Ala., 1927), p. 17.

The basic problem was to find a replacement for the traditional tutorial method of training ministers. The Baptist ministers in each state qualified to give systematic theological instruction were too few and too busy to handle all ministerial education for the rapidly growing denomination. Even these learned men could not, in an age of rising educational standards, be expected to provide as thorough a course of instruction as the faculty of an institution specially designed for this purpose. Some Baptist leaders thought that education societies ought to support beneficiaries at existing educational institutions, while others felt that a Baptist school was the best place for future ministers of the denomination. John Mason Peck promoted a Baptist theological school as a "labor-saving device...in comparison of which the mode of private instruction bears no proportion."[62]

Experience soon indicated that strictly theological institutions, although comparatively efficient in terms of teaching manpower, were usually far from economical when it came to finding enough tuition-paying students to balance the institutional budget. The only entirely separate Baptist

---

[62]Ryland, Virginia Baptist Education Society, p. 10; "Important Question," Latter Day Luminary, IV (May 1823), 131; Corey, "Historical Chronology," p. 10; Proceedings of the First Anniversary of the General Convention of Western Baptists at Cincinnati, Commencing on the Fifth of November, 1834 (Cincinnati, 1835), p. 27.

theological institution, except for a few on the academy

level, to achieve sustained successful operation prior to

the founding of Southern Baptist Theological Seminary in

1859 was Newton Theological Seminary, founded in 1825.

George Washington University was envisioned by some to be

an institution for ministerial training to which a college

would be added. The need for Congressional aid soon caused

priorities to be reversed and the theological department

lasted only a few years. Colgate managed to function for

two decades as an institution exclusively for ministerial

training, but in 1839, needing more tuition income to re-

duce the school's debt, the trustees voted to admit "a

limited number of young men...who may not have the ministry

in view."[63]

This evolution occurred much more rapidly at the Uni-

versity of Richmond. A literary department was planned but

was not to be undertaken "until the theological department

is adequately supported." The school opened in July, 1832,

as a theological seminary, but by the beginning of the second

session in February, 1833, tuition-paying nonministerial

students had to be admitted in order to pay faculty salaries.

---

[63]Robert B. Semple, "Address," Latter Day Luminary, II
(May 1820), 114; Irah Chase, "An Autobiographical Sketch,"
Baptist Memorial and Monthly Record, IX (March 1850), 81;
"The Exercises of Commencement-week," New York Baptist Reg-
ister, August 30, 1839,

Although the trustees in 1835 assured the denomination it
was not their "design so to extend the admission of literary students as to absorb the Theological character of the
institution," the following year an appeal was sent out for
still more literary students in order to support the faculty
and meet other institutional expenses. By 1842 the school
had enrolled 85 ministerial students and 351 planning for
other pursuits.[64]

In light of such experiences, most Baptist educators
chose to found colleges with affiliated theological "departments." Colleges proved to be the best means of financing
ministerial training, yet even with this backing theological
departments were in frequent trouble due to lack of students.
President John L. Dagg of Mercer University held hopes for
"greater prosperity," but admitted in 1845 that "the number
of students and our success in the theological department
have doubtless been much below what is desirable." Similar

---

[64] "Virginia Baptist Seminary," Christian Index, July 7,
1832; R.E. Gaines, "The Beginnings: The Seminary, the College,
1832-1866," The First Hundred Years: Brief Sketches of the
History of the University of Richmond (Richmond, Va., 1932),
p. 20; H.H. Harris, "Richmond College," in Herbert B. Adams,
Thomas Jefferson and the University of Virginia (Washington,
1888), p. 271; Virginia Baptist Education Society (n.p.,
1833), p. 4; Proceedings and Annual Report of the Va. Baptist Seminary, etc. etc. etc. (Richmond, Va., 1835), pp. 9-
10; "Virginia Baptist Seminary," Religious Herald, December
9, 1836; F.W. Boatwright, "The Beginnings of Higher Education Among Virginia Baptists," Religious Herald, August 13,
1931.

regrets were expressed in Indiana, where the multiplication of tiny rural churches unable to support full-time
pastors and the low salaries of those employed even by the
larger and wealthier churches provided little incentive for
young ministerial aspirants to invest in extensive training.
At Howard the professorship in the theological department
was endowed, and it was announced that the duties of the man
filling this position "will be wholly unconnected with the
other departments of the College," since "where the different
departments are blended, the Theological is almost invariably
lost sight of." Tuition from nonministerial students, however, was still essential to meet the other operating costs
of the institution. In order to retain the income from more
than 100 such students it was necessary in 1846 to meet
their demands for collegiate-level instruction. By 1849
the small number and lack of preparation of ministerial
students resulted in the theological professor's spending much
of his time teaching in the collegiate department. While
the shortage of Baptist ministers and missionaries was acute
in antebellum America, the rate at which fully trained ones
could be supplied was extremely slow.[65]

[65]"Mercer University and the Alabama Baptist," Christian
Index, January 17, 1845; letter from George C. Chandler, Bap-
tist Banner and Western Pioneer, July 16, 1840; Cady, Centen-
nial History, pp. 71-72; "Theological Department of Howard
College," Alabama Baptist, September 2, 1843; "Howard College,"
South Western Baptist, October 28, 1853; "Report," Alabama
Baptist, January 16, 1850; Robert Ryland, A Sermon Delivered
Before the Baptist Education Society of Virginia, June 4, 1836
(Richmond, Va., 1836), pp. 4-5.

At a time when "the obstacles to be overcome" were much greater in establishing a theological school or department than in founding a college, it was natural for a broader rationale of Baptist education to emerge from the struggles and strategies of men attempting to improve the quality of the Baptist ministry. "With me it is not very material," said President Robert Ryland of Richmond, "whether the school be strictly theological or purely literary, provided it be a place of resort for pious youth. The kind of knowledge is less important than the mental discipline to be imparted." If for some reason a choice had to be made between the scientific, literary, and linguistic studies and the sacred subjects, Ryland advised selecting the former. A supporter of Howard took a similar position, arguing that without the mental discipline of a college education one could not successfully pursue theological studies, while with a disciplined mind theological knowledge might be gained without formal instruction. William Carey Crane, who later became President of Baylor University, contended in the 1830's and 1840's that colleges were both directly and indirectly aiding "the cause of Christ" in areas other than just ministerial education. "By educating our sons, they making intelligent lawyers, physicians, merchants and planters," said Crane, "we should do more towards the spread of Baptist influence than by the efforts and preaching

of all the ministers at present living in our country combined." Stephen Taylor, in arguing for support of Bucknell,
agreed that Baptists "must act upon the community not through
the Gospel ministry alone, but through the agency, the personal everyday influence of educated men in all the learned
professions, and in all the great departments of useful industry."[66]

A few Baptist leaders dissented from both this rationale
and the strategy it was used to justify. In proposing a
"great Southern Baptist institution" exclusively for ministerial training, Basil Manly found "radically defective" the
"common expedient" of founding colleges in order to promote
and finance theological education. Manly learned from his
experience with Furman University that the classical department, because it was the key to survival, soon dominated
the alliance, and that money donated by Baptists to educate
young ministers was often "diverted in the mixed institution
from its principal design." R.B.C. Howell, arguing fourteen
years later for the same type of institution Manly had advocated, assessed the results of Baptist college founding.

---

[66]"Our University--No. 2," Christian Index, April 17,
1851; Ryland, Sermon, p. 15; "Howard College," South Western
Baptist, May 25, 1854; W. Carey Crane, "The Collegiate Education of the United States," Baptist, October 19, 1844; W.
Carey Crane, "Collegiate Education," Christian Index, January
11, February 1, 1838; Stephen Taylor, "U. at Lewisburg,"
Christian Chronicle, August 26, 1846.

Although originated for the stated purpose of improving
the ministry, Howell concluded, these schools had been
"allowed to take too much of a secular character, and to
lose sight to a painful extent of their original design."[67]

As these comments suggest, the arguments, alliances,
and strategies of Baptist educational leaders attempting
to arouse their denomination rarely brought the intended
results. As late as 1858 it was still being hopefully argued in Georgia that "as the people become generally educated, they will appreciate an educated ministry." Although some Baptist leaders viewed education as a means to
awaken the denomination from apathy toward such enterprises
as missions, the Maine Baptist newspaper could editorialize
in 1861: "We know of no Denomination so apt to neglect its
own interests as the Baptist. Their colleges and seminaries
of learning--their missionary societies, their periodicals,
their ministry, none of them receive that general and hearty
denominational support which they ought to have."[68]

---

[67]"Theological Education in the Southern States," Southern Baptist and General Intelligencer, March 13, 1835; "Central Theological Seminary," Religious Herald, August 2, 1849.

[68]"Mercer University," Christian Index, December 8,
1858; Riley, Memorial History, pp. 60, 62; "Denominational
Interests," Zion's Advocate, February 1, 1861.

Considering the many problems Baptist educational leaders faced in mobilizing their denomination to support ministerial education, perhaps anything more than the limited gains made on this point were not to be expected. Despite the gap between intentions and results concerning theological training, important foundations for increased learning among Baptists were established by 1861. More than two dozen Baptist-affiliated colleges were in operation. To understand this achievement, attention must be focused on the communities in which these schools were located.

CHAPTER III

COMMUNITY

Prospects for success in the new Baptist educational
venture were far from bright when Jeremiah Chaplin arrived
in Waterville, Maine, to initiate instruction at Colby College. The enterprise in 1818 lacked not only the organized
support of the Baptist denomination in the state, but also
"a well united body of inhabitants" of the town "who fondly
cherished the college as a rich blessing to themselves and
their children." A small group of community leaders had
persuaded the town to bid for the school, but when opening
of the literary department was delayed and concrete benefits of the institution for the town were slow in appearing,
whatever popular support existed at the time the bid was
made quickly evaporated.[1] Chaplin's task, and that of his
fellow Baptist educators at other colleges founded after
Colby, was to cultivate community as well as denominational
support.

Selection of the proper location for a college was an
important determinant of subsequent community support. The

_____

[1]Robert E. Pattison, Eulogy on Rev. Jeremiah Chaplin,
D.D., First President of Waterville College, Me., Delivered
in the Baptist Meeting House, Waterville, On the Evening Preceding Commencement, August 8, 1843 (Boston, 1843), p. 12.

size and economic promise of a town, its proximity to major
routes of travel, and its need for facilities of secondary
and collegiate education all were important considerations
in choosing the best site from among the bids of several
towns. It did not seem to be of particular consequence
that the one selected be a predominantly Baptist community.

Once a decision was made and an institution established,
the process of sinking roots into community life and binding
the cultural and economic fortunes of the town and immediate
vicinity with those of the college proceeded rapidly. Preparatory departments and special nonclassical courses served
many educational needs of the community. Graduates of normal courses and students working their way through college
helped staff local schools with unusually well-qualified
teachers. Companion institutions for female education were
frequently founded. The college president or some other
distinguished member of the denomination from the faculty
often filled the local Baptist pulpit. Public lectures by
faculty members, literary society exhibitions, and numerous
other influences emanating from the college also served to
augment local cultural resources. Some economic benefits
to the community, such as the boarding of students with
townspeople, might be matters of conscious policy. Others,
such as the money put into the local economy by students
and increases in land values near the college, were inevitable.

Communities responded to all these tangible benefits
of an educational institution by supporting their college
in several ways. The college town and nearby settlements
supplied a large percentage of each institution's students.
Citizens contributed liberally to meet operating expenses,
erect buildings, and create endowment funds. College events
such as the annual commencements were attended in great numbers by a broad spectrum of local residents. Throughout the
antebellum period the immediate vicinity of the college was
a crucial and generally dependable source of support for
Baptist colleges.

I

Selection of a college site was influenced by widespread contemporary distaste for cities. "Nearly all that
is desperate in guilt, expert in crime, and accomplished in
miscreancy," wrote one Baptist in 1829, "flows into a large
city, as into a common receptacle." A Baptist minister in
Boston found that "young men in cities are peculiarly exposed" to all the temptations of appetite, avarice, and
passion in the urban environment, "and thousands on thousands are ruined by them." Many similar observations
pointed to the conclusion expressed by one member of the
denomination in 1832, that Baptists locating educational

institutions should follow the maxim, procul ab urbe.
Some advised that colleges should be a moderate day's
journey from a city so as to be close enough to enjoy its
advantages but far enough to avoid its vices. Even this
suburban compromise was insufficient for others who advocated locations not only "remote from the distracting
influence of the city," but "equally free from the temptations usually presented to the young in country towns
and villages."[2]

Rural virtues abounded in the minds of antebellum
Baptists considering the location of their colleges. A
supporter of Wake Forest College argued that schools
should be "places of retirement...from the feverish strife
of life" where a young man could "break and harness his
mind for the tug and tear of life." Stephen W. Taylor
offered a host of reasons why a small town was selected
as the site for Bucknell University even though Baptist
numerical strength and wealth resided in the more urban
areas of Pennsylvania. In addition to making the all-
important point that "the morals of youth" were safest "in
our best country villages," Taylor enumerated the healthful

---

[2] "Immorality in Cities," Columbian Star and Christian
Index, September 19, 1829; Robert W. Cushman, Temptations
of City Life: An Address to Young Men on the Temptations
of Cities (Boston, 1847), p. 30; "Location of Our Institutions," Religious Herald, May 11, 1832; "Wake Forest College," Biblical Recorder, March 25, 1848.

"advantages of the pure air and water of the country, and
the peculiarly fine effect of rural beauty and sublimity
upon the spirits." The "retirement of a village" also
promoted "close and successful application to study."
Taylor noted both a parental and denominational preference for rural locations, observing in regard to the latter
that "while it would be utterly impracticable to unite the
country brethren in the support of a city College, there
are many strong inducements, such as have been suggested,
to influence those of larger towns to send their children
to the country to be educated."[3] Country colleges, in
short, were easier to sell.

Financial liabilities of too pastoral a site, however,
soon proved to be as threatening as the moral dangers of an
urban setting. When Rock Spring, Illinois, failed to grow
any larger than a dozen buildings, and resulting lack of
local support put the survival of John Mason Peck's school
there in doubt, plans were made in 1831 to relocate the institution "near some village or town in which the prospect
exists of a future dense population." Furman University
tried three different locations in or near towns of less

[3]"Wake Forest College," Biblical Recorder, November 23,
1850; Stephen W. Taylor, "A Brief History of the Origin of
the University at Lewisburg," manuscript dated April 18,
1850, in the Bucknell University Archives, p. 10; Stephen W.
Taylor, "University at Lewisburg," Christian Chronicle,
September 9, 1846.

than 500 inhabitants before locating among the more substantial number of citizens in Greenville, South Carolina.
When the population of Spring Arbor, Michigan, began level-
ing off as it approached 1,000, and the settlement seemed
destined to be "not much of a village," the Free Will Baptists moved their institution in 1853 to Hillsdale, a town
of little more than 1,000 at the time but growing rapidly
enough to exceed 2,000 by 1860.[4]

Not all Baptist colleges of this period sought the
congenial surroundings of a moderately small town. George
Washington University, the University of Richmond, and the
University of Rochester resided in urban areas. From these
quarters came an argument for the city. A proponent of
locating the proposed seminary of the Virginia Baptists
in Richmond argued that "whether temptations are less in
the country, is questionable." He asserted that students
could find more privacy in a city and fewer distractions

[4]David Wright, Memoir of Alvan Stone of Goshen, Mass.
(Boston, 1837), p. 164; J.M. Peck, A Guide For Emigrants, Containing Sketches of Illinois, Missouri, and the Adjacent
Parts (Boston, 1831), p. 291; "Record Book of the Rock
Springs Theological and High School, Rock Spring, Illinois,
1824-1831," typescript in the Dargan-Carver Library, Nashville, Tennessee, p. 98; for data on the populations of Edgefield, Stateburg, and Winnsboro, South Carolina, during this
period, see Robert Mills, Statistics of South Carolina, Including a View of Its Natural, Civil, and Military History,
General and Particular (Charleston, 1826), pp. 522, 743,
539. Except where other sources are cited, population statistics employed in this chapter are based on decennial reports of the United States Census Bureau. Letter from I.D.
Stewart, Morning Star, July 7, 1852.

than in a small community with all the pressures of everyone knowing everyone else. President Robert Ryland of the
University of Richmond observed from his own experience
that some rural schools could be quite "wicked" while certain urban institutions were "most orderly." The prosperity of a school, Ryland added, was greatly enhanced by
an urban location. George Washington University pictured
its proximity to the nation's capital as an asset rather
than a liability. Students had the opportunity "of wit-
nessing the highest exhibitions of talent in the Halls of
Congress and in the Supreme Court." Urban benefits in
Washington were not just political. President Joseph G.
Binney confidently contended in 1855 that "a city, where
life is seen in all its aspects, is the best location for
a college." Promoters of the University of Rochester in
1850 saw no contradictions in describing their city of
30,000 as a "rural, growing, and beautiful metropolis."[5]

---

[5]"The Education Society," Religious Herald, April 20,
1832; "Richmond College--No. 6," Religious Herald, January
4, 1844; Circular of the Columbian College, Washington, District of Columbia, 1853 (Washington, 1853), p. 11. For in-
stances of students attending sessions of Congress and the
Supreme Court when classes were dismissed for this purpose,
see W.I. Brooks to Iverson L. Brooks, December 1 and 16,
1845, Iverson L. Brooks Papers, Baptist Historical Collection, Wake Forest College Library. J.G. Binney, The Inaugural Address of the Rev. J.G. Binney, D.D., As President
of the Columbian College, D.C., Wednesday, June 17, 1855
(Washington, 1857), p. 39; "Circular," Annunciator, April
4, 1850.

Urban advocates, however, were a small minority, and even they made occasional concessions to the prevailing belief in rural virtues and city vices. George Washington University, overlooking the city from a high range of ground on its northern boundary, stipulated in the college rules that "visits to the city should be requested as rarely as possible; for, when frequent, they are obviously unfavorable to...habits of studiousness, sobriety, and good order." Students were not to "associate with vicious company; attend the theatre or any such place; visit any barroom or similar establishment; or visit any hotel but for special and adequate reasons." President Binney's advocacy of the city as a place where "life is seen in all its aspects" was thus qualified by the persistent belief that certain aspects of the city were too dangerous for student observation. After the University of Richmond moved from its original campus about five miles outside the city to within one-half mile of the city limits in 1834, the catalogue for the following year assured patrons of the institution that the new suburban site had "all the advantages of a location immediately in the city, with none of its evils." It was not until the founding of the University of Rochester and the old University of Chicago in the 1850's that Baptist institutions of higher education followed the example of colonial Brown and located themselves in the midst of an urban population.[6]

The record of antebellum Baptist college founding suggests that a large majority of the denomination's educators agreed with the judgment of Stephen W. Taylor of Bucknell concerning the best size for a college community. Taylor advocated Lewisburg, Pennsylvania, in 1846 as "a place of such an amount of business as to keep it sound and bright, yet a flourishing collegiate Institution would be its prominent object, and command the respect and liberal commendation of the citizens." He rephrased this reason for selecting Lewisburg a few years later, commenting that "in a village...a university may be the prominent object of public regard; (a circumstance highly conducive to its prosperity)."

---

[6]James D. Knowles, "History of the Columbian College, District of Columbia," Christian Review, II (March 1837), 130; "Columbian College," Columbian Star, February 23, 1822; Laws of the Columbian College in the District of Columbia (Washington, 1856), pp. 8, 16; "Richmond College--No. 1," Religious Herald, November 23, 1843; H.H. Harris, "Richmond College," in Herbert B. Adams, Thomas Jefferson and the University of Virginia (Washington, 1888), p. 271; Proceedings and Annual Report of the Va. Baptist Education Society, With the Rules and Regulations of the Virginia Baptist Seminary, etc. etc. etc. (Richmond, 1835), p. 12. The population of Providence when Brown University moved there from Warren in 1770 was about 4,000. Although Providence was not chartered as a city until 1830, Carl Bridenbaugh lists it among those towns which between 1743 and 1760 "became small cities and took on many of the attributes of urban life." The college was on a hill overlooking most of the town, but was only a few blocks from the business center. See Carl Bridenbaugh, Cities in Revolt: Urban Life in America, 1743-1776 (New York, 1955), p. 5; Walter C. Bronson, The History of Brown University, 1764-1914 (Providence, 1914), p. 50.

With this base of support and without any competing institutions in the area, Taylor anticipated that an institution would have sufficient time to "create most of its
own patronage."[7]

Nine out of the sixteen institutions in this study
selected settlements having a population of 1,000-2,000
in the town or township. Two others, Shurtleff and Colgate, placed themselves in populations falling just outside
this range. When chosen as the site for Shurtleff in 1831,
Upper Alton, Illinois, and its neighbor, Lower Alton, had
a combined population of only about 500. It was evident,
however, that the Altons were rapidly growing, and just a
few years later their population exceeded 1,000. Hamilton,
New York, numbered about 2,600 residents in the township
when Colgate University located there in 1819, but the
village of Hamilton consisted of only about forty buildings
and was hardly destined to become even remotely urban. A
town of approximately 1,000-2,000 was for a substantial
majority of Baptist colleges the most congenial home. Such
towns were, in the words of Ransom Dunn when seeking a new
site for Hillsdale College, small enough so "the people
can appreciate such an institution" yet large enough to

---

[7]Taylor, "University at Lewisburg,"; Taylor, "Brief
History," p. 10.

"do something handsome" for it in terms of buildings or
other forms of support.[8]

Two of the five clear-cut exceptions to this general
trend, Mercer University and Wake Forest College, selected
sites where there were no settlements at all. The remaining
three were the urban or suburban institutions of George
Washington, Richmond, and Rochester. In each case the exception can be quite easily explained and usually, at least
for the years prior to 1850, does not challenge the wisdom
of the majority. Mercer was a particularly well-financed
institution. Beginning with the Penfield bequest and greatly aided by the personal fortune Jesse Mercer acquired
through marriage, the institution by 1837 had over $80,000
in subscriptions, and school properties valued at $30,000.
Although plans were made that same year to create a town
around the college site, this was not a financial necessity.

---

[8]Sources of population data other than decennial census
reports: "Interesting Statistics," Regular Baptist Miscellany,
II (March 1831), 90 /re Granville/; Mitchell B. Garrett, Sixty Years of Howard College, 1842-1902, Howard College Bulletin, LXXXV, No. 4 (Birmingham, Ala., 1927), p. 18; Carlton
C. Sims, "Rutherford County from 1815 to 1946," A History
of Rutherford County, ed. Carlton C. Sims (n.p., ca. 1947),
p. 39; Prospectus and Course of Studies of Union University
of Tennessee (Nashville, Tenn., 1848), p. 3; Peck, Guide,
pp. 296-97; J.M. Peck, A New Guide For Emigrants to the West,
Containing Sketches of Michigan, Ohio, Indiana, Illinois,
Missouri, Arkansas, With the Territory of Wisconsin and the
Adjacent Parts (Boston, 1837), pp. 307-08; Horatio G. Spaf-
ford, A Gazetteer of the State of New York (Albany, N.Y.,
1813), p. 202; Ransom Dunn, "The Story of the Planting: A
Reminiscence of the Founding and Early History of Hillsdale
College," Reunion, May 6, 1885.

Lacking such sources of individual wealth and finding the anticipated denominational support developing only at a very slow pace, Wake Forest College was more than $20,000 in debt by 1839. Subsequent attempts to create a college town met with little success, and the college was not entirely free from debt until 1860. George Washington was founded with the anticipation of national Baptist support. But internal difficulties and competition from Baptist colleges founded in states where the University once drew its support created serious financial difficulties during its early decades. An assessment of local support in 1832 noted a disturbing urban indifference to the institution and attributed this to the fact that "business and politics are the absorbing things here." Five years later George Washington was struggling to raise the mere $15,000 that would keep it from being auctioned off to pay debtors. Where denominational support failed to meet the expectations of the founders of Wake Forest and George Washington, this was not the case with the University of Richmond. In 1832 Virginia was second only to New York in total Baptists and had over 15,000 more members of the denomination than third-ranking Georgia. For more than a decade, agents for George Washington University had been cultivating a favorable attitude toward education among this large Baptist population. Only a very small percentage of Baptists in

the state held anti-mission sentiments. The magnitude of
this denominational backing more than compensated for any
urban indifference encountered in the city of Richmond.
By the 1850's the demand for higher education in western
New York was sufficiently developed to make the University
of Rochester an almost instant success. Railroad facilities
and the Erie Canal permitted the new university to draw a
substantial number of students from far into the wealthy
countryside. About one-quarter of the students even came
from outside New York State. Encountering only one competing college within an area containing almost 600,000
inhabitants, the University of Rochester had little cause
to worry about any liabilities incurred in the choice of
an urban site.[9]

[9]B.D. Ragsdale, Story of Georgia Baptists, I (Atlanta,
1932), 24, 60; George W. Paschal, History of Wake Forest
College, I (Wake Forest, N.C., 1935), 48-51; Ragsdale, Story,
I, 13-14, 24-25, 60; Christian Index, History of the Baptist
Denomination in Georgia: With Biographical Compendium and
Portrait Gallery of Baptist Ministers and Other Georgia Bap-
tists (Atlanta, Ga., 1881), p. 156; B.M. Sanders to Samuel
Wait, June 13, 1838, Samuel Wait Correspondence, Baptist
Historical Collection, Wake Forest College Library; Paschal,
History, I, 223-24, 250, 185, 190, 455, 300; "Columbian Col-
lege," Christian Index, January 21, 1832; Ibid., March 23,
1837; American Baptist Register for 1852, ed. J. Lansing
Burrows (Philadelphia, 1853), p. 407; Robert Ryland, The
Virginia Baptist Education Society, The Society, the Semi-
nary, the College (Richmond, 1891), pp. 6-7; Baptist Almanac
and Annual Register, 1847 (Philadelphia, 1847), pp. 25-26;
"Removal and Endowment of Madison University," New York Bap-
tist Register, January 27, 1848; "Farmers Educate Your Sons,"
Annunciator, June 20, 1850; University of Rochester, Cata-
logue, 1850/51, pp. 7-13, and 1859/60, pp. 9-12; "To the
Friends of Madison University," Supplement to the Rochester
Daily Democrat, November 9, 1847.

An examination of the eleven typical college towns
reveals several important common characteristics in addition to their size. Rarely did a college promoter or
annual catalogue fail to emphasize that a given institution had a high and healthy location. A representative
passage, from the Bucknell catalogue of 1853, notes that
the town of Lewisburg "stands on high ground, is entirely
free from those fevers which prevail in some of the adjacent districts, and has always been regarded as not inferior in salubrity to any other part of the state." Most
of the other college sites were on high ground and none
would concede a better health record to any other place
in the state. All but three of the eleven towns were located at or reasonably near the geographical center of
their respective states. Murfreesboro, Tennessee, was
advertised in the Union University catalogue as being "within a few rods of the centre of the State itself." Of those
institutions not centrally located in terms of state geography, Hillsdale College was near the center of population
in antebellum Michigan, and Shurtleff College was strate-
gically located in the heart of the Mississippi Valley. A
majority of the eleven college communities were county seats.
In the early 1840's Murfreesboro almost became the state
capital of Tennessee. Alton, Illinois, was founded after
the county seat had already been located in Edwardsville,

but the "active, aggressive" merchants and financiers of
this newer settlement "pushing out for new business, for
their own enrichment, and for the upbuilding of the town,"
had secured the state penitentiary for their community in
1827.[10]

The local economies of almost all these college towns
were either enjoying considerable prosperity at the time
they were selected as college sites or anticipating significant future growth. Some, such as Waterville, Maine,
and Greenville, South Carolina, met both these criteria.
Waterville benefited from the power afforded by two rivers,
one with a drop of nearly forty feet and the other of about
one hundred feet. This power was being harnessed for manufacturing as early as the 1790's and by the mid-1820's there
were a dozen mills in town. Located at the head of navi-
gation, Waterville by 1818 was a distribution and trading
center for a growing agricultural community. Greenville for
several decades prior to 1850 had been a small but prosperous resort for people living in the low-country and a
trading center for farmers in the Southern backwoods. Near-

[10]University at Lewisburg, Catalogue, 1853, p. 30;
Union University, Catalogue, 1849/50, p. 13, as quoted in
Richard H. Ward, "The Development of Baptist Higher Education in Tennessee," unpublished Ph.D. dissertation, George
Peabody College for Teachers, 1953, pp. 12-23; Sims, "History," p. 37; Centennial History of Madison County, Illinois,
and Its People, 1812 to 1912, ed. Wilbur T. Norton (Chicago,
1912), I, 307, 472.

by water power and the coming of the railroad presaged
increased industrial development in the 1850's.[11]

Alton, Illinois, Marion, Alabama, and Lewisburg,
Pennsylvania, were primarily centers of trade, while
Georgetown, Kentucky, benefited from both commerce and
industry. In addition to its penitentiary, Alton had important natural advantages as a river port. John Mason
Peck predicted in 1831 that "Alton will yet be the Boston
of Illinois." Despite the strong competition from nearby
St. Louis for most of the river trade, Peck was convinced
that Alton would at least be "the commercial depot for an
extensive back country, now rapidly filling up with enterprising farmers, and a place of extensive business." Before the bubble burst with the panic and the murder of
Elijah Lovejoy in 1837, Alton was a booming "commercial
emporium." Marion, located on the edge of Alabama's Black

---

[11]Waterville, Fairfield and Winslow. Souvenir. Past
and Present. Progress and Prosperity, ed. J.H. Burgess
(Waterville, Me., ca. 1902), pp. 1-2; "Waterville," Water-
ville Intelligencer, November 2, 1826; Henry S. Burrage,
"The Beginnings of Waterville College, Now Colby University,"
Collections and Proceedings of the Maine Historical Society,
IV (N.S.) (April 1893), 133; Ernest C. Marriner, The History
of Colby College (Waterville, Me., 1963), p. 61; Alfred S.
Reid, "Literary Culture in Mid-Nineteenth Century Green-
ville," Proceedings and Papers of the Greenville County
Historical Society, 1962-1964 (Greenville, S.C., 1965),
p. 56; James C. Furman, An Historical Discourse, Delivered
Before the Charleston Baptist Association, At Its Hundredth
Anniversary, Held in Charleston in November, 1851 (Charles-
ton, S.C., 1852), p. 21; Laura S. Ebaugh, "A Social History,"
The Arts in Greenville, ed. Alfred S. Reid (Greenville, S.C.,
1960), p. 16.

Belt, was a thriving center of cotton and slave trading.
By the mid-1840's the town had eight dry goods stores with
estimated total annual sales of $180,000. Completion of
the cross-cut connection to the Pennsylvania Canal in 1834,
along with the opening of the Lewisburg and Mifflinburg
Turnpike four years earlier, helped make Lewisburg a prosperous shipping center for the farm products of the fertile
Buffalo Valley. Georgetown had enough water power nearby
for a paper mill supplying Lexington, Louisville, and Cincinnati, and when selected as a college site had "a number
of considerable manufacturing establishments." On the
northern rim of the Blue Grass Region, this town also
probably benefited from its proximity to Lexington (twelve
miles to the south), the center of a prosperous agricultural
area and the commercial capital of the state prior to 1830.[12]

---

[12]J.M. Peck, A Gazetteer of Illinois (Jacksonville, Ill.,
1834), p. 173; Matthew Lawrence, John Mason Peck, The Pioneer Missionary: A Biographical Sketch (New York, 1940),
p. 62; Peck, Gazetteer, pp. 175-76; Centennial History of
Madison County, p. 306; "Illinois," Baptist Advocate, II
(June 1836), 141; Peck, New Guide, pp. 307-08; item copied
from the Alton Observer in "Miscellany," Zion's Advocate,
March 22, 1837; S.A. Townes, The History of Marion, Sketches
of Life in Perry County, Alabama (Marion, Ala., 1844), reprinted in Alabama Historical Quarterly, XIV, Nos. 3 and 4
(1952), 211, 193, 202; Garrett, Sixty, pp. 3-4; J. Orin Oliphant, "How Lewisburg Became a Canal Port," Northumberland
County Historical Society, Proceedings and Addresses, XXI
(August 1957), 66; J. Orin Oliphant and Merrill W. Linn,
"The Lewisburg and Mifflinburg Turnpike Company," Pennsylvania History, XV (April 1948), 86; Lewis E. Theiss, Centennial History of Bucknell University, 1846-1946 (Williamsport,
Pa., 1946), pp. 19-21; Sherman Day, Historical Collections
of the State of Pennsylvania (Philadelphia, 1843), p. 633;
A History of Bourbon, Scott, Harrison and Nicholas Counties,

Four towns were enjoying bursts of prosperity at the
particular moment when they became college communities.
For a few years following the War of 1812, Hamilton, New
York, experienced an "upswing of various enterprises" which
manifested itself in the construction of several new commercial buildings in the village. Although it would soon feel
the effects of the Panic of 1837, Franklin, Indiana, was
pervaded by "a general spirit of prosperity" when it became a college town in 1835. Murfreesboro, Tennessee, also
prospered during the mid-1830's. In 1833 the town had two
cotton factories, two cotton gins, numerous craftsmen, and
about a dozen stores. Any effects of the national depression were not mentioned by a visitor to Murfreesboro in 1840
who noted "abundant and very generally diffused" wealth in
the town and the fertile surrounding farm region. One year
later, Union University was located there. Business in
Granville, Ohio, from 1827 through 1831 was flourishing,
largely due to construction of the Ohio and Erie Canal. A
second generation of Granville businessmen, possessing "an
unusual degree of enterprise," won large contracts for

Kentucky, ed. William H. Perrin (Chicago, 1882), pp. 180-81;
Timothy Flint, A Condensed Geography and History of the
Western States, or the Mississippi Valley (Cincinnati, 1828),
p. 191; William J. Black, "The History of Georgetown College,
Georgetown, Ky.," History of Higher Education in Kentucky,
ed. Alvin F. Lewis (Washington, 1899), p. 140; Francis G.
Davenport, Ante Bellum Kentucky, A Social History, 1800-
1860 (Oxford, Ohio, 1943), p. 24.

construction of the nearby section of the canal. While
construction was delayed by difficult terrain between
Newark and Columbus, Granville became a thriving terminal of traffic for the portion completed north to
Cleveland.[13]

Soon after being selected as the site for Denison
University, Granville was once again secluded from the
major routes of commerce. The canal was completed to
Columbus in 1833, and Granville was connected to it only
by a six-mile "navigable feeder." The Cumberland Road
also reached Columbus in 1833, bypassing the village about
eight miles to the south and having little effect on the
local economy. Granville's young entrepreneurs could not
have foreseen the rapid decline in local prosperity due to
the crop failures, flood, and epidemic of 1834 and the panic
of 1837. But it was quite apparent from the projected
routes of the canal and turnpike that most of the economic

[13]L.M. Hammond, History of Madison County, State of New
York (Syracuse, N.Y., 1872), p. 433; /David D. Banta et al./,
History of Johnson County, Indiana (Chicago, 1888), p. 505;
Baxter E. Hobgood, "Economic History of Rutherford County,"
History of Rutherford County, ed. Carlton C. Sims (n.p., ca.
1947), p. 213; Sims, "Rutherford," p. 39; R.B.C. Howell,
"Murfreesborough," Baptist Banner and Western Pioneer, April
9, 1840; Nathan S. Burton, "Granville's Indebtedness to Jere-
miah Hall," Old Northwest Genealogical Quarterly, VIII (Octo-
ber 1905); 380; "Granville Institution," Baptist Weekly Journal of the Mississippi Valley, December 2, 1831; William T.
Utter, Granville: The Story of an Ohio Village (Granville,
Ohio, 1956), pp. 106-11; Henry Bushnell, The History of Granville, Licking County, Ohio (Columbus, Ohio, 1889), p. 133.

gains induced by their construction were of a temporary nature. Beyond becoming a trading center for farmers in the vicinity, the outlook for Granville's economy was not very bright. Given this situation, Granville's warm reception to plans for locating Denison University there in 1831 may be partly understood in conjunction with the town's efforts the following year to change the county seat from Newark to Granville. Although the town was temporarily booming, there was a pressing need to find more permanent sources of local prosperity.[14]

A similar situation existed in Hillsdale, Michigan, two decades later when the Free Will Baptists surveyed it as a possible site for their college. Completion of the segment of what soon became the Michigan Southern Railroad connecting Hillsdale with Toledo in 1843 brought great prosperity to this young town. For most of the next decade further construction of the railroad stalled, and Hillsdale served as the storage and forwarding point for a large

---

[14]Ibid., p. 143; Francis P. Weisenburger, The Passing of the Frontier, 1825-1850, Vol. III of The History of the State of Ohio, ed. Carl Wittke (Columbus, Ohio, 1941), pp. 97, 108-09; G. Wallace Chessman, Denison: The Story of an Ohio College (Granville, Ohio, 1957), pp. 17-18; J.H. Young, Tourists Pocket Map of the State of Ohio (Philadelphia, 1842); Utter, Granville, p. 214; Bushnell, History, p. 149; Chessman, Denison, p. 34; Utter, Granville, pp. 214-15; Memorial Volume of Denison University, 1831-1906 (Columbus, Ohio, 1907), p. 52; Bushnell, History, p. 144; cf. Chessman, Denison, p. 18, concerning the probability of an awareness of this need in 1831.

domestic trade. In early 1853, less than a year after the
railroad was completed to Chicago, Ransom Dunn arrived in
town and proposed at a meeting of prominent citizens that
Hillsdale bid for the Free Will Baptist college planning to
move from Spring Arbor. Dunn later recalled that completion
of the railroad to Chicago and "the consequent depression
in business" experienced by Hillsdale "doubtless had some
influence in stimulating the interest to hear what this pro-
claimer of a new college would say." Badly in need of a
new local industry, Hillsdale citizens bid for and welcomed
their college with an enthusiasm comparable to that of Granville, Ohio. In both cases, despite the future prospects or
present state of the economy, Baptist educators found for
their college a population with particular reason to "appreciate such an institution."[15]

Dunn and his associates also sought "a location enjoying railroad facilities."[16] Transportation was a key both
to the health of the local economy and to the ease with which
a college could attract students. Eight of the eleven college towns were located directly on major routes of travel.

[15]Compendium of History and Biography of Hillsdale
County, Michigan, ed. Elon G. Reynolds (Chicago, 1903),
p. 55; Willis F. Dunbar, Michigan: A History of the Wolver-
ine State (Grand Rapids, Mich., 1965), p. 383; Dunn, "Story."

[16]Ibid.

The other three, Hamilton, Granville, and Lewisburg, were
close enough to such routes to benefit in terms of student
access, if not commercial gain.

At the time they were chosen to be college towns, all
but Hillsdale were served by major coach roads, turnpikes,
canals, or rivers. Georgetown, Marion, Murfreesboro, and
Greenville were each at the intersection of several important thoroughfares leading to centers of population such as
Lexington, Cincinnati, Mobile, Montgomery, Nashville, Columbia, and Charleston. Franklin was on the stage road to Indianapolis, and Hamilton was about six miles by coach from
the Cherry Valley Turnpike, a major route between Albany
and Buffalo. Granville and Lewisburg were near to both
turnpike and canal facilities. Except in winter, when it
was necessary to take the road along the Kennebec River,
the 180 miles between Waterville and Boston could be traveled completely by water, at a cost (in 1831) of $3.25.
Situated near the confluence of the Mississippi, Missouri,
and Illinois rivers, Alton could be easily reached by a
large portion of the population in the Mississippi Valley.[17]

[17]/Map of/ Kentucky (Philadelphia: A. Finley, 1823);
David H. Burr, /Maps of the United States, Exhibiting the
Post Offices and Post Roads/ (n.p., 1839); Tourists' Pocket
Map of the State of Indiana (Philadelphia: S. Augustus Mitch-
ell, 1835); John H. Eddy, The State of New York With Part of
the Adjacent States (New York: Samuel Maverick, 1818); Chess-
man, Denison, pp. 17-18; Reuben W. Dunn, "The Manufacturing
Industries of Waterville," The Centennial History of Water-

Hillsdale was the one town which already had railroad
facilities when selected as a college site. In the 1840's
train service came to Franklin and Waterville. Railroad
lines arrived in Murfreesboro, Alton, and Greenville in
the early 1850's and reached Marion later in the decade.
Although direct service did not reach them until the 1870's
and 1880's, Georgetown was within six miles of a depot as
early as 1835, and stations were located even closer to
Granville and Lewisburg in the 1850's. Hamilton was the
only college town without at least limited access by rail
prior to the Civil War. Denison's promoters might try to
make a virtue out of being close enough to gain the advantages yet sufficiently removed to avoid "the attendant evils,
especially to the young, of railroad depots." James Furman
could envision his institution of "Sacred Learning" as pro-
tector of Greenville against the "Vice" brought by the railroad. Yet such transportation facilities were so important
and college sites were so shrewdly selected that even the
tiny communities of Penfield, Georgia and Wake Forest, North

ville, Kennebec County, Maine, ed. Edwin C. Whittemore
(Waterville, Me., 1902), p. 340; Moses Greenleaf, Map of
the District of Maine (n.p., 1815); Waterville College:
Origin, Progress, & Present State of the College (Portland,
Me., 1822), p. 3; "Waterville College," Zion's Advocate,
January 27, 1831; Justus Bulkley, Historical Sketch of
Shurtleff College, Upper Alton, Illinois (Upper Alton, Ill.,
1865), p. 2.

Carolina, had railroad service at hand before 1850.[18]

In most cases a town was selected in which formal agencies of male secondary education were either nonexistent or
ready to be relinquished so that the new college was assured
of quickly becoming the community's sole institution for
instructing boys on this as well as the collegiate level.
In 1817 there was no academy within ten miles of Waterville.
Other than the preparatory department of Denison, Granville
had no institution of formal secondary education until 1833.
An "Advanced School," separate from Shurtleff, was not opened
in Alton until 1858. Hillsdale built a new schoolhouse in
1848 and had many pupils ready for secondary education by
the time its college arrived. Facilities of the county academies in Georgetown and Murfreesboro were turned over to the

---

[18]Crisfield Johnson, "History of Hillsdale County," His-
tory of Hillsdale County, Michigan, With Illustrations and
Biographical Sketches of Some of Its Prominent Men and Pio-
neers (Philadelphia, 1879), p. 45; W.R. Holloway, Indianapolis: A Historical and Statistical Sketch of the Railroad
City (Indianapolis, 1870), pp. 41-42, 69; Franklin College,
Catalogue, 1845/46, p. 11; Waterville, Fairfield, p. 2; Sims,
"Rutherford," pp. 38-39; Centennial History of Madison County,
p. 96; Arthur C. Cole, The Era of the Civil War, 1848-1870,
Vol. III in The Centennial History of Illinois, ed. Clarence
W. Alvord (Springfield, 1919), p. 42; Ebaugh, "Social His-
tory," p. 16; Albert B. Moore, History of Alabama (Univer-
sity, Ala., 1934), pp. 313-15; B.O. Gaines, The B.O. Gaines
History of Scott County, I (Reprint of original, 1904 edi-
tion; Georgetown, Ky., 1957), 128; "Granville College,"
Journal and Messenger, July 25, 1851; W. Williams, Appleton's
Railroad and Steamboat Companion (New York, 1848), map facing
p. 249; J. Orin Oliphant, The Rise of Bucknell University
(New York, 1965), p. 26; Jesse L. Rosenberger, Rochester and
Colgate: Historical Backgrounds of Two Universities (Chicago,

new colleges when they located in these towns. With Franklin College on the scene, the county academy planned for
the town of Franklin was never established.[19]

Contrasting with the numerous similarities in size of
population, avowed salubrity, central location, economic
prosperity, ease of access, and need for secondary education, is the lack of unusual Baptist strength in most of
the towns where members of the denomination located their
colleges. The college community was usually noted for its
piety, but seldom was this a predominantly Baptist piety.
Only four of the eleven college towns--Marion, Hamilton,
Georgetown, and Greenville--were clearly Baptist strong-
holds. The company of migrating New Englanders which

1925), p. 24; "Granville College," Journal and Messenger,
July 25, 1851; Furman, Historical Discourse, p. 21; "Access
to Penfield," Christian Index, January 23, 1846; Paschal,
History, I, 52, 189; Hugh T. Leffler and Albert R. Newsome,
North Carolina: The History of a Southern State (Rev. ed.;
Chapel Hill, N.C., 1963), p. 347.

[19]Raymond S. Finley, The History of Secondary Educa-
tion in Kennebec County in Maine, University of Maine
Studies, 2nd series, No. 54 (Orono, Me., 1941), chap. ii;
Howard L. Bowen, The History of Secondary Education in
Somerset County in Maine, University of Maine Bulletin,
XXXVIII, No. 1 (Orono, Me., 1935), p. 23; Utter, Gran-
ville, p. 156; Centennial History of Madison County, p. 331;
Compendium of...Hillsdale, p. 55; Black, "History," p. 142;
Frank E. Bass, "Education in Rutherford County," A History
of Rutherford County (n.p., ca. 1947), p. 147; advertisement
in the Tennessee Telegraph (Murfreesboro), October 23, 1841;
"Union University," Tennessee Baptist, May 22, 1847; /Banta
et al./, History, p. 384.

settled Granville in 1805 brought with it a fully constituted Congregational church, and contained just one
Baptist family. At the time Denison was founded the town
had a growing group of Baptists in the process of constructing their first church edifice, but Congregationalism was
to prevail as the majority local religion for many more
decades. Episcopalians constituted a church the same year
as the Baptists, and the Methodists had organized in town
over a decade earlier. Considering these facts, one college historian found the selection of Granville as home
for a Baptist college so unlikely that he felt at least a
partial role must be attributed to "the Providential plan."
Presbyterians were the largest single denomination in both
Franklin and Lewisburg. The Franklin Baptist Church strug-
gled into existence only a few years before the town was
designated as college site. When it was organized in 1844,
the Baptist church in Lewisburg was the only church of that
denomination in the entire county. Methodists and Presbyterians were the leading denominations in both Murfreesboro
and Alton. Not until after the arrival of the denomination's
college was a Baptist church formed in Waterville and a Free
Will Baptist church founded in Hillsdale.[20]

[20]Benjamin F. Riley, History of the Baptists of Alabama,
1808-1894 (Birmingham, Ala., 1895), p. 124; Townes, History,
p. 200; Julia M. Lovelace, A History of the Siloam Baptist
Church, Marion, Alabama (Birmingham, Ala., ca. 1958), p. 10;
Howard D. Williams, First Baptist Church, Hamilton, New York:

160

College communities often possessed a modicum of culture as well as piety. All but Alton, Franklin, and Hillsdale were settled for more than twenty years before they
became college towns. Four had histories of more than
forty years. A large majority were not fledgling frontier
towns but rather well-established communities within the
context of their respective regions. Granville in the 1830's
has been described as "an oasis of New England traditions
and spirit in the midst of the shifting sands and turbulence
of the New West." Summer visitors brought to Greenville
homes the culture and polish of Charleston and even Europe.
Marion had so many families with well-stocked libraries that
by rolling a wheelbarrow from house to house in the early

Historical Sketch, 1796-1961 (n.p., n.d.), pp. 1, 7; "The
Church at Georgetown," Baptist Chronicle and Literary Reg-
ister, II (April 1831), 58-59; Seventh Census of the United
States; 1850 (Washington, 1853), pp. 349-51; Bushnell, His-
tory, p. 37; Utter, Granville, pp. 120-21; Chessman, Denison,
p. 19; Utter, Granville, p. 113; Jacob Little, A New Year's
Sermon, Delivered in Granville, Licking County, Ohio, On the
First Sabbath of January, 1849 (Newark, Ohio, 1849), p. 13;
Bushnell, History, pp. 131, 222-23; Francis W. Shepardson,
Denison University, 1831-1931, A Centennial History (Gran-
ville, Ohio, 1931), pp. 17-19; John F. Cady, The Centennial
History of Franklin College (n.p., 1934), p. 33; Theiss,
Centennial History, p. 27; W.T. Stott, History of Fifty Years
of the First Baptist Church of Franklin, Indiana (n.p., n.d.),
pp. 4-5; "Biographical," Baptist Memorial and Monthly Chron-
icle, I (March 1842), 79; J. Orin Oliphant, The Beginnings of
Bucknell University: A Sampling of the Documents (Lewisburg,
Pa., 1954), p. 23; R.B.C. Howell, "Murfreesborough," Baptist
Banner and Western Pioneer, April 9, 1840; Peck, Gazetteer,
pp. 174-75; Centennial History of Madison County, pp. 337-
41; Minnie S. Philbrick, Centennial History of the First Baptist Church of Waterville, Maine (Waterville, Me., 1925), pp.
5-6; Windsor H. Roberts, A History of the College Baptist
Church, 1855-1955 (n.p., n.d.), pp. 5-7.

1840's, President Samuel Sherman was able to collect "a
respectable nucleus of a library" for his college.[21] Thus
in many cases towns were selected that were well-suited not
only to feel and appreciate the economic benefits of a college but also to welcome the cultural benefits brought by
institutions of higher education.

II

A few years after Lewisburg became the site of Bucknell a letter in the local newspaper assessed the impact of
"this literary enterprise, undertaken by a few of our public spirited citizens, but in which thousands are now co-
operating." The author claimed that the new college "has
done more to spread the knowledge of a town that map pub-
lishers have but recently deigned to notice, than any other
event in its somewhat long but peaceful history." Apparently
finding them too obvious to enumerate further, the author
concluded that "the incidental and increasing advantages of
such an institution to the town may easily be conceived."[22]

---

[21]Memorial Volume of Denison, p. 7; Ebaugh, "Social
History," pp. 11-13; Benjamin F. Riley, A Memorial History
of the Baptists of Alabama (Philadelphia, 1923), p. 77.

[22]"Education in Pennsylvania," Lewisburg Chronicle,
September 15, 1848.

Local cultural and economic benefits such as those here
alluded to were rapidly and forcefully experienced by college communities.

The process of interweaving the fortunes of college
and community had important cultural dimensions. Substantial contributions were made by colleges in the area
of local secondary and elementary education. Most institutions initially functioned on only a preparatory level,
and some even had elementary departments. Preparatory instruction continued to be offered long after these schools
became full-fledged colleges. Between 1820 and 1861 Baptist colleges educated as many, if not more, students in
their preparatory departments than in their collegiate
courses. Hillsdale during the 1858/59 school year had
632 preparatory and 37 college students. At Shurtleff,
Denison, and Franklin throughout most of this period the
number of preparatory students each year was about double
the college course enrollment. Numbers were more evenly
balanced at the other institutions, but data on student
residences indicates that all Baptist colleges provided
terminal secondary education for local students.[23]

---

[23]These generalizations are based on data taken from a
total of 234 catalogues issued prior to the Civil War by
the 16 colleges included in this study. Almost 75% of all
catalogues published between 1825 and 1862 have been located
and examined. All but a few contain lists of students and
their homes. Totals of the preparatory department lists,
including figures from other sources and estimates for years

Preparatory or "academical" departments were designed
not only to prepare boys for college entrance, but also "to
impart to those contemplating no such connection, a good
common education, in some degree polished and finished by
the facilities arising from the relation which this department bears to the college." The quality of secondary education offered by many colleges to their communities is more
explicitly suggested by the claim of Mercer's trustees that
"the large share of attention which the preparatory classes
in this Institution will receive from the Professors, will
give it a preference over any of the County Academies." In
the mid-1840's Hamilton Academy experienced a damaging decline in enrollment due to competition from high-grade instruction offered in Colgate's preparatory department.[24]

---

when no catalogue was published or located, indicate that
approximately 10,000 individuals received secondary instruction at these institutions. This estimated total
assumes the average length of study to be about two years
per student. Analysis of student origins based on a sample
of 26 catalogues issued by 12 different institutions shows
an average of 40% of the preparatory enrollment drawn from
the college town, another 10% from elsewhere in the county,
and an additional 20% from outside the county but within 60
miles of the college. Since the number of students from
the college town is usually more than double the number of
local boys enrolled in college courses, a significant portion of the students from the town and nearby were probably
receiving terminal education.

[24]Wake Forest College, Catalogue, 1848/49, p. 12;
"Mercer University," Christian Index, January 27, 1843;
Williams, "History," p. 147.

Quality, however, was not usually the issue when competitors began to appear. Academies founded by Congregationalists in Granville, Unitarians in Waterville, and
Episcopalians in Marion produced declines in preparatory
department enrollments of the Baptist colleges in these
towns. Rival Baptist academies in the vicinity drew potential students away from the preparatory departments of
Shurtleff and Union. Another source of competition appeared
in the late 1850's with the development of public high
schools. Despite some declines in enrollment due to people
sending their sons to secondary schools a little nearer
home or of their own denomination, most preparatory departments continued to provide secondary education for
significant numbers of local boys.[25]

Partial collegiate courses were another educational
benefit for residents of the college environs. Such a
course was cited in 1849 as evidence of Georgetown College's
"peculiar adaptation to the wants of the community in which
it is located." Students in these programs recited with

---

[25]Shepardson, Denison, pp. 49, 72; Ernest C. Marriner,
Kennebec Yesterdays (Waterville, Me., 1954), p. 213; "Re-
port," Alabama Baptist, January 16, 1850; Austen K. deBlois,
The Pioneer School: A History of Shurtleff College, Oldest
Educational Institution in the West (New York, 1900), p. 118;
W.G. Inman, "The History of Union University," Baptist and
Reflector, August 13, 1891; "Schools and Colleges," Journal
and Messenger, July 16, 1858; Cady, Centennial History,
p. 87.

many of the regular college classes but generally pursued
a shorter and less classical course of studies. At the
end of a year or two they received, in lieu of a degree,
"full testimonials of their respective attainments." This
option was frequently used by ministerial students, but
student lists giving residence data indicate partial
courses were also appealing to young men of the college
town or nearby. Although President George C. Chandler
expressed concern over the number of students leaving
school during the middle of the spring session, part-time
education remained available to youth living in the vicinity of Franklin College.[26] This opportunity was vigorously
promoted by the local newspaper:

> Young men of Johnson County, don't let the
> golden opportunity - the long winter - slip
> away unimproved! You have an institution of
> learning almost right in sight of your own
> homes, and how easily you could spend this
> Winter within its walls, and take the plow
> next Spring, physically refreshed, and if
> industrious, mentally grown.[27]

In addition to "the education of all classes in the
best manner possible" and the training of ministers,

---

[26]Anonymous letter to the editor, Georgetown Herald,
August 15, 1849; Waterville College, Catalogue, 1834/35,
p. 9; "Waterville Commencement," Zion's Advocate, August 10,
1836; "Franklin College," Christian Messenger, August 21,
1849.

[27]"Proposed Endowment of Franklin College, $100,000,"
Weekly Democratic Herald (Franklin, Ind.), November 24,
1859.

promoters of Shurtleff College planned to "extend the
blessings of instruction to every settlement, by aiding
those who wish to become well-qualified to teach common
schools." Claiming that "professional teachers should be
ranked next to good ministers of the Gospel," Stephen W.
Taylor envisioned Bucknell as, among other things, "a
nursery for competent teachers." President Jonathan Going
of Denison considered academies and colleges such as his
own "necessary for the training of teachers of common
schools until appropriate institutions shall be provided
for that purpose." In an address delivered at Wake Forest
in 1854, Basil Manly, Jr., found that colleges were still
meeting "the greatest present necessity for our schools,
by furnishing a supply of competent teachers." With no
state normal schools in the Mississippi Valley until the
late 1850's and none functioning in a state such as Maine
until the 1860's, denominational colleges were important
sources of skilled teachers for local schools.[28]

Only a few schools offered specific normal courses
such as those established at Bucknell and Furman in the

[28]"Alton Seminary," Cross and Baptist Journal of the
Mississippi Valley, June 13, 1834; Taylor, "University at
Lewisburg," Christian Chronicle, December 9, 1846; Jonathan
Going, Inaugural Address at the Anniversary of the Gran-
ville Literary and Theological Institution, August 8, 1838
(Columbus, Ohio, 1839), p. 15; Basil Manly, Jr., A Plea for
Colleges (Philadelphia, 1854), p. 20; John W. Cook, Educa-
tional History of Illinois (Chicago, 1912), chap. viii;
Edward W. Hall, History of Higher Education in Maine (Wash-
ington, 1903), p. 188.

mid-1850's. Unsuccessful in their attempts to gain state
approval and support for teacher training programs, Franklin
and Wake Forest abandoned efforts to establish such departments on a formal basis. But in the various scientific,
English, and preparatory courses of most antebellum Baptist colleges, "special attention" was given "to that class
of young men, who wish to qualify themselves to become skillful instructors of common schools."[29]

Pedagogical concerns and benefits were both regional
and local. Georgetown's trustees were disturbed by "the
great destitution felt throughout the South-west in regard
to an adequate supply of competent teachers." To help
alleviate this situation, the college catalogue of 1856/57
offered free tuition and guaranteed placement in a good
teaching job to anyone who promised to teach for five years
after completing either the regular or scientific course.
Young men attracted to the college from a distance by such
an offer might leave the college environs upon graduating.
But at least while attending college they were likely to
join the sizable number of their fellow students providing

[29]Oliphant, Rise, p. 68; William J. McGlothlin, Baptist
Beginnings in Education: A History of Furman University
(Nashville, Tenn., 1926), p. 117; Cady, Centennial History,
p. 53; Paschal, History, I, 372; Annual Meeting of the Trustees of the Granville Literary and Theological Institution
and of the Ohio Baptist Education Society, August 14th and
15th, 1833 (Cincinnati, 1833), p. 5; Paschal, History, I,
372.

local schools with valuable teaching talent. One of the
reasons advanced for founding a Baptist college in Indiana
was that in sending boys to colleges of the denomination
in other states "we must lose their instructions in common
schools during their vacations." Soon after Franklin was
founded students from this "infant college" began teaching
in the district schools of the county.[30]

An increase in the local opportunities for secondary
and in some cases higher education of women was also likely
to follow the founding of a college, even though all in this
study except Hillsdale were never or only briefly coeduca-
tional before 1860. Waterville Academy, an adjunct to the
College managed by the college faculty, had seventy-four
women students in 1834. Professor Jonathan Farnham of
Georgetown College established a "seminary for young ladies"
near the college campus in 1846. The wife of Union's president added the Tennessee Baptist Female Institute to Murfreesboro's educational facilities in 1851. Bucknell
opened its University Female Institute in 1852 under the
supervision of the University's president and trustees.
More than half of the students came from Lewisburg. The

[30]Georgetown College, Catalogue, 1856/57, p. 16; Henry
D. Kingsbury, "City of Waterville," Illustrated History of
Kennebec County, Maine, eds. Henry D. Kingsbury and Simeon
L. Deyo (New York, 1892), I, 584; Shepardson, Denison, p. 37;
"To the Baptists of Indiana," Cross and Baptist Journal of
the Mississippi Valley, April 11, 1834; /Banta et al./,
History, pp. 284-85.

South Carolina Baptist Convention founded a women's college in Greenville soon after Furman moved there.[31]

In 1831 the Baptist church of Granville extended a call to Jonathan Going, who was in the sixteenth year of a highly successful pastorate in Worcester, Massachusetts. Going did not accept the call from Granville's young church of fewer than one hundred members. Six years later the preaching of this nationally prominent Baptist came to the Granville church when Going entered its pulpit as Denison University's new president. Going was but one of a succession of Denison presidents and faculty members supplying the local pulpit during a considerable number of the pre-Civil War years. Students from Denison also "added much to the strength of the church and the interest of their meetings." The distinguished abilities of presidents and faculty members from many other Baptist colleges of this period were made available to local churches of the denomination.[32]

[31]Vivian L. Moore, The First Hundred Years of Hillsdale College (Ann Arbor, Mich., 1944), p. 7; Cady, Centennial History, p. 88; Marriner, History, p. 326; "Waterville Academy," Zion's Advocate, August 6, 1834; Black, "History," p. 154; advertisement, Tennessee Baptist, August 23, 1851; Oliphant, Rise, pp. 72, 75; University at Lewisburg, Catalogue, 1850/51, pp. 15-17; University Female Institute, Catalogue, 1860, pp. 7-11; Robert N. Daniel, Furman University: A History (Greenville, S.C., 1951), pp. 72-73.

[32]Memorial Volume of Denison, p. 41; Kate S. Hines, "The Story of the Granville Baptist Church, Commemorating Its First Century, 1819-1919," typescript, ca. 1919, Denison University Archives, p. 56; Bushnell, History, p. 219; Hines, "Story," p. 94; Williams, "History," p. 302; History of

Non-Baptists as well as Baptists had frequent access
to college talent. Numerous public lectures and addresses
were presented by faculty members. Colorful annual exhibitions of student literary societies were well attended by
townspeople. Discussing the effect of local literary institutions on the children of Marion, the town newspaper
observed that "association with students who are students
incites the youth to mental improvement." The impact of
Franklin students teaching in district schools before the
development of a well-supported public school system in
Indiana was assessed by a contemporary historian who was
born and raised in Johnson County during the 1830's and
1840's. He recalled that "they taught in such a spirit of
enthusiasm as to implant in the minds of their scholars
far higher ideals of education than had been the case before. They did much to leaven the lump and prepare the
people of the county for what was to follow."[33]

Bourbon, Scott, p. 192; J.M. Bradley and Ellis M. Ham, History of the Great Crossings Baptist Church (Georgetown, Ky.,
1945), pp. 34, 36; H. Farr Waggener, The First Baptist Church
of Upper Alton: A History of One Hundred Years (Alton, Ill.,
ca. 1930), pp. 4-5; Stott, History, p. 40; Ragsdale, Story,
I, 65; Paschal, History, I, 468.

[33]Howard D. Williams, "The History of Colgate Univer-
sity to 1869," unpublished Ph.D. dissertation, Harvard Uni-
versity, 1949, p. 129; "The Lewisburg Course of Lectures,"
Lewisburg Chronicle and West Branch Farmer (Lewisburg, Pa.),
April 11, 1852, and February 2, 1855; "Lectures on the Nat-
ural Sciences," Alabama Baptist, March 20, 1850; E.W. Sikes,
"The Genesis of Wake Forest College," Publications of the
North Carolina Historical Commission, I (1907), 555;

Of the many broad cultural functions performed by
Baptist colleges, the education of full-time college students was the least local in nature. Yet even in this role
colleges served a large number of young men living in the
immediate vicinity. Colgate and Union drew close to one-
half of their college students from outside the state in
which the school was located, and a large portion of George
Washington's students came from well outside the District
of Columbia. But the remaining thirteen institutions found
a majority of their students within a sixty-mile radius of
the campus. An average of 20% of the enrollment in college
courses during the antebellum years came from the college
town itself; another 5% came from elsewhere in the county.
Approximately 30% of the student body was drawn from outside the county but within sixty miles of the college.
Only about 10% had homes outside the state.[34]

D.P. Baldwin, "Madison University Thirty Years Ago," Madisonensis, October 10, 1885; "Literary Exercises," Democratic
Reflector (Hamilton, N.Y.), January 29, 1845; "Marion and
Its Schools," Tri-Weekly Commonwealth (Marion, Ala.), May
21, 1859; Charles W. Taylor, Biographical Sketches and Review of the Bench and Bar of Indiana (Indianapolis, 1895),
pp. 675-77; /Banta et al./, History, pp. 284-85.

[34]These generalizations are based on an analysis of student lists from 36 catalogues. This sample, taken from 234
catalogues, consists of catalogues selected from 13 different
institutions at five-to ten-year intervals, and spans the
years between 1825 and 1862. A sixty-mile radius was a yard-
stick sometimes used by antebellum Baptist educators themselves in defining a college's constituency. See, "Richmond
College--No. 4," Religious Herald, December 21, 1843.

Provision of board and sometimes rooms for the more
than three-quarters of the college students who came from
a distance created one of the several economic ties quickly
formed between college and community. Noneconomic reasons
for employing the resources of the town in this respect
were stated in the catalogue of Georgetown College:

> The students do not board in commons:
> (a plan which though somewhat cheaper is
> productive of disorder,) but are received
> into the families of the citizens, where
> they retain propriety of manners, enjoy a
> constant and parental supervision, escape
> numerous temptations, and in case of sick-
> ness receive proper attention.[35]

The building committee of Bucknell's board of trustees expressed a more practical reason in their argument for de-
laying construction of additional dormitory rooms and a
commons. The committee calculated that "boarding and
lodging the Students with the Citizens of the Town, will
interest them in the College, by the strongest plea, self-
interest." By boarding eighteen different students for
varying periods of time during the 1851/1852 school year,
one Lewisburg woman had a profit margin (not counting her
own labor) of more than 30%. It was estimated in 1856 that
from student board "more than $200 are poured...weekly into
the pockets of the residents."[36] A majority of the other

[35]Georgetown College, Catalogue, 1845/46, p. 11.

[36]Quoted in Theiss, Centennial History, pp. 63-64; Eric
G. Stewart, "Living in Lewisburg in the 1840's and Early 1850's,"
term paper written for History 221, May 17, 1934, Bucknell
University Archives, pp. 6-7; "The University at Lewisburg—
No. 1," Christian Chronicle, August 13, 1856.

antebellum Baptist college towns received this same form
of income.

Adding to the money spent for student board all the
other local expenditures by University of Richmond students,
President Robert Ryland estimated in 1844 an annual total
exceeding $15,000, "an amount which would seek other channels
but for the existence of such an institution." In 1852 it
was claimed that Denison brought "at least $10,000" into
Granville and that "the net profits on this sum must be at
least $2,000." At the end of the decade about the same
total was projected for Franklin College. Going beyond
student spending to calculate the total amount put into
Greenville's economy by Furman during 1854, the University
treasurer arrived at a figure of $75,000. Marion's news-
paper found in 1859 that Howard College and Judson Female
Institute "bring here and put in circulation hundreds and
thousands of dollars that would never reach us otherwise."
Rochester's return on money contributed by citizens to the
University was determined in the mid-1850's as comparable
to the annual interest on $1,000,000.[37] In terms of regular

[37]"Richmond College--No. 10," Religious Herald, February
1, 1844; Silas Bailey, Mr. Little's New Year's Sermon: Review
of Mr. Little's Twenty-Fifth New Year's Sermon (Columbus,
Ohio, 1852), p. 15; "Proposed Endowment of Franklin College,"
Weekly Democratic Herald (Franklin, Ind.), November 24, 1859;
"The University and College," Southern Baptist, February 28,
1855; "Marion and Its Schools," Tri-Weekly Commonwealth (Marion, Ala.), May 21, 1859; Martin B. Anderson, The End and Means
of a Liberal Education: An Inaugural Address, Delivered July
11, 1854 (Rochester, N.Y., 1855), pp. 63-64.

cash revenue alone, colleges were a profitable community investment.

Broader economic benefits were suggested by the local newspaper in promoting Franklin College's drive for an endowment of $50,000, the first $10,000 of which was to be secured from Johnson County. "Certain persons," the paper reported, "paid not less than $10,000 in order to secure a branch of the Bank of the State, in one locality; and why? Businessmen know why." A subsequent editorial told how enterprising men in young towns "labor just as hard and diligently to secure the location of a College, as they do to secure the location of a Railroad, knowing that the one pays just as well as the other."[38]

An important part of the payment came in terms of land values. "What does the man do," the same newspaper asked, "who wants to sell his farm? He advertises it as lying within a certain distance of the Franklin College. Why? Because it enhances the value. Just so it is with our town property." At Georgetown in late 1829, anticipation of the opening of the college with a distinguished denominational leader as its president resulted in rising property values and sale of land "with unusual rapidity." Even before construction of college buildings started, the

---

[38]"Proposed Endowment of Franklin College," Weekly Democratic Herald (Franklin, Ind.), November 24, 1859; "Franklin College," ibid., April 26, 1860.

relocation of Hillsdale College had a similar effect on real estate within a ten-mile radius of the town. Because the college would "enhance the value of their real estate," founders of Bucknell who resided in Lewisburg felt it necessary to argue that "self-interest had not determined the location." Justifying expenditures for buildings to house the many denominational colleges in America, President Justin R. Loomis of Bucknell contended that any excessive proliferation of college facilities was "more than refunded by the additional value given to property by the proximity of a college."[39]

Institutions themselves as well as local citizens reaped the benefits of college-induced land appreciation. The great contemporary faith in education's effect on land values and the success attendant upon this faith can be seen in two Baptist educational efforts which did not result in regular collegiate institutions. In 1839 plans were formed for a collegiate and theological institution in western Pennsylvania under the auspices of the Free Baptists, a group "engaged in purifying the Church from the accursed influences of slavery." A joint-stock company

---

[39]Ibid., February 2, 1860; "Dr. William Staughton," Baptist Herald and Georgetown Literary Register, I (January 1830), 10-11; Moore, First Hundred, pp. 24-25; Stephen Taylor, "University at Lewisburg," Christian Chronicle, September 2, 1846; J.R. Loomis, An Inaugural Address Delivered July 27, 1859 (Philadelphia, 1860), p. 36.

was formed to sell $80,000 worth of shares at $500 each.
From the capital thus raised, $60,000 was to be used for
the purchase of 3,000 - 4,000 acres of land. Most of the
remaining capital would be used to erect college facilities
on 200 acres of the tract set aside for that purpose. The
rest of the land would then be distributed equitably among
the shareholders. It was expected that as soon as the college went into operation the value of the land would double
or triple. For some reason this scheme was never fully implemented, but a similar approach did result in large
profits for a contemporary institution, the Western Baptist
Theological Institute in Covington, Kentucky. Totally
lacking funds for a theological seminary, the Executive
Committee of the Western Baptist Education Society began
in 1835 to purchase on credit contiguous tracts of land
near Covington. After accumulating over 350 acres, the
Committee publicized their plans to found a school on the
site and began to sell off a portion of their purchases in
order to meet payments as they came due. By 1843 enough
was realized from land sales to pay for the original purchases, erect buildings for the Institute, and still have
almost $100,000 worth of land for an endowment.[40]

---

[40]"Western Education Society," Christian Reflector,
June 12, 1839; "First Annual Report of the Western Baptist
Education Society," Baptist Advocate, I (December 1835),
301; "Western Theological Institute," Baptist Memorial and
Monthly Chronicle, II (July 1843), 196-98.

More modest profits from nearby land were frequently
realized by Baptist colleges. Mercer University in the
early 1830's quickly bought up close to 1,000 acres adjacent
to the institution. By 1837 the school was selling some
lots from this land and had already realized almost four
times the total original purchase price. The Town Lot Fund
created by these sales continued to grow, and in the mid-
1840's helped finance several new college buildings. During the same period Wake Forest achieved a more than three-
fold gain from sale of college land. Sale of about 50 acres
near the college in the 1850's brought Bucknell a profit of
over $10,000. On the same day in 1832 that Shurtleff's
Board of Trustees was organized, arrangements were made to
purchase a college tract of 362 acres. By 1836 about
$4,000 had been received from sale of lots laid off near
the college and gradual sale of the remainder helped to
meet pressing expenses throughout the next decade. Although
college lots were put on the market as soon as instruction
began at Franklin, it was too late to profit from the pre-
1837 boom in land values. Some proceeds were received from
land sales, however, in the mid-1840's. Both Colby and the
University of Rochester also realized some income from sale
of college lands.[41]

---

[41]Plan, History and Terms of the Mercer Institute, Prepared and Published by the Teachers and Trustees of the Executive Committee of the Baptist Convention for the State of
Georgia, Who Have the Supervision of the Institution. July,

Drawing upon their own experience as well as that of
many of their local associates, Baptist educational leaders
could convincingly affirm that colleges were good for the
economy. "Considered then simply as a pecuniary question,"
Justin Loomis concluded in 1859, "the heavy pecuniary out-
lay of establishing local colleges is not a tax upon the
community. Regarded as a question of Political Economy, it
is capital profitably invested." Five years earlier Basil
Manly stated this principle in more general form before an
audience at Wake Forest: "...whatever multiplies and cheapens
the means of education and elevates its character in any
region, enhances the material prosperity of that region."
This faith in the cash value of formal education was well-
founded in local realities. Fully aware of the tens of
thousands of dollars Denison and several lesser institutions
brought annually into town, a Congregational minister could
state as literal truth in 1851 that "schools are the staple
of Granville." Five years later in a neighboring state it

1834 (n.p., n.d.), pp. 2-3; "Mercer University," Southern
Baptist and General Intelligencer, November 17, 1837; Ragsdale, Story, I, 80, 99; Paschal, History, I, 190-91; Oliphant, Rise, p. 38; /Adie K. Bell/, Report of the Board of
Trustees of the University at Lewisburg to the Patrons and
Friends of the University (Philadelphia, 1858), p. 7; Bulk-
ley, Historical Sketch, p. 3; "Illinois," Baptist Advocate,
II (June 1836), 142; "Shurtleff College," North-Western Bap-
tist, January 1, 1844; deBlois, Pioneer, p. 98; W.C. Thompson,
"The Board of Directors," First Half Century of Franklin College, Jubilee Exercises (Cincinnati, 1884), p. 33; Cady, Cen-
tennial History, pp. 36, 45; Marriner, History, pp. 18, 34;
Jesse L. Rosenberger, Rochester:The Making of a University
(Rochester, N.Y., 1927), pp. 113-14.

could be unequivocally asserted with reference to Bucknell
that "pecuniarily considered, the establishment of the University...has done more for Lewisburg than any other event
in its history."[42]

III

After enumerating the cultural and economic benefits
emanating from the University of Richmond, President Robert
Ryland asked in 1844: "Is it not then in the interest of
Richmond to cherish the youthful college situated in its
vicinity and called by its name? This question, I believe,
will be answered affirmatively by an enlightened self-love
and a liberal public spirit." A decade later Henry Whipple,
professor, trustee, and agent of Hillsdale College, suggested
to the citizens of Hillsdale County: "Every man who owns a
farm or an acre of land, or has a growing family in this
vicinity will be benefited pecuniarily by the success of
the enterprise, and should contribute of his influence and

[42]Loomis, Inaugural Address, p. 36; Manly, Plea, p. 11;
Jacob Little, Twenty-fifth New Year's Sermon. A Discourse
Preached in Granville, Ohio, on the First Sabbath of January,
1852 (Granville, Ohio, 1852), p. 29; Jacob Little, Twenty-
fourth New Year's Sermon. A Discourse Delivered at Granville,
Ohio, on the First Sabbath of January, 1851 (Granville, Ohio,
1851), p. 40; "The University at Lewisburg--No. 1," Christian
Chronicle, August 13, 1856.

his means toward its accomplishment."[43] The response anticipated by Ryland and urged by Whipple soon developed in their
own and other college communities once the tangible results
of having collegiate institutions nearby were experienced.

With denominational support slow in developing, a favorable community response was essential to the survival of
most Baptist colleges during their early years. Tuition
fees were an important source of revenue, especially those
derived from the more populous preparatory departments, but
rarely were they sufficient even to pay faculty salaries.
Sale of college land, collections of agents in areas of the
state outside the immediate vicinity of the institution,
occasional grants of state aid, and expedients such as the
granting of M.D. degrees on an examination and fee basis
provided some additional income. Yet the expenses of
founding and sustaining colleges were met only in small
part by support from these sources.[44]

---

[43]"Richmond College--No. 10," Religious Herald, February 1, 1844; "Our College," Morning Star, September 20, 1854,
copied from the Hillsdale Gazette (Hillsdale, Mich.).

[44]Ryland, Virginia Baptist, p. 14; Shurtleff College:
Its Financial Concerns, Condition and Prospects, broadside
dated August 1, 1845 (Upper Alton, Ill., 1845); Letter from
D.R. Campbell, Christian Repository, V (January 1856), 50.
The activities of agents and the state are discussed below,
chap. iv. Marriner, History, pp. 65-66; deBlois, Pioneer,
pp. 90-91, 104. Some alumni societies were formed prior to
1861, but they were not strong enough to offer substantial
financial assistance. See Chessman, Denison, p. 35.

In the early years some colleges drew effectively on the resources of the East. This was especially true in terms of personnel. Baptist Yankees were among the founders of Wake Forest, Mercer, and Baylor, and occupied the presidencies of Howard, Union, and Georgetown. Wake Forest, Georgetown, and Denison almost immediately sought faculty, funds, and equipment in the East. John Mason Peck made a highly successful trip eastward in the mid-1830's to bolster the finances of Shurtleff. By the end of the decade, however, it was becoming apparent that New England would no longer provide substantial support. The depression following 1837 and the fact that "New England is growing comparatively poor" convinced Jonathan Going in the late 1830's that Denison must be sustained almost exclusively by the people of Ohio. Unsuccessful fund-raising trips by agents of both Shurtleff and Denison in the mid-1840's signaled the end of major contributions from the East. A few years later the slavery issue began to take its toll. Upon returning from New England with books contributed to the college library, President Howard Malcom of Georgetown was accused of importing abolitionist literature which would have a disturbing influence on the students. A highly successful presidency of more than eight years was terminated soon afterward for this native of Philadelphia when it became known locally that he had recently voted

for an "Emancipation candidate."[45] The days when the East
played an important role in the life of a Baptist college
were limited in almost every case to its initial decade.

The major reason for financial distress among Baptist
colleges prior to 1850 was the pressure of debts incurred
while acquiring facilities and a corresponding lack of endowment. Hillsdale, Bucknell, Rochester, and Furman, all
of which did not begin operating as colleges at their permanent sites until the late 1840's or early 1850's, started
with at least subscriptions to an endowment fund in hand.
But their predecessors, except for Mercer, did not acquire
any significant endowment before 1845 and had to operate
in most cases for several decades without this important
source of income. Endowment fund drives at Howard, Union,
and Georgetown in the 1840's reached totals of about $50,000
in subscriptions by 1850. Campaigns launched in the early

[45]George Washington University even dispatched agents
to obtain gifts, apparatus, and endorsements from England.
See "The Columbian College in the District of Columbia,"
Latter Day Luminary, IV (March 1823), 91-94; "Substance of
the Proceedings," ibid., V (June 1824), 176; Rufus Weaver,
"The Invasion of the South by the Sainted Baptist Yankees,"
Chronicle, VII (October 1944), 165; Sikes, "Genesis," p. 552;
Leland W. Meyer, Georgetown College: Its Background and a
Chapter in its Early History (Louisville, Ky., 1929), p. 37;
Chessman, Denison, pp. 23-24; deBlois, Pioneer, p. 70;
letter from Going quoted in Willis A. Chamberlin, "Dr. Jonathan Going's Impress Upon the Midwest," Chronicle, VIII (July
1945), 113; deBlois, Pioneer, p. 103; Shepardson, Denison,
p. 60; Meyer, Georgetown, p. 73; "Georgetown College," Georgetown Herald (Georgetown, Ky.), August 15, 1849, clipping in
the "Howard Malcom Memorial Scrapbook," American Baptist Historical Society, Rochester, New York, p. 32.

1850's to endow George Washington, Richmond, Wake Forest,
Colgate, Franklin, and Denison brought in total subscriptions ranging from about $50,000 to $75,000 by 1857. Subscriptions toward an endowment for Shurtleff in the late
1850's probably did not exceed $50,000 until after 1860.
Colby had an endowment of less than $10,000 in 1857.[46]

Even the more successful of these endowment fund
drives did not produce a steady income for more than a few
Baptist colleges prior to 1860. Although some of the subscriptions bore interest until being paid in full, collections were extremely costly and uncertain. Bad harvests or
a business depression such as that of 1857 caused numerous
delays and defaults in payment. Of the $50,000 subscribed
for Wake Forest's endowment between 1850 and 1857, only
about $19,000 had been collected by the spring of 1860.

---

[46]John C. Patterson, "History of Hillsdale College,"
Collections and Researches Made By the Michigan Pioneer and
Historical Society, VI (1883), 151, 155; Oliphant, Rise,
p. 35; Rosenberger, Rochester: The Making, p. 47; McGlothlin,
Baptist Beginnings, pp. 100-104; Georgia Baptist Convention,
Minutes, 1839, pp. 7-8; Garrett, Sixty, pp. 24, 29, 60-61,
64; W.G. Inman, "The History of Union University," Baptist
and Reflector, September 10, 1891; "Georgetown College,"
Baptist Banner, January 17, 1849. Georgetown's reported
endowment seems to have vanished by 1856, and a new campaign
was launched in that year. By September, 1857, $100,000 was
subscribed. See letter from D.R. Campbell in the Christian
Repository, V (January 1856), 50, and "Georgetown College,"
Western Recorder, September 23, 1857. Earlier endowment
fund drives were conducted at George Washington, Richmond
and Colgate, but they did not raise any significant amounts.
U.S., Congress, House, Financial Condition of the George
Washington University, 61st Cong., 3rd Sess., 1910, House

In 1863 one-half of the $82,000 in pledges to Denison during
the previous decade were still outstanding and of dubious
value. Much of the money actually collected for endowments
was used to pay off old debts, construct and repair buildings,
or meet other pressing needs.[47]

Amid all the expedients and uncertainties, one source
of support provided the margin for survival. Starting with
their original bids and continuing up through their gifts
to the endowment fund drives of the 1840's and 1850's, college communities proved to be both generous and consistent
contributors to Baptist colleges. Local appeals to "an enlightened self-love and a liberal public spirit" by Baptist
educators such as Whipple and Ryland were answered affirmatively. Presented with arguments closely resembling those
advanced by Ryland, the city of Richmond subscribed the first
$38,000 toward the University's $100,000 endowment fund drive.
Soon after the appeal by Whipple, citizens of Hillsdale

Doc. 1060, pp. 9-11; The Claims of the Columbian College as
Seen in Its Past History and Present Condition (Washington,
1857), p. 10; Harris, "Richmond," p. 275; F.W. Boatwright,
"The Beginnings of Higher Education Among Virginia Baptists,"
Religious Herald, August 13, 1931; Paschal, History, I, 298;
Williams, "History," pp. 183-88, 280-82; Cady, Centennial
History, pp. 59-65; "Facts! Facts!," Journal and Messenger,
April 2, 1852; "Granville College Endowment," ibid., Septem-
ber 30, 1853; Chessman, Denison, p. 91; deBlois, Pioneer,
pp. 322-26, 142; "Educational Convention at Alton," Christian
Times, November 12, 1856; Marriner, History, p. 146.

[47]Cady, Centennial History, pp. 66, 81; Paschal, History,
I, 298, 300; Chessman, Denison, p. 91.

185

County exceeded by $7,500 their goal of $30,000 for college buildings.[48]

The dependability of support from college communities was frequently demonstrated throughout the antebellum years. Despite their early expectation that Baptists outside Ohio would assume an equal share of Denison's support, the citizens of Licking County had contributed more to the college by 1843 than either the eastern states or the rest of Ohio. Although actions to alleviate Colby's financial troubles of 1839-40 were slow in developing elsewhere, over $10,000 was quickly subscribed in Waterville. After Howard's building was destroyed by fire in 1844, the people of Marion immediately came to the rescue. Citizens of Lewisburg provided the first $20,000 in subscription to Bucknell's original endowment fund drive. A decade later they supplied almost half the money needed for new buildings. Even though Baptist wealth in Pennsylvania was concentrated in the Philadelphia area, nearly 20% of all contributions to the University prior to 1858 came from Lewisburg. By July, 1850, close to one-third of the subscription to Colgate's $60,000 endowment fund drive had been obtained in Hamilton alone. Lack of outside support for Shurtleff caused a temporary loss of faith among local backers in the early 1840's, but

[48]"Richmond College," Religious Herald, October 30, 1851, December 25, 1851, and April 15, 1852; Patterson, "Hillsdale," p. 151.

a resurgence of community support occurred in 1856 when
more than $35,000 was received from the Alton area toward
the goal of $50,000 endowment. Franklin County's quota of
$10,000 in the 1859-60 endowment fund drive of Franklin
College was oversubscribed by 100% in less than a year.
Georgetown and vicinity contributed more than half the
subscriptions reported in early 1849 by J.M. Frost, the
college agent. Seven years later President Duncan Campbell
proposed to a public meeting of Scott County residents that
they supply the first $25,000 of a $100,000 endowment fund
drive. Scott County subscribed its portion in a matter of
months, but this example was slow to "prompt liberality in
other sections."[49]

This record of local financial support reveals as much
strength in communities where Baptists did not predominate
as in those few places where they did. A few pieces of

[49]Annual Meeting of the Trustees of the Granville Literary and Theological Institution, and of the Ohio Baptist
Education Society, August 13th and 14th, 1834 (Cincinnati,
1834), pp. 8-9; "Granville College," Cross and Journal,
August 4, 1843; "Waterville College," Zion's Advocate and
Eastern Baptist, May 13, 1840; Garrett, Sixty, pp. 26-27;
Oliphant, Rise, p. 29; John H. Harris, Thirty Years as Presi-
dent of Bucknell, With Baccalaureate and Other Addresses,
compiled and arranged by Mary B. Harris (Washington, 1926),
p. 178; /Bell/, Report, p. 5; "Madison University," New York
Chronicle, II (June and July, 1850), 258; "Shurtleff College,"
Western Star, February 16, 1847; "Educational Convention at
Alton," Christian Times, November 12, 1856; Cady, Centennial
History, pp. 83-84; "Communications," Baptist Banner, January
10, 1849; "Educational," Western Recorder, December 19, 1855;
Letter from D.R. Campbell, Christian Repository, V (January
1856), 51; "Georgetown College," Western Recorder, April
16 and June 11, 1856.

evidence added to those already cited further suggest that
the contributions of people living in the vicinity of Baptist colleges were not merely based on denominational affil-
iations. After Licking County subscribed the first $25,000
in Denison's 1853 endowment fund drive, the college agent
explained why the next $25,000 was to come from counties
adjoining Licking. This decision was made, he said, not
because "the numerical or pecuniary strength of our denomination in them required them to raise that sum, but their
proximity to the College did require them to do it." Enough
subscriptions were already reported from these counties to
indicate that some of their residents were assuming this
geographical as well as denominational responsibility. Members of the Congregational church in Granville evidenced
similar feelings of local obligation with their substantial
contributions to Denison. The $14,340 provided in 1857 by
Lewisburg toward Bucknell's $30,000 building fund came from
155 local contributors. Families belonging to the town's
Baptist Church at this time probably numbered less than 75.
A prominent Catholic judge in North Carolina took an active
and deep interest in Wake Forest. Colgate received an important contribution from a wealthy Presbyterian. A devoted
historian of the Baptists in Alabama found that during the
antebellum years in Marion "all classes irrespective of

name or denomination became enlisted in the success of
Howard."[50]

Assessment of community responses in less economic
terms also points to the broad appeal of denominational
colleges. College commencements can be particularly revealing from this point of view. These "literary festivals"
lasted several days and usually featured student orations,
band music, distinguished guests, and a "President's levee."
Open to the public and promoted in the local newspapers,
these events were well attended by "friends of the college."
In 1850, when there were but five graduates, "some five or
six hundred persons,...Students and Faculty, Trustees and
Patrons, parents and children, brothers and sisters, citizens and strangers," attended the public levee following
Howard's commencement exercises. At Georgetown's commencement in 1859 about 3,000 people came to see 20 young men
graduate. Ceremonies involving a dozen or less graduates

---

[50]"Our Educational Enterprises in Ohio and Indiana,"
Journal and Messenger, September 16, 1853; "Granville College Endowment," ibid., September 30, 1853; Little, Twenty-
fifth, p. 10; Harris, Thirty Years, p. 178; Jubilee Anniversary of the First Baptist Church of Lewisburg, Pa.,
1844-1894 (Lewisburg, Pa., 1894), p. 40; Paschal, History,
I, 132-33; Williams, "History," p. 44; Riley, History,
p. 77.

attracted 4,000 - 5,000 spectators to the Bucknell campus in the late 1850's.[51]

Reports from Georgetown and Colby suggest that commencements were enthusiastically attended by the lower as well as the upper ranges of local society. A correspondent to the state Baptist newspaper who attended Georgetown's exercises in 1847 was disturbed by the hearty applause from the gallery, whose occupants "seemed to suppose that the louder the pounding, the stronger was the testimony of the excellence of the speech." By 1828, Colby's commencements were attended by a more orderly assemblage than "the motley collection that assembled en masse in 1822" and created "scenes of great confusion." Yet it could still be reported in 1845 that "our farmers, mechanics, and other laborers, gather at these anniversaries....On the present occasion... the house was crowded with what might strictly be called a popular audience. The people were there."[52]

[51]Anonymous letter in the Georgetown Herald (Georgetown, Ky.), June 16, 1847; "Howard Examination," South Western Baptist, July 31, 1850; "Georgetown College Commencement," Christian Repository, IX (August 1859), 629; "The Commencement Week," Lewisburg Chronicle (Lewisburg, Pa.), August 17, 1855; "University at Lewisburg," Baptist Family Magazine, I (September 1857), 283.

[52]"Georgetown Commencement," Baptist Banner and Western Pioneer, July 1, 1847; "Waterville College," Waterville Intelligencer (Waterville, Me.), September 25, 1828, copied from the Kennebec Journal; "Commencement at Waterville," Zion's Advocate, August 19, 1845.

Literary festivals were an important means of increasing and rallying local support for a college. They
were, as an observer of Colby's commencement in 1842 commented, well "calculated to produce a favorable impression
on the numerous friends of the institution, as well as to
awaken in the public generally a powerful interest in its
growing prosperity and usefulness." The need to bolster
local confidence was especially important during the earliest years of a college. After struggling through its first
school year in a tiny frame house, Franklin had a special
stage constructed, printed up programs, and held an "Exhi-
bition." The college's first bachelor's degree was not
granted until almost a decade later. Large crowds attending
commencements from outside the vicinity provided local merchants and keepers of boarding houses with "their annual
harvest seasons," forcefully reminding them of the economic
benefits emanating from the college. Even the music of "an
excellent brass band" such as that engaged for the Richmond
University commencement in 1852 helped to create a festive atmosphere which would leave "a strong impression upon the
public mind in favor of the College." Occasionally attention was given exclusively to those attending from the immediate vicinity, as when Howard's president employed the
occasion to deliver an address on "the advantages a

community derives from good Literary Institutions."[53]

The very fact that so many from such a broad spectrum
of the community attended may be attributed at least in
part to their appreciation of these "advantages." Literary festivals provided Baptist educators with a means of
assessing as well as further cultivating local support.
The huge crowds at Georgetown's commencement in 1845 were
regarded as evidence of the "increased interest the community is taking in education." A long anonymous letter to
the Baptist newspaper in Georgia criticised these exhibitions as superficial, contrived, "literary shows" but was
unable to explain why they succeeded in attracting both
parents and the general public year after year. One answer
to this question is suggested by an article on the commencement exercises at Mercer in 1857. By gathering annually at
"the source of science and literature," it was reported,
the community was "doing court to mental culture."[54] The
college was a source of more than just science and literature in the eyes of nearby residents, and they may not have

[53]"Commencement," Yankee Blade (Waterville, Me.), August
13, 1842; Cady, Centennial History, pp. 30, 35, 85; "Commencement Week at Mercer," Christian Index, July 22, 1857; "Literary," Western Recorder, August 4, 1852, copied from the Richmond Whig; "Howard College," South Western Baptist, July 30, 1851.

[54]"Commencement Exercises of Georgetown College, Ky.,"
Baptist Record, July 16, 1845; anonymous letter, Christian
Index, August 11, 1843; "Commencement Week at Mercer," ibid.,
July 22, 1857.

192

fully understood the values of mental culture, yet they were paying respects to an educational institution which played a tangible and important role in community life.

In 1832 Denison's trustees stated that their major objective was "to build up a useful Institution--suited to the wants and calculated to promote the welfare of a rapidly growing and free country." Examination of the relations between institutions and communities provides ample testimony that Denison and other Baptist colleges were highly successful in achieving this goal on the local level. What Marion's newspaper affirmed in regard to Howard College and the companion Judson Female Institute could be applied to antebellum Baptist colleges in general: "There is no class of persons in the community but feels the influence of these institutions pecuniarily, morally, and intellectually." A British visitor to Colby was quick to observe that "the sympathies of every class of the community" were enlisted on behalf of the college.[55] Having proved themselves useful

[55]Annual Meeting of the Ohio Baptist Education Society and of the Trustees of the Granville Literary and Theological Institution, October 6, 1832 (Cincinnati, 1832), p. 20; "Marion and Its Schools," Tri-Weekly Commonwealth (Marion, Ala.), May 21, 1859; Francis A. Cox and James Hoby, The Baptists in America: A Narrative of the Deputation From the Baptist Union in England to the United States and Canada (New York, 1836), p. 342.

to the community and successfully cultivated it as a base
of support, Baptist colleges could reach out to provide
benefits for and attract sustenance from a larger portion
of the "rapidly growing and free country."

CHAPTER IV

PUBLIC EDUCATION

Several decades after the ambitious educational plans
of America's revolutionary generation were first proposed,
reformers were struggling to create support for a system
of common schools. "Much has been said and written upon
the subject of education," remarked one observer in 1836,
"but still its importance does not appear to be so fully
realized, by the majority of people, as its incomparable
value would seem to demand." "The number of those who
have deliberately calculated the benefits of an extensive,
sound, intellectual and moral cultivation," noted the
Alabama Baptist in 1844, "is comparatively small. The
mass of people do not bestow sufficient attention on the
matter, to become thoroughly interested." These hard facts
were soon encountered by the "few active and influential
men" who founded Baptist colleges. Like contemporary common
school reformers, this group was "in advance of public
opinion."[1]

---

[1]J.M. Austin, "Education," Evangelical Magazine and Gospel Advocate, February 27, 1836; "An Appeal to the People of Alabama on Popular Education," Alabama Baptist, January 6, 1844; David Benedict, Fifty Years Among the Baptists (New York, 1860), pp. 314, 226; B.D. Ragsdale, Story of Georgia Baptists, I (Atlanta, 1932), 8-9, 68-69.

Slowly developing denominational support plus the more
rapidly tapped but also limited resources of the small college community were insufficient to sustain the substantial
institutions envisaged by Baptist educators. In addition
to cultivating special group interests, these men had to sell
education to the individual citizen. Even Baptists were more
often addressed as citizens than as members of a denomination.
Reaching out beyond the confines of denomination and community
for funds and students, promoters of Baptist colleges disseminated an early-nineteenth-century gospel of education
among the general public.

Baptist higher education also contributed to the development of American culture through active support of publicly
financed and controlled schools and through students educated at the denomination's colleges. Viewing their colleges
as contributors to the public good, Baptist educators both
supported the development of a state system of common schools
and sought assistance from the state for their own institutions. In this same nondenominational spirit, Baptist colleges recruited students from all possible sources and obtained enrollments characterized as much by secular ambition
as by denominational affiliation or religious zeal. Many of
those persuaded to attend college were drawn from obscure
origins and equipped not only for personal success but also
for cultural leadership within their professions and communities.

I

The principal means by which antebellum colleges solicited support was through the activities of college agents.
These men may be described as educational salesmen. They
were usually employed to canvass the entire state in which
a college was located. In some cases they literally sold
shares in their college which entitled stockholders to vote
for trustees and send sons and wards to the school at reduced costs. At other times market conditions required
that agents offer complete scholarships to contributors of
a specific sum, generally ranging from $100 to $500.[2] Their
objective was to create a demand for education and a desire
to support educational institutions, especially the ones
they represented.

The scope and intensity of college agencies is im-
pressive. On behalf of George Washington University, Luther
Rice "was continually employed in traveling from place to
place, and conducting a correspondence with persons in all
parts of the United States." Bradley Kimbrough, an agent
for Union University in the mid-1840's, traveled on horse-

-----

[2]J.M. Peck, "Rock Spring Theological School," American
Baptist Magazine, VII (May 1827), 156; "Treasurer's Report
from 1844 to 1856," Tennessee Baptist, May 10, 1856; Vivian
L. Moore, The First Hundred Years of Hillsdale College (Ann
Arbor, Mich., 1944), p. 27; "New Colleges," Waterville Intel-
ligencer, May 30, 1823.

back "night and day, in heat and frost, snow and rain, through dismal wilds and unbroken roads, oftentimes hungry wet and cold," but "he persevered with a steady, unostentatious zeal that knew no discouragement." During the mid-1850's Ransom Dunn conducted an agency for Hillsdale College which covered 10,000 miles by horse and carriage. Similar journeys were made by agents for other colleges as these men went not only from church to church and public meeting to public meeting, but frequently from house to house advocating education and their college. With the position requiring certain physical as well as moral qualifications, some men refused to accept agencies because they could not bear "the exposure, irregularity, and excitement."[3]

---

[3]James B. Taylor, Memoir of Rev. Luther Rice, One of the First American Missionaries to the East (Baltimore, 1840), pp. 194-95, 225; "Columbian College," Columbian Star, April 24, 1824; "Rev. Luther Rice," Zion's Advocate, November 9, 1836; W.G. Inman, "Planting and Progress of the Baptist Cause in Tennessee," microfilmed typescript, ca. 1920, Dargan-Carver Library, Nashville, Tennessee, p. 199; "Lives of the Founders and Builders of Hillsdale College," Advance, January 27, 1886; Francis W. Shepardson, Denison University, 1831-1931, A Centennial History (Granville, Ohio, 1931), p. 60; Samuel Wait, "Journal, December 27, 1826-July 1, 1827," Baptist Historical Collection, Wake Forest College Library, passim.; Samuel Wait to S.M. Wait, June 2, 1844, Samuel Wait Correspondence, ibid.; Ransom Dunn, "The Story of the Planting: A Reminiscence of the Founding and Early History of Hillsdale College," Reunion, May 27, 1885; "Wake Forest College," Biblical Recorder, May 9, 1846; Stephen W. Taylor, "A Brief History of the Origin of the University at Lewisburg," manuscript dated April 18, 1850, Bucknell University Archives, p. 7; "Bethel College Agency--A Mistake Corrected," Western Recorder, January 25, 1859.

An agent's commitment to the cause of education was also tested on another level. "The difficulties of an agency," wrote N.W. Hodges while in the field for Furman University, "are such that no one can conceive of them properly, without an actual experience. To labor and enlarge the views of contracted and illiberal minds--make explanation and overcome prejudices--be disappointed in four cases out of five,...requires an exercise of patience and an ardor of pursuit which it is difficult to command." Samuel Wait, who solicited funds for Wake Forest College in the 1830's, probably exemplified the attributes of the most successful agents: "He was simple in his language, had conciliatory manners and a great amount of tact, and...a stern sense of Christian duty."[4]

Since the agency method was a common means of acquiring support for all benevolent enterprises, some college funds came from agents employed by state conventions to solicit for missions as well as education. But usually the college appointed an agent to work exclusively for its own benefit. Sometimes the position was assumed by a professor or the college president. Occasionally colleges hired a man such as Elon Galusha, who served many institutions and could

---

[4]"Furman Theological Institute," Southern Baptist and General Intelligencer, September 25, 1835; George W. Paschal, History of Wake Forest College, I (Wake Forest, N.C., 1935), 38-39.

almost be termed a professional agent. Whatever their backgrounds and other functions, however, most agents were unusually talented and influential members of the denomination. Luther Rice's conversion from Congregational to Baptist beliefs while en route to the foreign mission field
and his leading role in founding the Baptist General Convention gave him a national reputation. In 1815 he declined
an invitation to become   president of Transylvania University and spent most of the remaining twenty years of his
life as an agent for George Washington University. Jonathan Going, who traveled extensively in Ohio to create
support for Denison University, was a well-known leader of
Baptist home missions. "One of the best preachers in the
State," James De Votie, interrupted his ministerial career
to serve as agent of Howard College. Dr. William Shadrach,
pastor of the First Baptist Church of Philadelphia, resigned
this prominent position to put his reputation and persuasive
skills to work for Bucknell University between 1847 and
1853. His colleague in this agency was the "hero missionary,"
Eugenio Kincaid.[5]

---

[5]Ohio Baptist Convention, Minutes, 1843, p. 12, and
1847, pp. 14-15; Paschal, History, I, 601, 606; John F. Cady,
The Centennial History of Franklin College (n.p., 1934),
p. 57; Howard D. Williams, "The History of Colgate University to 1869," unpublished Ph.D. dissertation, Harvard University, 1949, p. 53; James B. Taylor, Memoir, p. 301; Elmer
L. Kayser, The George Washington University, 1821-1966

Luther Rice and his fellow agents were "ardent, enterprising" men whose efforts evoked a powerful grass-roots response. Appeals for Franklin College emphasized that gifts of $10 from "the many" would "be of great use," in "establishing an institution for their sons," and even smaller contributions came from the most humble levels of society. Many of the subscribers to Colby College planned to pay their subscriptions in labor on the college buildings and grounds. A farmer in North Carolina set aside a baby pig for Wake Forest. When fully grown, he estimated, it would sell for $2 or $3. Donations to Mercer University in the mid-1830's included $40\frac{1}{2}$ bushels of corn, 4 pairs of socks, $2\frac{1}{4}$ gallons of vinegar, and an empty barrel. A subscription of 50 cents to Bucknell's $100,000 endowment fund drive was paid in installments of $12\frac{1}{2}$ cents.[6]

(Washington, D.C., 1966), p. 9; Shepardson, Denison, p. 50; "Rev. James H. DeVotie," Alabama Baptist Advocate, April 27, 1849; Lewis E. Theiss, Centennial History of Bucknell University, 1846-1946 (Williamsport, Pa., 1946), pp. 35, 50-51, 25.

[6] "Rev. Luther Rice, A.M.," Southern Baptist and General Intelligencer, December 9, 1836; "Franklin College," Christian Messenger, November 13, 1845; Ernest C. Marriner, The History of Colby College (Waterville, Me., 1963), p. 35; "The College Pig," Biblical Recorder, November 13, 1856; Plan, History and Terms of the Mercer Institute, Prepared and Published by the Teachers and Trustees of the Executive Committee of the Baptist Convention for the State of Georgia, Who Have the Supervision of the Institution, July, 1834 (n.p., n.d.), p. 7; Justin R. Loomis, An Address Delivered June 9, 1865, in Commencement Hall of the University at Lewisburg, Pa., Before the Students of the Several Departments, On the Occasion of Their Celebrating the Completion of the Endowment Fund (Lewisburg, Pa., 1865), pp. 10-11.

Most contributions, however, probably came from the
broad range of middle-class Americans--professional men,
those in business pursuits, and "substantial farmers, with
means to live comfortably and independently, yet apprehen-
sive that they were not equal to the cost of a liberal education for their children." Despite pleas emphasizing that
even contributions of $10 would be very helpful, Franklin
reported in 1852 that of the $35,000 pledged for endowment,
over 300 of the subscriptions were for $100 each. "Those
who have given their obligations," said the report, "are
mostly farmers and mechanics; a few are merchants and professional men--by no means can they be called rich--the
valuation of their property ranging between fifteen hundred and ten thousand dollars; the greater part falling
under four thousand dollars."[7]

Traveling widely and reaching into almost all segments
of society, agents carried their message to large numbers
of people. In one year on horseback in the late 1830's,
Rockwood Giddings obtained 480 subscriptions for Georgetown
College. The agent for Mercer during the same period reported 600 - 700 pledges. Almost 4,500 subscribers were

[7]J.L. Orr, An Address Delivered Before the Philosophian
and Adelphian Societies of the Furman University at Their
Annual Meeting, Greenville, S.C., July 18, 1855 (Greenville,
S.C., 1855), p. 10; "Facts! Facts!" Journal and Messenger,
April 2, 1852.

enlisted by Bucknell's agents in the late 1840's. Many times more than the number of contributors must have at least been exposed to the pleas of each agent.[8]

The agency system was an expensive but necessary and fruitful means of sustaining Baptist colleges in their early years. Almost half of the money collected by Shurtleff College agents went to pay their own salaries, and the college considered their efforts so important that agents were paid more than professors. Without agents in the field, it was found that interest in an institution soon dwindled; when unusually active and able agents were at work, a college prospered.[9]

The long-range influence of college agents is suggested by the sharp increase in educational concern among Baptists which was widely noticed by the 1850's. In 1826 the national convention of Baptists abandoned educational activities in favor of exclusive support for missions. As late as 1847

---

[8]"Georgetown College," Baptist Memorial and Monthly Chronicle, V (April 1846), 113; "Notice to College Subscribers," Christian Index, October 24, 1839; Theiss, Centennial History, p. 52.

[9]Shurtleff College: Its Financial Concerns, Condition and Prospects, broadside dated August 1, 1845 (Upper Alton, Ill., 1845); Austen K. deBlois, The Pioneer School: A History of Shurtleff College, Oldest Educational Institution in the West (New York, 1900), pp. 120, 125; "Mercer University - Endowment," Christian Index, March 25, 1857; Theiss, Centennial History, pp. 50-52, 120.

the President of Colgate University complained that the
churches were more interested in missions than education.
By the end of the antebellum period, however, it was lamented that missions were being crowded out by a concern
for education. Missionary zeal was now subordinated to
educational projects, which "have had in their service
much of the best talent. Our most persuasive men have
carried them to the Association; to the church-meeting, to
the fireside, and preached and talked Education till it has
become a cardinal point of Baptist faith."[10]

The faith in education preached by college agents, however, had surprisingly little denominational emphasis. Almost all Baptist educators and agents were ministers. They
were deeply interested in "securing to the Baptist denomination...the requisite number of competent ministers." Yet to
gain the greatest patronage for their institutions, especially in areas of strong anti-mission sentiment, and to satisfy
their personal commitment to education in general, they
usually promoted their colleges in nondenominational terms.
Even in the Baptist press few appeals were made to purely
denominational motives. Baptists were urged by college
agents to do their "duty as citizens." An agent for Union

[10]"Institution at Hamilton," New York Baptist Register,
May 14, 1847; "Missions and Education," Baptist Champion,
March 22, 1860; "Denominational Education Vs. Missions,"
Biblical Recorder, June 30 and July 14, 1859.

solicited his "brethren" as "individual Christians, as
patriots, and philanthropists" as well as members of Baptist churches. Georgetown's contributors were reminded of
"the importance of general education /and/ the necessity
of raising up school masters" in addition to "the value of
a learned ministry."[11]

Agents sought support from "the enlightened public"
and not just loyal Baptists. While conducting an agency
for George Washington University, William Staughton preached
before Methodist and Presbyterian congregations in Norfolk,
Virginia. An agent for Howard was recommended to "friends
of education." "The Patriot, the Christian, and the lover of
learning" were entreated by Franklin's agent to aid the college. Before beginning a one-year tour to raise endowment
for Georgetown, Duncan Campbell argued that "the permanent
endowment of a first class institution of learning is a
State interest that rises above all local or sectarian
interests. Our denomination, it is true, has a peculiar
interest in it; still it is an interest of common concern
to every man in the State." Campbell laid claim to "the

---

[11]J.H. Eaton, "Introductory Address," Baptist, June 14,
1845; "Theological Seminaries," Christian Index, June 13,
1839; H. Bradley, "To the Board of Trustees of the I.B.M.L.
Institute," Baptist Banner and Western Pioneer, August 5,
1841; "Address to the Friends of Union University, Murfreesborough, Tennessee," Tennessee Baptist, August 30, 1856;
H.S. Malcom, "To the Contributors to Georgetown College,"
Baptist Banner and Western Pioneer, June 23, 1842.

aid of every lover and friend of education in the State."[12]

At times Baptist college agents employed arguments
strikingly similar to those of the common school reformers.
Education was promoted as a check upon the disruptive
effects of "the vast emigration from Europe of the lower
order of society." In appealing to "Christian friends in
every religious denomination /and/ fellow citizens of every
calling," Bradley Kimbrough contended that Union provided
equal educational opportunities and benefits for all classes
of society. A frequent theme of this agent's message to
potential contributors is suggested by the question he
stressed in announcing his itinerary for mid-1846: "Without intelligence how are we to sustain our liberties?"
General education was promoted by college agents as essential to the preservation of the republic.[13]

An antebellum Baptist college sometimes had as many as
five agents in the field. Few were the years when a college

---

[12]"Wake Forest College," Biblical Recorder, May 9, 1846;
Wait, "Journal," entry for January 21, 1827; "Agency of the
Howard," Alabama Baptist, August 17, 1844; "Franklin College,"
Christian Messenger, February 28, 1844; letter from D.R.
Campbell, Christian Repository, XLIX (January 1856), 50-51.

[13]P.S. Gayles, "Address," Baptist, II (October 1836),
343; Bradley Kimbrough, "Address to the Churches and Citizens of the States of Tennessee, North Alabama, and North
Mississippi," Baptist, August 2, 1845; letter from Bradley
Kimbrough, Baptist, March 28, 1846; D.R. Campbell, "Education and Its Claims," Christian Repository, III (July 1853),
70.

did not have at least one agent conducting what was recalled by a contemporary as being a "crusade for education."
Considering the numbers of these men, their talents, their
zeal, and the scope of their efforts, college agencies must
be considered as an important factor in the cultural history
of this period. When Samuel Wait traveled throughout North
Carolina "calling attention to the subject of education,"
he conducted the first comprehensive educational campaign
ever made in the state. Agents "awakened...zeal in behalf
of education" primarily within their own denomination, but
their gospel of education transcended denominational interests in its content and audience. Their objective was to
enlist the support of any potential "friends of education"
whether they be Baptist or not. It was said that Jeremiah
Chaplin, who traveled extensively in Maine to raise money
for Colby, "exerted a wide influence over the public mind,
in favor of science and literature." A similar claim could
be made for Baptist college agents in general.[14]

[14] "Mercer University," Christian Index, June 27, 1845;
L.R. Mills, as quoted in Paschal, History, I, 301; Samuel
Wait, "The Origin and Early History of Wake Forest College,"
Wake Forest Student, II (October 1882), 51; George W.
Paschal, "President Samuel Wait," Wake Forest Student,
XLIV (January 1927), 189; "How Are the Mighty Fallen!"
Baptist Banner and Western Pioneer, November 7, 1839;
Nathaniel Kendrick, A Discourse Delivered in the Chapel of
the Hamilton Literary and Theological Institution, On the
Death of Rev. Jeremiah Chaplin, D.D., June 6, 1841 (Utica,
N.Y., 1841), p. 17; Basil Manly, A Plea for Colleges (Phila-
delphia, 1854), p. 20.

II

Promoters of Baptist colleges translated their broadly
conceived belief in education into support for a wide variety
of institutions. Agents tried to "advance the cause of education" on all levels, beginning with the Sabbath school
and ranging up through the common school, academy, and college to the theological seminary.[15] Baptists were particularly active on behalf of the contemporary common school
movement. A surprising number of Baptist leaders also endorsed an active role for the state in higher education.
Baptist encouragement was given both to state universities
and to the principle of state aid for denominational colleges.

"If we cast our eyes over the length and breadth of
the land," reported a group of Indiana Baptists in 1839,
"we shall readily perceive that science and literature have
been propelled and carried forward by different religious
denominations. They have not only originated colleges and
theological seminaries, but they have also been assiduously
engaged in promoting common schools." In 1854 Basil Manly
told an audience at Wake Forest that "the warmest advocates

---

[15]J.B. Taylor, Memoir, p. 255; Lucille W. Wilkinson,
"Early Baptists in Washington, D.C.," Columbia Historical
Society Records, XXIX-XXX (1928), 246; Howard F. King,
"Adie Kyle Bell," L'Agenda (n.p., 1899), p. 9.

of colleges have been always and everywhere the most zealous
and efficient promoters of common schools." Evidence for
these claims was abundant within the Baptist denomination.
Prominent Baptists such as John Mason Peck, Jonathan Going,
and Silas Noel provided important leadership for the movement to establish a system of free public schools. In
Illinois Peck promoted common schools at many large religious and agricultural gatherings and through his contacts
with members of the state legislature. Going aided the
cause of primary public education both in Massachusetts and
the Midwest. While helping to establish Georgetown College,
Noel was an officer of the Kentucky Common School Society.[16]

Common schools were promoted by Baptists in their newspapers, public addresses, and conventions. Numerous articles and editorials in the Baptist press concerning common

<hr>

[16]"Report of the Committee on Education of the General
Association of Baptists in Indiana," Baptist Banner and Wes-
tern Pioneer, October 24, 1839; Manly, Plea, p. 21; Helene
L. Jennings, "John Mason Peck and the Impact of New England
on the Old Northwest," unpublished Ph.D. dissertation, Uni-
versity of Southern California, 1961, p. 244; John W. Cook,
Educational History of Illinois (Chicago, 1912), p. 300;
Paul E. Belting, "The Development of the Free Public High
School in Illinois to 1860," Journal of the Illinois State
Historical Society, XI (January 1919), 481; Worcester Bap-
tist Association, Mass., Minutes, 1845, p. 25; Willis A.
Chamberlin, "Dr. Jonathan Going's Impress Upon the Midwest,"
Chronicle, VIII (July 1945), 115; Edmund Turney, The Pros-
pect of Death an Incentive to Christian Consistency and Faith-
fulness: A Discourse Delivered on the Occasion of the Death
of Rev. Jonathan Going, D.D., President of Granville College,
With a Sketch of His Life (Hartford, Conn., 1845), p. 13;
Leland W. Meyer, Georgetown College: Its Background and a
Chapter in Its Early History (Louisville, Ky., 1929), p. 48.

schools urged "a more liberal patronage on the part of our
State Legislature and a more zealous support among the
people." Arguments of common school reformers were widely
disseminated through such media. A system of public education was found to be "absolutely essential for the very
support and existence of our civil government." It was
contended that education of a child was far less expensive
than support of a criminal or pauper whose condition resulted from lack of education. Sometimes a Baptist paper
reprinted the entire text of a state superintendent's
annual report or a piece of educational legislation. New
common school readers received lengthy reviews. A baccalaureate speaker at Howard in 1850 quoted extensively from
Horace Mann's _Eleventh Annual Report_. Baptist conventions
and societies enthusiastically endorsed educational legislation and encouraged members of the denomination to help
establish and improve common schools.[17]

---

[17]"New England Common Schools," _Southern Baptist_, Febru-
ary 22, 1854; "An Appeal to the People of Alabama on Popular
Education," _Alabama Baptist_, January 6, 1844; "Educate the
Masses," _Christian Index_, April 13, 1854; Joel S. Bacon, _An
Inaugural Address, Delivered in Georgetown, Ky., July 26,
1830_ (Georgetown, Ky., 1830), p. 4; "General Education in the
West," _Baptist Weekly Journal of the Mississippi Valley_, No-
vember 8, 1833; S. Baker, "The Advantages of Education,"
Christian Repository, III (November 1853), 283; "Common
Schools," _Cross and Baptist Journal of the Mississippi Valley_,
February 2, 1838; "Common School Law," _ibid._, March 23, 1838;
"Report of the Superintendent of Common Schools," _Baptist
Banner and Western Pioneer_, February 8, 1844; "Comprehensive

Support for common schools was based on a conception
of Baptist colleges as integral parts of an educational
structure serving the public good. Within this structure
the various levels of education were viewed as essentially
interdependent. "Our district schools, academies and colleges," declared a young graduate of Colby in 1829, "all
form one chain, from which if one link be taken, the whole
is broken." The University of Rochester's president re-
affirmed this sentiment twenty-five years later: "Our
American system of education is one whole," stated Martin
B. Anderson. "Each department has a common interest with
the others." In addition to supplying common schools with
competent teachers and providing educational opportunities
for their graduates, Baptist colleges educated men who became "the authors of our schoolbooks, the devisers and up-
holders of the school system in our Legislatures, and the
favorers of it in all our towns and boroughs." With "many
districts that do not know what qualifications a teacher
should possess in order to teach their children" college
graduates were seen as essential to the "elevation and
efficiency" of local schools. Common schools, in return,
helped to sustain colleges. "An interest created in behalf

Series of New School Books," ibid., August 13, 1840; "The
Bible a Classic," South Western Baptist, October 30, 1850;
Ohio Baptist Convention, Minutes, 1838, p. 5; Illinois Bap-
tist Convention, Minutes, 1838, p. 7; Pennsylvania Baptist
Education Society, Reports and Minutes, 1857, p. 5.

of one," said the editor of a Baptist newspaper, "is so much done for the other." The future prosperity of colleges, observed Jonathan Going, "will depend on the efficient action of the common schools and Academies, which must furnish their pupils, and diffuse throughout the community a taste for reading, a desire for general knowledge, and an interest in education, and create a demand for thorough education in the professions and in candidates for public office."[18]

All educational agencies functioning in the public interest received Baptist support. Because of their constant experimentation with new methods to facilitate the learning process and their development of materials appropriate to a child's level of understanding, Sunday schools exerted "a manifest influence upon the interests of general education." These institutions thus contributed to the

---

[18]"Education in the South," Christian Index, February 18, 1847; A. Sanborn, An Oration Delivered on the Anniversary of the Literary Fraternity of Waterville College, in Waterville, July 28th, 1829 (Waterville, Me., 1829), p. 16; Martin B. Anderson, The End and Means of a Liberal Education: An Inaugural Address, Delivered July 11, 1854 (Rochester, N.Y., 1855), p. 51; "Granville Institution," Cross and Baptist Journal of the Mississippi Valley, February 24, 1837; J. R. Loomis, An Inaugural Address, Delivered July 27, 1859 (Philadelphia, 1860), p. 38; "Commencement at Waterville," Zion's Advocate, August 19, 1845; letter to the editor, Baptist Banner and Western Pioneer, January 6, 1842; Manly, Plea, p. 20; "Common Schools," Watchman of the Prairie, November 14, 1848; Jonathan Going, Inaugural Address at the Anniversary of the Granville Literary and Theological Institution, August 8, 1838 (Columbus, Ohio, 1839), p. 16.

general welfare and deserved public approbation. At least
partly due to this reasoning, even advertisements for and
endorsements of state universities appeared in the columns
of Baptist newspapers.[19]

Because they were parts of an educational system
serving the public good, Baptist colleges were considered
by some denominational leaders and others to be worthy of
financial assistance from the state. "A college is a public charity," asserted an agent for Colby in 1831, "and this
College has all the claims to support from the public which
that character gives." Concentrating state aid to education
on common schools to the exclusion of denominational colleges,
argued President Rufus Babcock a few years later, would be
"as wise and consistent as it would be to sever the head
from the human body, in order to favor the limbs." A commencement speaker at Furman in 1855 contended that denominational colleges had "multiplied extensively the facilities
for general education." Since these colleges thus promoted
"the good, greatness and glory of South Carolina, why does
the State neglect to aid them, by annual appropriations from

---

[19]"Sunday Schools and General Education," Christian In-
dex, March 10, 1832; advertisements for the University of
Alabama and the University of Georgia in ibid., September
24, 1831, March 30, 1833, et passim; "University of Alabama,"
Alabama Baptist, June 5, 1850; "Wisconsin University,"
Watchman of the Prairies, November 7, 1848.

the Treasury, in their useful and benevolent and patriotic
mission of educating, exalting and refining her citizens?"[20]

At least seven out of the sixteen Baptist colleges in
this study subscribed to such arguments by seeking state aid
in the form of grants or loans. Colby's charter of 1813 gave
the college a township of land, and two additional half-
townships were granted in 1861. Net proceeds from stumpage
and sale of this land eventually reached close to $75,000.
Annual cash appropriations to Colby by the state legislature
between 1821 and 1832 totaled almost $15,000. George Wash-
ington University began appealing to Congress for assistance
in the early 1820's. In 1828 Congress released the college
from a debt to the government amounting to about $30,000.
Four years later Congress was successfully solicited for
$25,000 worth of city lots to endow faculty salaries. Deni-
son's trustees sought "pecuniary aid" from the state legislature in 1836 on the grounds that "colleges...are indispensable to a general system of public education" and are
most efficiently and beneficially operated when sponsored
by individual denominations. Their petition was denied the
following year by legislators wary of establishing connections between church and state. One reason why the University

[20]"Waterville College," Zion's Advocate, September 1,
1831; Rufus Babcock, Jr., The Teacher's Office: Inaugural
Address of Rev. Rufus Babcock, Jr., President of Waterville
College, July 29, 1834 (Augusta, Me., 1834), p. 20; Orr,
Address, pp. 10-11.

of Richmond obtained a college charter in 1840 was the hope
of obtaining a portion of the state literary fund. During
the following year Wake Forest received a loan of $10,000
from the state literary fund and remained a debtor to the
state until 1860. The legislature refused Colgate's request
in 1840 for an annual appropriation of $5,000, but between
1847 and 1850 the college received annual appropriations
totaling $8,500. In 1854 President Martin B. Anderson ex-
pressed a desire for state aid to the University of Rochester. His wish was fulfilled in 1857 and 1858 with successive grants of $12,500 each for the University.[21] Thus
right up to the eve of the Civil War some Baptist colleges
sought and received legislative recognition of their contributions to the public good.

---

[21]Marriner, History, pp. 9, 137, 47, 85-86; J.T. Champlin, A Historical Discourse Delivered at the Fiftieth Anniversary of Colby University, August 20, 1870 (Waterville, Me.,
1870), p. 20; "Columbian College," Christian Secretary, May
10, 1828; Luther Rice to Adoniram Judson, March 3, 1823, in
Luther Rice Letter Book, January 6 - June 2, 1823, Baptist
Historical Collection, Wake Forest Library; "Tenth Annual
Report of the Board," Latter Day Luminary, V (June 1824),
173-76; Leland W. Meyer, The Life and Times of Colonel Richard
M. Johnson of Kentucky (New York, 1932), pp. 384-85; "Colum-
bian College," Christian Secretary, May 10, 1828; Luther Rice
to Obadiah B. Brown, November 4, 1831, Luther Rice Letters,
Office of the University Historian, George Washington Univer-
sity; James D. Knowles, "History of the Columbian College,
District of Columbia," Christian Review, II (March 1837),
128; "Granville Institution--Legislative Aid," Cross and
Baptist Journal of the Mississippi Valley, December 30, 1836;
"Granville Institution," ibid., March 31, 1837; "Richmond
College--No. 5," Religious Herald, December 28, 1843; Paschal, History, I, 205-10; Williams, "History," p. 194; Sta-
tistics of College Aid (n.p., 1851), p. 2; Anderson, End and
Means, p. 59; Jesse L. Rosenberger, Rochester: The Making of
a University (Rochester, N.Y., 1927), pp. 127-28.

III

The nondenominational character of antebellum Baptist
colleges can be most clearly seen by examining the methods
they used to recruit students and the nature of the institutions' clientele. In keeping with the conception of their
responsibility to the commonweal and in response to a
pressing need for tuition revenue, these denominationally
affiliated colleges sought and obtained students from a
broad range of the general public. Several institutional
devices and a variety of arguments were employed to increase public demand for collegiate education.

College agents were as active in securing students as
in acquiring contributions. A former student at Hillsdale
wrote Ransom Dunn concerning his agency: "I well remember
you, when I was a boy, at Johnston, Wisconsin, pleading for
Hillsdale College and preaching in the old stone schoolhouse.
I then made up my mind that I should attend college at Hillsdale." Since student fees were for most colleges the only
major source of income other than voluntary contributions,
institutional prosperity and sometimes survival depended on
such recruiting. Tuition revenue from each student at Mercer was estimated to be equivalent to the interest from
$600 of endowment. Without an endowment and with "its very
existence...contingent on the number of its students," Wake

Forest urged friends of the college to "show their friend-
ship by making it the place of education for their sons
and wards." A skillful agent in the field could substantially alleviate the continuous and urgent need for increased enrollment at antebellum Baptist colleges.[22]

Manual labor programs proved to be less effective devices for increasing enrollment and courting public favor.
Of the eleven Baptist colleges in operation prior to 1840,
only George Washington and Georgetown did not join the
nationwide manual labor movement which flourished during
the 1830's and then quickly died out. Colby's workshop
manufactured doors, blinds, sashes, bedsteads, tables,
chairs, carriages, and boxes. Students at Franklin and
Denison spent several hours out of each school day making
barrels and tubs. Corn, cotton, potatoes, and oats were
grown on the manual labor farm at Mercer. Some of these
experiments in part-time student labor lasted about a

[22] "Erroneous Statements Corrected," New York Baptist
Register, February 17, 1848; Samuel Wait to S.M. Wait, June
2, 1844, Wait Correspondence; letter from Eugenio Kincaid,
Christian Chronicle, April 5, 1848; "Lives of the Founders
and Builders of Hillsdale College," Advance, June 23, 1886;
Helen D. Gates, A Consecrated Life: A Sketch of the Life and
Labors of Rev. Ransom Dunn, D.D., 1818-1900 (Boston, 1901),
p. 120; "Mercer University," Christian Index, June 8, 1848;
"To the Patrons of Wake Forest College," Biblical Recorder,
May 1, 1847; H.H. Harris, "Richmond College," in Herbert B.
Adams, Thomas Jefferson and the University of Virginia
(Washington, 1888), p. 276.

decade, but most were abandoned after five years or less.[23]

There were many dimensions to the rationale for manual
labor. The widely acknowledged faculty psychology of the
period gave strong endorsement to the movement. To preserve a "healthy and pleasant action in the system," students must cultivate "the physical as well as the intellectual and moral powers." Because of the "intimate connection between the mind and the body," it was frequently
asserted, "whatever contributes to corporeal vigor contributes also to vigor of mind, and consequently to the progress
of the student in the acquisition of useful knowledge."
Physical health as well as mental vigor was a common concern of educators and parents. It was frequently the son
with the "naturally delicate constitution" and "not fit for
much farmwork" to whom a family gave the opportunity of
attending college. Death was such a common visitor to colleges that the agent of Mercer considered it a strong point
in his institution's favor "that as few students have died
to the number in College as in any other institution throughout the South." Manual labor was also designed to cultivate
"habits of industry" and instill business acumen. After

---

[23]Charles E. Hamlin, untitled sketch of Colby College's
Department of Manual Labor in the Twelfth Annual Report of
the Secretary of the Maine Board of Agriculture (Augusta, Me.,
1867), p. 189; Cady, Centennial History, p. 36; Plan, History and Terms of Mercer, p. 3.

218

encountering the difficulties and hardships of combining
work with study, the student could "hardly fail of being
an active, enterprising...man." From the college's point
of view, there was a good chance of gain and little risk
of loss in the purchase of large tracts of land for manual
labor farms, even if the experiments were soon abandoned.
And often the manual labor energies of students were profitably directed toward the construction of college buildings.[24]

Important denominational interests were served by
manual labor, but the basic objective of the movement was
to enlist a broad patronage for Baptist colleges irrespective of denominational lines. Some Baptists viewed manual
labor as a device to remove the "formidable opposition" to

[24]T. Meredith, Address Delivered Before the Literary
Societies at the Wake Forest Institute, North Carolina, Nov.
24th, 1836 (Newburn, N.C., 1837), p. 9; "Wake F. Institute--
No. 8," Biblical Recorder and Southern Watchman, March 24,
1838; "Mechanical Labor Combined with Study," Christian Index, March 12, 1831; Constitution of the Manual Labor Association Connected With Waterville College; With an Address to
the Public (Augusta, Me., 1832), p. 6; Samuel Wait, "Origin,"
p. 50; William Cathcart, The Baptist Encyclopaedia (Rev. ed.;
Philadelphia, 1883), p. 120; William Hague, Christian Greatness in a Scholar: A Discourse on the Life and Character of
Rev. Irah Chase, D.D. (Boston, 1866), p. 6; Samuel S. Sherman, Autobiography of Samuel Sterling Sherman (Chicago, 1910),
p. 19; "Mercer University," Christian Index, November 24,
1858; "Wake F. Institute--No. 8," Biblical Recorder and Southern Watchman, March 24, 1838; Constitution of the Manual
Labor Association, p. 6; Paschal, History, I, 79; "Theological Institution," Southern Baptist and General Intelligencer,
December 4, 1835; "Mercer University and the Alabama Baptist,"
Christian Index, January 17, 1845; Jennings, "John Mason Peck,"
p. 113; Edwin C. Whittemore, Colby College, 1820-1925: An
Account of its Beginnings, Progress and Service (Waterville,
Me., 1927), p. 46.

ministerial education within their own ranks. Arguments of anti-mission Baptists that education of young ministerial candidates "had a tendency to render them vain and self-sufficient...proud or foppish" might be met by having such students engage in some hard physical work. Manual labor also could test the sincerity of those preparing for the ministry and "qualify them to endure hardships...as mission-aries and pastors in new settlements." Yet those Georgia Baptists who were most interested in ministerial education were sharply divided on the desirability of manual labor, and at Furman the system was not obligatory for the theo-logical students while it was for the others. In these states and others such as South Carolina, Indiana, and Maine the most consistently pursued common purpose of manual labor advocates was to encourage widespread patronage from the general public for Baptist colleges. President Jere-miah Chaplin recommended the plan to Colby's trustees be-cause it would "contribute more to the increase of your number of students than all other causes combined." Non-denominational concerns also held sway in Alabama. "The manual labor plan," stated a circular for Howard's pre-decessor at Greensboro, "is happily adapted to all classes, and to pour knowledge upon the whole horizon of every man's station. It gives habits of industry to the idle; economy to the wasteful; strength to the feeble; means of knowledge to the indigent; and the prospects of usefulness to all."[25]

The initial public response to manual labor at Colby, Denison, Richmond, and Furman was encouraging, but problems were soon encountered. Expecting and willing to sustain small annual losses in manual labor operations for the sake of increasing patronage and tuition income, institutions soon found any such gains to be meager when compared to the large losses sustained by student farms and workshops. Much of the return on sale of goods went to pay the supervisor of the farm or shop. Colby guaranteed students a fixed price for articles produced and then had difficulty finding a market for them. Unskilled hand labor was unable to compete favorably in Maine with craftsmen employing water

---

[25]"Plan of General Education," Christian Index, July 28, 1832; "Manual Labor System," New York Baptist Register, February 22, 1823; "Furman Academy, S.C. and Manual Labor," Columbian Star and Christian Index, August 14, 1830; Carl B. Wilson, The Baptist Manual Labor School Movement in the United States: Its Origin, Development, and Significance, Baylor University Bulletin, XL, No. 4 (Waco, Texas, 1937), p. 51; "Virginia Baptist Education Society," Religious Herald, April 27, 1832; "Education of Ministers," Christian Index, July 16, 1831; Benjamin F. Riley, A Memorial History of the Baptists of Alabama (Philadelphia, 1923), p. 59; "Manual Labor System," New York Baptist Register, February 22, 1833; Rufus W. Weaver, "The Presidents of Mercer During Its First Half Century," Christian Index, February 18, 1926; "Furman Institution," Christian Index, January 23, 1840; Harvey T. Cook, Education in South Carolina Under Baptist Control (Greenville, S.C., 1912), pp. 70-71; "Baptists in Indiana," Cross and Baptist Journal of the Mississippi Valley, June 20, 1834; Cady, Centennial History, p. 24; Jeremiah Chaplin, "To the Trustees of Waterville College," manuscript dated 1833, Jeremiah Chaplin Papers, Colby College Archives; "Baptist Manual Labor School," Christian Index and Baptist Miscellany, November 25, 1834.

power. The cultivating and harvesting seasons in Virginia did not coincide with the academic calendar of Richmond College.[26]

Even when subsidized by the college, a manual labor enterprise rarely provided more than a small portion of a student's educational expenses. Although he was skilled as a cooper, a student at Denison found the shop facilities and the earnings disappointing.[27] The hard economic facts encountered by the student who was one of the unskilled majority were described by an article in the New York Baptist Register:

---

[26]Hamlin, untitled sketch, p. 191; G. Wallace Chessman, Denison: The Story of an Ohio College (Granville, Ohio, 1957), p. 62; Robert Ryland, The Virginia Baptist Education Society. The Society, the Seminary, the College (Richmond, Va., 1891), p. 11; "Manual Labor School for South Carolina," Southern Baptist and General Intelligencer, May 1, 1835; "Furman Theological Institute," ibid., September 25, 1835; B.M. Sanders, Valedictory Address, Delivered Before the Trustees, Faculty, Students, and Friends of the Mercer University, Greene County, Ga., Dec. 12, 1839 (Washington, Ga., 1840), p. 11; Constitution of the Manual Labor Association, p. 9; Marriner, History, p. 68; Ryland, Virginia Baptist, p. 11; "To the Trustees of the Wake Forest Institute," Biblical Recorder, October 12, 1836; Whittemore, Colby, p. 45; "Manual Labor Institutions," Zion's Advocate, August 29, 1832; Hamlin, untitled sketch, p. 191; "Richmond College--No. 1," Religious Herald, November 23, 1843.

[27]Virginia Baptist Education Society (n.p., 1833), p. 7; Annual Meeting of the Trustees of the Granville Literary and Theological Institution, and of the Ohio Baptist Education Society, August 14th and 15th, 1833 (Cincinnati, 1833), p. 11; Shepardson, Denison, p. 28; Paschal Carter to John Stevens, October 18, 1835, and Charles Stevens to John Stevens, January 24, 1836, John Stevens Papers, American Baptist Historical Society, Rochester, New York.

But if he has a <u>trade to learn</u>, how is he
to pay the expenses in college by working
<u>three hours</u> when he could generally do no
more than earn his living in a cabinet-
maker's shop by working <u>all the time</u> of
the first whole year of his apprenticeship? And everybody knows that the price
of a year's labor on the farm, if a young
man work the <u>whole time</u>, will not more
than cover the most economical expenses
of a college year. How, then, is he to
earn the amount by working two or three
hours in a day at college?[28]

Small returns probably played an important role in

dampening student enthusiasm for manual labor at schools

such as Denison. A somewhat different problem predominated

in the South, where it was circumspectly observed that "the

style of agriculture" and "the peculiar kind of domestic

polity...furnish barriers" to the success of manual labor

experiments. Many planters in North Carolina and Alabama

sent their sons to Baptist manual labor schools to acquire

industrious ways, learn some scientific farming techniques,

and gain experience generally applicable to management of

the plantations which they would some day inherit. Un-

accustomed to hard work, these students soon rebelled against

the system and some withdrew from the colleges. When the

system became voluntary at the University of Richmond, fewer

than one-third of the students participated.[29]

---

[28]"Manual Labor Schools," <u>New York Baptist Register</u>,
March 20, 1835, copied from the <u>Connecticut Observer</u> (Hartford).

[29]"Furman Academy and Theological Institution," <u>Colum-
bian Star and Christian Index</u>, November 13, 1830; George
Stevenson, <u>The Educated Farmer: An Oration Before the</u>

Colleges responded to this problem by arguing that
the "habits of order and self-denial" taught by manual
labor were essential to combat "that indolence and those
false notions of honor, which naturally arise from a state
of slavery." They also assured parents that the tasks of
students did not involve "anything justly considered dis-
honorable" and that "no dirty or degrading kind of labor
is required of them." Yet student aversion to manual labor
persisted and was by no means limited to the South or to an
affluent family background. "The young man who goes to college," John Mason Peck observed in 1840, "is taught to look
forward to the learned professions, to merchandising, or to
some petty clerkship for his future business. The son of
the farmer or mechanic rarely looks back to the farm and
the workshop as the business of life. These pursuits are

Euzelian and Philomathesian Societies of Wake Forest Col-
lege, North Carolina. Delivered June 13, 1855 (Raleigh, N.C.,
1855), p. 4; Mitchell B. Garrett, Sixty Years of Howard
College, 1842-1902, Howard College Bulletin, LXXXV, No. 4
(Birmingham, Ala., 1927), p. 12; Paschal, History, I, 80;
Cook, Education, pp. 58-59; B.M. Sanders to Samuel Wait,
November 3, 1836, Wait Correspondence; F.W. Boatwright,
"The Beginnings of Higher Education Among Virginia Bap-
tists," Religious Herald, August 13, 1931; William T.
Brooks, An Address Delivered Before the Alumni of Wake
Forest College, On the Afternoon of June 18th, 1859
(Raleigh, N.C., 1861), p. 10; "Annual Report," Religious
Herald, June 18, 1840.

left to the illiterate vulgar. He has been to college--
therefore he expects to be a gentleman."[30]

Baptist educators soon found that the expensive device
they were employing to increase patronage was in fact reducing it. A few individuals urged that manual labor be
continued because of its other functions, but by the early
1840's Baptist educators were forced to conclude that "the
system has become extensively unpopular."[31] Since public
appeal was essential to the early success of Baptist colleges, manual labor was rapidly abandoned.

Student literary and debating societies proved to be
much more effective in attracting public interest and support. Societies were founded within a year after formation
of the first college classes at twelve of the sixteen Baptist colleges included in this study. Only a few years
more passed before societies appeared at the remaining four
institutions. Meeting rooms were soon elaborately furnished

---

[30]"Fairfield Manual Labor School," Biblical Recorder and
Southern Watchman, October 19, 1839; "Mercer Institute,"
Christian Index and Baptist Miscellany, February 18, 1834;
"Virginia Baptist Education Society," Religious Herald, April
27, 1832; "Wake Forest Institute--No. 8," Biblical Recorder
and Southern Watchman, March 24, 1838; Benedict, Fifty Years,
pp. 210-11; J.M. Peck, "Department of Agriculture in Shurtleff College," Baptist Banner and Western Pioneer, April 9,
1840.

[31]"Mercer University," Christian Index, September 23,
1842; "Mercer University," ibid., January 27, 1843; Weaver,
"Presidents"; Paschal, History, I, 85; "Furman Institution,"
Christian Index, January 23, 1840.

and stocked with large collections of books and periodicals.
Considerable assistance in these enterprises came from the
general public.[32]

Baptist educators gave their wholehearted assistance to
these popular organizations. Faculty members often helped
to found and foster societies. A professor at Shurtleff
"very materially assisted" the Alpha Zeta Society in its
early years. The Literary Fraternity of Georgetown College
was named by Professor J.E. Farnham, who also wrote its constitution. Membership in Wake Forest's societies was originally open to professors as well as students, and faculty
members provided advice on the purchase of books for the
society libraries. Meeting rooms were frequently provided
for the societies within college buildings. College catalogues advertised societies as integral parts of a complete
college education and as "valuable auxiliaries" to the formal curriculum. While much of this aid to societies was
based on an appreciation of the ways in which they stimulated student intellects and supplemented classroom

---

[32]Paschal, History, I, 505-12, 527; Marriner, History,
pp. 450, 454-55; Garrett, Sixty Years, pp. 12, 150; William
W. Greene, Semi-Centennial History of the Alpha Zeta Society
of Shurtleff College, Together With Complete Rosters of Active and Honorary Members (Alton, Ill., 1898), pp. 12, 28.
For a general history of student societies during this
period, see Thomas S. Harding, "College Literary Societies:
Their Contribution to the Development of Academic Libraries,
1815-76," Library Quarterly, XXIX (January and April 1959),
1-26, 94-112.

subjects,[33] it is unlikely that Baptist educators overlooked
the important role these organizations played in making colleges more attractive to many potential students and contributors.

The inclusiveness of Baptist higher education's search
for support was most explicit in the arguments used to interest parents and attract students. Appeals to denominational
motives were rare, and even general religious considerations
received little emphasis beyond the level of moral training.
From a religious point of view, college education was pictured as "a season of comparative retirement from the world"
and "the grand climacteric" of a young man's development,
during which his character was given its final shape and
tested. Because of the undergraduate malleability assumed
in this theory, the college years could also be a "dangerous
period for a young man's existence," when good morals might
be "exchanged for a show of science and literature." Baptist educators shared the contemporary belief that "home is
the abode and citadel of virtue," but assured parents that

[33]Greene, Semi-Centennial History, pp. 11, 19; Hul-Cee
M. Acton, History of the Tau Theta Kappa Society of George-
town College (Georgetown, Ky., 1918), pp. 5-6; Paschal,
History, I, 146, 490, 503, 525-26; Marriner, History, p. 454;
Garrett, Sixty Years, p. 150; Georgetown College, Catalogue,
1847/48, p. 14; Denison University, Catalogue, 1854, p. 21;
Richmond College, Catalogue, 1855/56, p. 16; Mercer Univer-
sity, Catalogue, 1857/58, p. 35; J. Orin Oliphant, The Rise
of Bucknell University (New York, 1965), p. 43; deBlois,
Pioneer, p. 107; Williams, "History," p. 174.

students leaving the domestic circle for the relative "perils of College intercourse" would be surrounded at their college by "such influence as will best substitute the influences of the home." Students would board with pious families and teachers would "endeavor to act the part of the affectionate Christian parent." It was the "ardent desire" of Georgetown's president, Howard Malcom, that residence at his college "should be attended by as few temptations as are incident to a parent's fire-side." Colleges were to complete the process of bringing children up "in the nurture and admonition of the Lord" said Stephen Taylor in promoting Bucknell, but his concept of Christian nurture in higher education was essentially nondenominational.[34]

---

[34]Franklin College, Catalogue, 1850/51, p. 14; Bacon, Inaugural Address, pp. 6-7; E.T. Winkler, Religious Liberty: An Address Delivered Before the Philosophian and Adelphian Societies of the Furman University, At Their Annual Meeting, Greenville, June 24th, 1853 (Charleston, S.C., 1853), p. 5; Laws of the Columbian College in the District of Columbia (Washington, 1856), p. 9; B.M.B., "Does It Pay to Go to College?" Ciceronian Magazine, I (December 1856), 289; Robert W. Cushman, Temptations of City Life: An Address to Young Men on the Temptations of Cities (Boston, 1847), pp. 7-8; "Reply to J.E.," New York Baptist Register, March 16, 1848; Meyer, Georgetown, p. 71; Stephen W. Taylor, Motives: An Inaugural Address Delivered in the Chapel of the Hamilton Literary and Theological Seminary, August 19, 1835 (Utica, N.Y., 1835), p. 9; "Going to College," Religious Herald, September 17, 1857; James C. Furman, "To the Baptists of South Carolina," Southern Baptist, April 24 and May 1, 1850; Franklin College, Catalogue, 1860/61, p. 19; "Georgetown College," Baptist Banner and Western Pioneer, January 8, 1846; Stephen Taylor, "The University at Lewisburg," Christian Chronicle, November 25, 1846; Taylor, Motives, p. 3.

More frequently stressed than the religious and moral
reasons for attending college was the proposition that "knowledge is power and wealth and influence." Education had
secular value for all segments of society. Confronted with
"the immense influx of the laboring population of Europe"
and the resulting "displacement of American manual labor"
during the 1840's, parents from the middle ranges of society
must begin "increasing the intellectual cultivation of their
sons...to qualify them for directing and using this manual
labor." And since "the mass swells up from the bottom,...
woe to those who are on the top unless they keep their
balance well" and support "more perfect systems, and better
applied systems of education." Even the "son of the immi-
grant of today who excavates our hills for the tracks of
the iron horse" could, by "attending...schools which lie
along the line of his father's toils, /become/ the engi-
neer and director of the labors of the race of immigrants
which next comes over the water." In such a fluid society
a college education was a "profitable investment" which
conferred "a higher elevation...in social position than a
similar amount of money invested in any other form would
do." One thousand dollars invested in a college education,
it was claimed in 1854, would double a man's annual income.[35]

[35]"Education," Baptist, June 29, 1844; Stevenson, Educated Farmer, p. 5; "Triumph of Knowledge," Howard College
Magazine, I (December 1858), 65; "Educate Your Sons and

Arguments for the practical benefits of a college education were usually based on the pervasive contemporary belief in faculty psychology. Man was viewed as possessing "corporeal, mental and moral faculties capable of improvement" and thus was "at any given stage of his existence, exclusively the creature of education." Despite a few unsuccessful attempts to reform the curriculum which it supported, and occasional isolated challenges to its psychological assumptions, the theory of mental discipline persisted as the foundation of Baptist educational theory throughout the antebellum years. The college's primary function was to develop and discipline all the faculties of the mind in just proportion.[36]

The resulting "symmetry of intellectual character" and development of "the whole person" had certain religious connotations, especially in the sphere of morality. Faculty

---

Daughters," New York Recorder, January 2, 1850; "Union University," Tennessee Baptist, December 22, 1860; "Education," Biblical Recorder, March 23, 1850; Stephen Taylor, "The University at Lewisburg," Christian Chronicle, December 9, 1846; Manly, Plea, pp. 8-10.

[36]Going, Inaugural Address, p. 3; S.W. Lynd, Address Delivered Before the Ohio Baptist Education Society, At the Annual Meeting Held in Granville, October 6, 1832 (Cincinnati, 1832), p. 5; George B. Taylor, The Thinker, An Address Delivered in Richmond, Va., Monday, June 30, 1856, Before the Society of Alumni of Richmond College, At Their First Annual Meeting (Richmond, Va., 1856), pp. 32-33; Bacon, Inaugural Address, pp. 10-11; "Educational Reform," Christian Contributor and Free Missionary, December 8, 1847; Babcock, Teacher's Office, p. 4; General Information Respecting the Internal Arrangements of the Granville Literary and Theological Institution (Columbus, Ohio, 1836), p. 5; Manly, Plea, p. 4.

psychology also supported a philologically oriented curriculum particularly useful to ministers. Yet the arguments
for attending college primarily spoke to "the mechanical
and utilitarian spirit of the times," and asserted that
mental discipline would make a man more "active, vigorous,
and useful" in terms of secular success.[37]

In a country where "no hereditary rights, no conven-
tional forms, no exclusive privileges" determined career
patterns, and where "every individual is liable to be called
upon to act in various capacities," a general rather than
vocational college education was seen as especially appropriate and eminently practical. The mental discipline of
collegiate study, it was argued, "fits the individual for
enjoying subsequent study, and thus lays the foundation for

---

[37]J.M. Pendleton, Education (Nashville, Tenn., 1854),
p. 10; Edward Baptist, Address Delivered Before the Trustees, Faculty and Students of Howard College, Marion, Perry
County, November 16, 1846 (Tuskaloosa, Ala., 1846), pp. 5,
8. Rooted in faculty psychology, the term "whole man" was
frequently used during the 1850's. For an examination of
its use in the late nineteenth century, see George E. Peter-
son, The New England College in the Age of the University
(Amherst, Mass., 1964), chap. 11. Pendleton, Education,
p. 12; "Original Language of the Scriptures," Christian
Index, February 1, 1838; William R. Williams, The Conservative Principle in Our Literature: An Address Before the
Literary Societies of the Hamilton Literary and Theological
Institution (Madison County, N.Y.), Delivered in the Chapel
of the Institution, On the Evening of Tuesday, June 13,
1843 (New York, 1844), p. 10; "Wake Forest Institute--No. 8,"
Biblical Recorder and Southern Watchman, March 24, 1838. For
an interesting argument that mental discipline even promoted
good health and longevity, see Stephen W. Taylor, Inaugural
Address Delivered at the Commencement of the University at
Lewisburg, Pennsylvania, On Wednesday, August 28, 1850 (n.p.,
n.d.), pp. 2-3, 9-10.

indefinite improvement." A man "with intellectual faculties properly strengthened" could "readily acquire the necessary amount of practical knowledge in any calling he may select." A college education would equip a person for mobility in a fluid society and improve his chances of controlling his own destiny. Mental discipline would also produce a "vigorous will" and a capacity for hard work which could compensate for any lack of "extraordinary genius." "We want no loungers here," warned Franklin's catalogue. The practical aim of higher education was to inculcate "habits of studiousness, sobriety, and good order" which formed "the purest presage of future eminence."[38]

Eminence in the professions, it was contended, would be extremely difficult without such general training. The rigors of a classical curriculum were also assumed to have value for "the boy who is to be a farmer, or a mechanic, or

[38]T.G. Keen, Characteristics of the Times, Strong Incentives to Intellectual Effort: An Address Delivered Before the Franklin & Adelphi Societies of Howard College, At Their Anniversary, Held at Marion, Alabama, July 24, 1850 (Tuskaloosa, Ala., 1850), pp. 24-25; Simon Colton, An Address Delivered Before the Philomathesian & Euzelian Societies in Wake Forest College, June 16, 1842 (Fayetteville, N.C., 1842), p. 15; "College Education--Its Advantages," Zion's Advocate, February 13, 1844; "Schools and Colleges," Journal and Messenger, July 16, 1858; Taylor, Inaugural Address, p. 1; Keen, Characteristics, pp. 25-27; Pendleton, Education, p. 14; Loomis, Inaugural Address, p. 22; Stephen Chapin, Triumphs of Intellect, A Lecture Delivered October, 1824, In the Chapel of Waterville College (Waterville, Me., 1824), pp. 13-15; Baptist, Address, p. 13; Franklin College, Catalogue, 1845/46, p. 11; Laws of Columbian, p. 11.

a merchant." But the college usually addressed itself to
the student aspiring to the learned professions and functioned as "vestibule to their temple." Since those in the
professions must be able to think quickly, logically, and
patiently, argued President Daniel Read of Shurtleff, the
traditional college studies "do 'pay' professional men...
a large dividend, and that immediately." Read found the
abstract subjects in a liberal education to be "of immediate
practical utility."[39]

IV

Arguments of college promoters apparently made good
sense to thousands of young men in antebellum America.
Evidence that the decision to attend college was a carefully and maturely calculated one can be found in the ages
of students enrolled in college classes. The average age
of a class of college freshmen at Colby in the mid-1830's
was not quite twenty-two. All four college classes at
Georgetown in 1844 yielded an average age of close to

[39]"College Education--What It Is," _Zion's Advocate_,
February 6, 1844; "Responsibilities of Educated Men," _Bap-
tist Messenger_, November 25, 1859; Sherman, _Autobiography_,
p. 27; Stevenson, _Educated Farmer_, pp. 6, 11; "Shurtleff
College," _Christian Times_, February 23, 1859.

twenty, and that at Bucknell a decade later was twenty-four. The first graduate of Franklin was thirty-three years old. These high averages and the age spans which compose them suggest, as a graduate of Colby concluded, "that many more came than were sent--that is,...many more were there of their own choice, than were _placed_ there by parents or guardians."[40]

The professional aspirations of such students are reflected in the fact that a majority of the graduates of pre-Civil War Baptist colleges entered one of the three major professions. And this majority contained almost as many lawyers and physicians as ministers. Sizable groups also pursued careers in education, agriculture, and business. The distribution for the 1621 antebellum graduates of ten Baptist colleges which began granting degrees prior to 1850 is as follows:

---

[40] /John Stevens/, "Denison University, Items in Its Character and History," ca. 1868, manuscript in the John Stevens folder, Denison University Archives, pp. 7-8; Hubbel Loomis, A Documentary History of Alton Seminary to March 7, 1835... (Alton, Ill., 1854), p. 16; "Mercer Institute," Christian Index and Baptist Miscellany, February 18, 1834; Joseph Ricker, Personal Recollections: A Contribution to Baptist History and Biography (Augusta, Me., 1894), p. 81; "Georgetown College," Baptist Banner and Western Pioneer, July 11, 1844; University at Lewisburg, "Minutes of the Board of Trustees," typescript in the Bucknell University Archives, entry for August 15, 1854; Wallace, "Alumni," p. 86; Ricker, Personal Recollections, p. 81.

```
ministers:  Baptist        27%
            non-Baptist     2
            total                    29%
lawyers                              18
educators                            13
physicians                            8
agriculture                           7
business                              7
other                                 3
occupation unknown                   15
```

Less complete reports on graduates of colleges which began

granting degrees in the 1850's indicate that a similar dis-

tribution would be found among the just over 2,500 graduates

of all 16 antebellum Baptist colleges in this study. Limited

data on all matriculants at Colby and Wake Forest suggest

that a considerably lower percentage of ministers would be

found among the probably close to 5,000 nongraduates of the

16 institutions.[41] Twenty-five reports on the number of

---

[41]*General Catalogue of the Officers, Graduates and Former Students of Colby College: Centennial Edition, 1820-1920*
(Waterville, Me., 1920), pp. 25-75; *Historical Catalogue of
the Officers and Graduates of the Columbian University*, Wash-
ington, D.C., 1821-1891, comp. H.L. Hodgkins (Washington,
1891), pp. 85-96; *General Catalogue of Wake Forest College,
North Carolina, 1834/35-1891/92*, comp. C.E. Taylor (Raleigh,
N.C., 1892); "Seventh General Catalogue of the Alumni of
Denison University," *Memorial Volume of Denison University,
1831-1906* (Columbus, Ohio, 1907), pp. 199-209; *Triennial
Register and Annual Catalogue, Mercer University, 1897-98*
(Macon, Ga., 1898), pp. 16-28; *Historical Catalogue of
Georgetown College, 1829-1917*, Georgetown College Bulletin,
XIV, No. 4 (Georgetown, Ky., 1917), pp. 25-38; "Semi-
Centennial and General Catalogue of the Officers and Stu-
dents of Shurtleff College for 50 Years--1827-77," *Jubilee
Memorial of Shurtleff College, Upper Alton, Ill.* (Alton,
Ill., 1877), pp. 19-29; Greene, *Semi-Centennial History*,
pp. 192-234; *Alumni Number, 1910*, Franklin College Bulletin,
I, No. 3 (Franklin, Ind., 1910), pp. 15-17; Barnett Wallace,

students "intending for the ministry" found in the Baptist
press from 1820 through 1861 also yield generally lower
percentages than those in alumni records. Rarely are more
than 30% reported in this category and usually the portion
is less than 20% of total enrollment.

The importance of denominational motivations among
those enrolling at Baptist colleges can be explored through
reports to Baptist newspapers on campus piety and on the

"Alumni and Society of Alumni," First Half Century of Franklin College, Jubilee Exercises (Cincinnati, 1884), pp. 87-
102; Memorial Catalogue: Fiftieth Annual Catalogue and Register of Howard College, East Lake, Alabama, For the Academic
Year 1891-92 (Birmingham, Ala., 1892), pp. 44-46; Roll of
Students of Richmond College, 1865 to 1905, With List of
Graduates, 1849 to 1861, Richmond College Bulletin, VII,
No. 2 (Richmond, Va., 1905), pp. 5-7. Although its graduates
began receiving degrees in 1844, Colgate was not included in
this analysis. For its first two decades, Colgate functioned
exclusively for ministerial training, and the persistence of
this tradition, even after nonministerial students were admitted, resulted in 70% of all antebellum degree recipients'
entering the ministry. At no other college included in this
study did more than 43% of all graduates become pulpit ministers. Some graduates counted as educators were licensed
or ordained ministers, but teaching was their primary pro-
fession. For data on alumni of the colleges not included
in the occupational analysis see: Colgate University: General
Catalogue Number, ed. Elmer W. Smith, Colgate University
Publication, XXXVII, No. 2 (Hamilton, N.Y., 1937), pp. 61-
125; "Sketches of Alumni," The First Half Century of Madison
University (1819-1869), or the Jubilee Volume (New York,
1872), pp. 226-335; "Alumni Association of Union University,"
Union University, Catalogue, 1910/11, pp. 94-98; Alumni Catalogue of Bucknell University, Lewisburg, Pennsylvania, 1851-
1910, Bucknell University Bulletin, X, No. 3 (Lewisburg, Pa.,
1910), pp. 20-22; General Catalogue of the University of
Rochester, 1850-1911, University Bulletin, VII, No. 2 (Rochester, N.Y., 1911), pp. 1-22; C.C. Brown, General Catalog of
Furman University...1852-1899 (Sumpter, S.C., n.d.). No alumni catalogue was located for Hillsdale, but this college probably granted about 20 degrees up through 1861. See Moore,
First Hundred, pp. 20, 52-53. On the nongraduates, see General Catalogue of Colby, pp. 245-69 and Paschal, History, 1,
601-52.

number of students belonging to Baptist churches. Of
eighteen scattered estimates concerning the proportion
of students who had experienced conversion, few substantially exceed 50% while one-third amount to 30% or less.
Less numerous reports on the denominational affiliation
of students indicate that only occasionally did Baptists
comprise a majority of students attending the denomination's colleges.[42] When juxtaposed with records of subsequent careers, these data strongly suggest that a large
number of students were attracted to Baptist colleges for
other than religious reasons. For these students, the
career advantages advertised by college promoters probably
exerted a major influence upon the decision to attend college.

Concern over social and economic mobility can also be
inferred from data on the family backgrounds of students.
Although sons of the wealthy comprised a substantial portion of the enrollment at most colleges, there is evidence
that those from the lower levels of society were also present. The Maine Farmer in the early 1840's found Colby to
be "emphatically a poor man's college" where students with

---

[42]It should be noted that the percentage of students
from Baptist families, and the portion of any given college
class which, largely due to annual days of prayer and revivals, experienced conversion before graduating or with-
drawing, probably exceeded by a considerable amount the percentage of students belonging to Baptist and other churches
at the time each estimate and report was made.

very limited means could work their way through. In the
1830's and 1840's most of the students at Denison wore
homespun and some even went barefoot. Howard De Votie
wrote to his father from Mercer in the late 1850's that
most of his fellow students were "rough uncouth looking
fellows" who lacked good manners. The majority of students
and the majority of contributions seem to have come from
what President George Chandler of Franklin termed "the
many." Chandler defined this majority group in pre-Civil
War America as those with "small but well cultivated farms"
and "economical shops."[43]

The quality of education which ambitious students
sought and received was sufficient to serve both their
aspirations and their abilities. Although the level of
instruction may have been quite low during the early years
of an institution such as Georgetown, by the mid-1840's the
college had adopted a "resolute adherence to the usages and

[43]C.D. Armstrong, "College Aristocracy," *Ciceronian
Magazine*, 1 (October 1856), 219-22; Rufus W. Weaver, "The
Future of Mercer University," *Christian Index*, December 20,
1920; "The Struggles of a Poor Student," *Baptist Weekly
Journal of the Mississippi Valley*, January 24, 1834; "Mer-
cer Institute, Ga.," *Christian Index*, November 10, 1832;
Sanborn, *Oration*, p. 17; editorial from the *Maine Farmer*
(Winthrop), quoted in Marriner, *History*, p. 110; "Waterville College," *Watervillonian*, September 4, 1841, copied
from the *Maine Farmer*; Chessman, *Denison*, pp. 63-64, 89;
J. Howard De Votie to James H. De Votie, September 12,
1858, James H. De Votie Letters, Duke University Archives;
"Waterville College," *Yankee Blade* (Waterville, Me.), July
30, 1842; Paschal, *History*, I, 458, 464; Sherman, *Autobiography*, p. 26; "Franklin College," *Christian Messenger*, November 13, 1845.

course of study of the best Eastern colleges" and was
losing many prospective students who sought a quicker and
easier path to the bachelor's degree. A similar regard
for high degree standards at the University of Richmond
delayed the granting of a B.A. until nine years after its
first college classes were organized. Located in regions
usually lacking a well-defined or well-administered educational ladder below the college level, Baptist schools
admitted students with widely varying degrees of preparation and educated each individual as far as he was willing
or able to go. The vast majority who did not qualify for
a formal degree received certificates signed by the college
president which specified their attainments.[44]

A few surviving reminiscences and other bits of data
indicate that many students found "it does pay to go to
college." One reward they perceived was the mental discipline, "beneficial to the pursuit of all the occupations."

[44]"Georgetown College," Baptist, August 2, 1845; R.E.
Gaines, "The Beginnings: The Seminary, the College, 1832-1866,"
The First Hundred Years: Brief Sketches of the History of the
University of Richmond (Richmond, Va., 1932), pp. 25-26;
Daniel H. Brush, Growing Up With Southern Illinois, 1820-1861
(Chicago, 1944), p. 64; Granville Literary and Theological
Institution, Catalogue, 1846/47, p. 11. A Canadian who was
critical of the classical curriculum made a tour of American
colleges in the mid-1830's and reported that although "many
students just drift through," probably a majority emerged
well educated. See Doctor Charles Duncombe's Report Upon the
Subject of Education, Made to the Parliament of Upper Canada,
February 25, 1836... (Toronto, 1836), pp. 33-36.

Another benefit came from the "atmosphere of letters," to
which a Wake Forest graduate attributed considerable importance "in giving direction to my development and advancement." Those planning careers in law and politics saw
"immense practical value" in literary society debates.[45]
The basic advantage of attending college, however, was suggested by Isaiah Booth, who recalled the following experience when he returned home from Denison during a summer
vacation in the early 1840's:

> I remained two weeks visiting friends
> and relatives.... Here for the first
> time did I begin to feel how perceptibly
> education separated those of equal age.
> Though I had been but two years at col-
> lege, it seemed that my schoolmates had
> gone backward half a century. I saw
> there was a wide difference between us.
> I supposed that society was becoming
> rough and going back to heathenism as
> fast as possible. But the fact was that
> my comrades were where I left them and
> I had gone forward.[46]

Booth's observations suggest that for many ambitious young
men a college education, traditional classical curriculum
and all, had great practical value. At a time when few men
obtained a college education but many took advantage of the

[45]B.M.B., "Does It Pay," pp. 290, 287; D.R. Wallace,
"Reminiscences of Old Wake Forest," Wake Forest Student,
XXVIII (January 1909), 28-29;   Greene, Semi-Centennial
History, p. 25.

[46]Isaiah Booth, "Reminiscences," undated typescript in
the Isaiah Booth folder, Denison University Archives, p. 8.

loosely controlled access to the professions, higher education could differentiate a man from many of his professional
competitors. A college education might also confer superior
qualifications to act as an arbiter of local culture.

The role of Baptist colleges in American cultural
development can be seen most clearly in terms of individual
students like Isaiah Booth and within the local context.
Booth happened to be from Syracuse, New York, but lists of
student homes in college catalogues reveal that a majority
were from tiny settlements, hamlets, and villages such as
Black Creek, Ga., Sabbath Rest, Pa., Burnt Hills, N.Y.,
Liberty Corners, Ohio, and Broad Ripple, Ind. The local
character of Baptist colleges, President Justin Loomis of
Bucknell perceptively observed, provided "precisely the
stimulus...necessary to bring the largest possible proportion
of young men to receive their advantages." "Little colleges"
such as those affiliated with the Baptists, noted another
contemporary, "are the means of affording liberal education
to numerous youth...within forty miles of /their/ walls,
who would never go to Cambridge." This was especially true
for the less wealthy students. "Men with their thousands,"
commented an article on Franklin College, "can send their
sons where they please; but men with only their hundreds

must have a place near home, and where expenses will be at
least reasonable." Various reminiscences attest to the
accuracy of the claim made in 1853 that "men of limited
means have by the opportunities thus afforded been elevated
out of the obscurity to which they seemed hopelessly con-
demned."[47]

Brought into contact with the world of learning and
with teachers and students from a variety of social, religious, and geographical backgrounds, many of those who attended Baptist colleges "went forward" enough to become
cultural leaders in their professions and communities. The
trustees of Wake Forest hoped their institution would play
a role in "elevating the literary character of North Carolina." Since 18% of its graduates became educators and
only slightly more than 10% of all matriculants moved from
the state before 1861, their college probably achieved this
goal. Over 100 Colby graduates who did not make teaching
a career taught for at least a year or two. Classrooms were
supplied at one time or another by more than 60% of the
Franklin alumni who did not become professional educators.

[47]Loomis, Inaugural Address, p. 34; "The Columbian College, D.C.," Christian Index, January 16, 1846; "Franklin
College," Christian Messenger, November 13, 1845; reminiscence
of William H. Rider, quoted in deBlois, Pioneer, p. 39;
Brush, Growing Up, pp. 63-64; Wallace, "Reminiscences,"
p. 320; "Notes on Collegiate Education," Southern Baptist,
March 2, 1853.

Achievements in the field of government and law are indicated by the fact that at least 11% of Colby's antebellum
graduates occupied judgeships or held public office. And
of course the many ministers educated at Baptist colleges
were in a position to "educate" their congregations and
communities. Mercer graduates and former students, it was
reported in 1852, "may be found along the lines of our rail-
ways, in the retired villages and neighborhoods of our commonwealth, everywhere elevating the standard of education
and ministerial usefulness."[48] Despite its perhaps excessive
enthusiasm, the Baptist newspaper in Maine made a highly sug-
gestive assessment of the cultural impact of college-trained
men:

> There is no class of men which exerts so
> powerful an influence on society as that
> which is every year sent out from these
> Institutions. How much do our Lawyers,
> Physicians, Preceptors of Academies, and
> Teachers of High Schools...do in giving
> tone to public sentiment. Who can tell
> what a single Lawyer in a country village
> can effect? or a Physician? or a Precep-
> tor of an Academy?...It is a notorious
> fact, that in almost every country, a
> considerable portion of the community,
> are in the hands of a class of men,

[48]Stephen Taylor, "The University at Lewisburg," Chris-
tian Chronicle, September 9, 1846; Wake Forest College, Cata-
logue, 1836, p. 3; General Catalogue of Wake Forest; Paschal,
History, I, 656; General Catalogue of Colby, pp. 25-75;
Wallace, "Alumni," pp. 87-102; Sylvanus Landrum, Sermon on
Ministerial Education Preached Before the Georgia Baptist
Convention (Penfield, Ga., 1852), p. 11.

> distinguished for talent and learning,
> much as clay in the hands of the potter.[49]

Due to the nature of their origins and sources of support, and through their agents, promotion of common schools, and recruitment of students, Baptist colleges exerted an essentially nondenominational influence on American cultural development prior to the Civil War. In addition to the decidedly nonsectarian stimulus they gave to the local economies and cultures in their immediate vicinities, these broadly functional institutions provided educational opportunities for thousands of future cultural leaders. The nondenominational impact of antebellum colleges affiliated with the Baptists may also be viewed in a larger perspective. Basically inclusive in their nature and functions, these colleges widely disseminated a gospel of general education which ranged from support of common schools to advocacy of the classical college curriculum. At a time in the development of American society when higher education might have turned to more specifically vocational or scholarly aims and left liberal education to a few institutions serving the cultural desires of a particular class, denominational colleges and their promoters helped to perpetuate and augment a public faith in general education which was to remain a salient characteristic of American culture for more than a century.

---

[49]"Prayer for Colleges," _Zion's Advocate_, February 10, 1831.

CHAPTER V

CROSSCURRENTS

Throughout the antebellum years, Baptist higher education was largely nondenominational in its aims and its functions. Sectarian sentiments were notably absent in the recruitment of students and solicitation of funds, even when these objectives were pursued in the Baptist press. Contributions of Baptist colleges to the general public were of greater significance than their service to denominational interests. Yet by the late 1840's and increasingly so in the 1850's forces were at work which presaged a change in the nature of these institutions. Sectionalism and denominationalism began to erode the inclusive character which predominated prior to the Civil War.

Disintegration of allegiances to the public good was noticed within the whole of American society in 1844 by a commencement speaker at Denison University. He defined this breakdown in terms of a rapidly growing "horizontal division of the elements which compose our public and private welfare. From harmonious action has arisen discordant opposition; without appreciating the dependence which each part has upon its opposite, to produce a combined, a useful

244

effort, every power has its individual impulse, and oper-
ates without sympathy in its own narrow sphere." Sectional
divisions, part of this general phenomenon, soon made their
way into the realm of Baptist higher education. In 1846,
one year after the denomination split over the slavery
issue, a speaker at Howard College warned against "sending
our youth abroad into distant States" for their education.
The geographical provincialism of denominational colleges
had previously been a matter of necessity or expediency;
now it could be regarded as a virtue. Editorials in the
denominational newspapers of southern states began in the
late 1840's to assert with increasing frequency that the
South must end its "vassalage to the North in literary
matters."[1]

The tendency toward increasing exclusiveness also
derived in part from anti-Catholic sentiments which flourished during the 1830's. Baptist educators were greatly
disturbed when they found sons of their brethren attending
Catholic schools such as Georgetown University. By the
mid-1840's parents were urged not only to stop "cruelly"

---

[1]Bellamy Storer, An Address Delivered Before the Literary Society of Granville College, Ohio, At the Annual Commencement, July 17th, 1844 (Cincinnati, 1844), p. 14; Edward Baptist, Address Delivered Before the Trustees, Faculty and
Students of Howard College, Marion, Perry County, November
16, 1846 (Tuskaloosa, Ala., 1846), p. 8; "Why Should We Educate Our Sons and Daughters at Home?" Christian Index, April
1, 1847.

consigning children "to the management of Catholic priests and priestesses," but also to avoid "surrendering" students to schools of any other denomination.[2]

Logical steps from the rationale of sectionalism and anti-Catholicism to that of denominationalism were quickly and easily taken by some college promoters in the 1850's. The progression is clearly illustrated in the following argument for increased Baptist patronage of Howard:

> Who would risk the education of his son
> in the hands of an adroit abolitionist?
> Who would commit the mental training of
> his child to the hands of a Jesuit? The
> error, however, is only modified in degree
> by committing that child to the hands of
> one who either has no fixed religious prin-
> ciples, or whose principles are adverse to
> our own.[3]

Sectarian influence upon students attending a denominational college came to be regarded by some Baptists as inevitable, even at institutions where such a goal was not actively pursued. From this type of reasoning the conclusion began to emerge that Baptists "must patronize their own schools."[4]

---

[2] "Collegiate Education," Christian Index, January 11, 1838; Stephen Taylor, "The University at Lewisburg," Christian Chronicle, December 9, 1846.

[3] "Endowment of Howard College," South Western Baptist, February 12, 1851.

[4] "Education, No. 3," Baptist, March 29, 1845; "Georgetown College," Western Recorder, August 25, 1852.

Increased denominationalism in Baptist higher education, although related to broad social forces, had its roots in certain institutional problems. By the 1850's interest in education which Baptist colleges helped to arouse among the general public was frequently focused on competing institutions. Preparatory department enrollments declined as local academies and high schools multiplied. With state universities becoming strong rivals in some states, colleges of other denominations appearing nearby, and transportation facilities greatly improved, it became increasingly difficult to tap customary local sources for increased college enrollments sufficient to compensate for reduced revenues from preparatory departments. College communities, which provided so much of the initial support for Baptist institutions, often proved unable or unwilling to sustain their original level of contributions. Forced to develop new sources of students and support, college promoters began to address themselves more exclusively to a denominational audience. They found the denomination increasingly interested in adopting and controlling each local enterprise.

The transition from denominationally affiliated community enterprise to state denominational college, which began for some institutions as early as the late 1840's, frequently included proposals for the removal of institutions to sites where they could better serve denominational

interests. In the resulting controversies and conflicts
the initial nondenominational aspects of Baptist colleges
were vividly illustrated and the more exclusively denominational identities many would later assume were foreshadowed.
Viewed within the context of a developing denominationalism,
removal controversies of the 1850's highlight an early phase
in the transition of Baptist colleges from an inclusive to
a more exclusive nature and function. Removal proposals
were generally unsuccessful, but the denomination continued
to strengthen its hold on most colleges, and the days of the
predominant antebellum emphasis on public service were numbered.

I

Events surrounding the severing of ties between the
Baptist General Convention and George Washington University
in 1826 form an important early episode in the erosion of
concern for the commonweal by sectionalism and denominationalism. In 1820 a close relationship between the institution
and the national organization was projected, with the convention expecting to provide buildings, screen beneficiaries,
appoint faculty, and determine their salaries. Finding that
the charter granted by Congress in 1821 did not permit them
to control college affairs, and unwilling to assume any

responsibility for the college's mounting debts, the members
of the Convention voted in 1826 to devote themselves exclusively to missionary concerns. At the request of the college trustees, the Convention as "a friendly expression of
countenance" continued until the mid-1840's to supply the
school every three years with a list of nominees from which
the trustees would be selected by vote of representatives
from Baptist churches and organizations contributing to the
college.[5] But 1826 terminated all hope for any other form
of official support from this denominational body.

Several immediate issues were involved in the Convention's decision. Faculty and student unrest, related in
part to serious financial problems, threatened the survival
of the college. Questions were raised as to the financial
abilities and even the honesty of Luther Rice, the college
and Convention agent. Suspicions and conflicts over the
collection and distribution of denominational funds had been

---

[5]"Proceedings of the General Convention at Their Second
Triennial Meeting, and the Sixth Annual Report of the Board,"
Latter Day Luminary, II (May 1820), 124; Proceedings of the
Fifth Triennial Meeting of the Baptist General Convention,
Held in New York, April, 1826 (Boston, 1826), p. 19; "Baptist General Convention," American Baptist Magazine, VI (July
1826), 209-10; Proceedings of the Sixth Triennial Meeting of
the Baptist General Convention Held in Philadelphia, 1829
(Boston, 1829), p. 23; James C. Welling, Brief Chronicles
of the Columbian College From 1821 to 1873 and of the Columbian University From 1873 to 1889 (Washington, 1889),
pp. 11, 14-17, 19.

building up for several years and pitted those primarily
interested in missions against those more concerned with
promoting education. The Convention's casting off of the
college, attack on Rice, and decision to pursue exclusively
missionary ends was also related to disputes over church
polity and represented a victory for those wishing to thwart
any movement toward a representative and comprehensive
national Baptist convention.[6]

Two broad issues of particular relevance to the future
nature of Baptist colleges can also be seen in the George
Washington University controversy. The first of these
issues concerned sectional tensions within the denomination.
Almost two-thirds of the delegates to the Convention of 1826
were from New York and Massachusetts. With a Baptist school
already well established at Hamilton, New York, and one just
opened near Boston, this majority block of delegates had
little reason to continue supporting an insolvent college
in Washington. Desiring to attain undisputed leadership of

[6]Luther Rice to O.B. Brown, April 19, 1826, Luther Rice
Letters, Office of the University Historian, George Washing-
ton University; Welling, Brief Chronicles, p. 11; Elmer L.
Kayser, Luther Rice, Founder of Columbian College (Washington,
1966), pp. 18-21; Richard Furman to Luther Rice, November 21,
1822, Rare Book Room, Boston Public Library; "Columbian Col-
lege," American Baptist Magazine and Missionary Intelligencer,
III (July 1821), 159; "Substance of the Proceedings," Latter
Day Luminary, V (June 1824), 181; "Business Before the Baptist
General Convention in the United States," American Baptist
Magazine, VI (April 1826), 115; "Baptist General Convention,"
Columbian Star, April 15, 1826; Winthrop S. Hudson, "Stumbling
into Disorder," Foundations, I (April 1958), 55-58.

a powerful missionary enterprise, the New England delegates and their New York neighbors supplied the votes needed to reduce the Convention to a missionary body and locate its Board of Managers in Boston.[7]

Prior to 1826 George Washington quite accurately viewed itself as a national institution fulfilling many of the "essential objects" embodied in secular proposals for a national university. It was anticipated in 1822 that students "meeting here from every quarter of the Union" would experience "a conforming and harmonizing influence /which/ results from the mutual surrendering of sectional pre-possessions." With "religious and political party dis-crimination...unknown in the proceedings and discipline of the College," it was reported two years later that students had been "collected from seventeen of the twenty-four states of the Union, embracing the wide extremes of Maine and Lou-isiana." Robert Ryland, a student during the mid-1820's, recalled that "boys from the North, South, East and West were brought together, and had their respective provincial-isms subjected to comparison and mutual criticism." In this process the fallacies of sectional stereotypes were quickly exposed. George Washington functioned during this period as a contributor to "the permanence and strength of

---

[7]Ibid., pp. 51-54.

our Union" and was supported in this effort by a great many
leading political figures in the city, including President
Monroe.[8]

After 1826 the college was still promoted as one of
the nation's "public charities," serving all citizens in the
city of Washington and accomplishing all "the essential good
which would be effected by a National University." Despite
claims made throughout the 1830's that George Washington was
a place where young men would "learn to bury their sectional
prejudices" and "strengthen the bonds of national union,"
however, the college quickly became a predominantly southern
institution. There had always been strong support from this
region, but prior to 1826 many contributions had also come
from the northern states. Although some gifts continued to
come from the North, and particularly from New York, Rice by
late 1827 was "disposed to believe it practicable to save
the College without New England, and even without New York."
Rice found that "everything indicates the faithlessness of
New England and that even New York may possibly follow the
example." Having previously traveled North as well as South

        8Welling, Brief Chronicles, p. 9; "The Rev. Luther Rice,
A.M.," Southern Baptist and General Intelligencer, December
9, 1836; "Columbian College," Columbian Star, February 23,
1822 and March 13, 1824; Robert Ryland, "Reminiscences,"
Ford's Christian Repository, XLVI (July 1888), 38; "Columbian College," Columbian Star, March 5, 1825; "Columbian
College," Latter Day Luminary, VI (January 1825), 21.

on behalf of George Washington, Rice now conducted his
agency exclusively in the South and spread his anti-Northern
sentiments while doing so. The high proportion of Southern
students was given special consideration by keeping classes
in operation from July through September with vacations
scheduled for the fall and spring. "This arrangement," an
advertisement emphasized, "gives Students from the South the
advantage of spending the sickly season on College Hill."
Except for relatively unproductive solicitation in the District of Columbia, the endowment fund drive of 1845-1848
drew solely upon resources of the South. As late as 1849
a desire was still expressed for significant numbers of
Northern students so that George Washington could help
"bind the Union together," but this hope was not fulfilled
before the Civil War.[9]

[9]Elon Galusha, The Crisis Is At Hand (Whitesborough,
N.Y., 1826), p. 1; "College Hill, D.C." Religious Herald,
July 1, 1831; "Commencement at Columbian College," Christian Index, November 15, 1838; Galusha, Crisis, p. 2;
"Columbian College," Zion's Advocate, November 20, 1828,
copied from the Columbian Star, November 8, 1828; James D.
Knowles, "History of the Columbian College, District of
Columbia," Christian Review, II (March 1837), 135; "Columbian College," Christian Index, December 5, 1839, copied
from the Washington City Globe; Donald Keyser, "A History
of Baptist Higher Education in the South to 1865," unpublished Th.D. dissertation, Southern Baptist Theological
Seminary, 1955, p. 5; "Proceedings of the...Second Triennial," pp. 146-50; "Seventh Annual Report of the Board,"
ibid., II (May, 1821), 365, 376; "Substance of the Proceedings," ibid., IV (June 1823), 202-12; Circular of the
Columbian College, D.C., broadside dated March 26, 1827;
Luther Rice to O.B. Brown, October 1, 1827, Rice Letters;

The comprehensive conception of George Washington University was shattered in the mid-1820's by denominational as well as sectional sentiments. To guard against further mismanagement of the school's finances and restore public confidence after the Convention action of 1826, supporters of the University elected a new board of trustees that year which included a group of men who were prominent in the political and financial life of Washington. Although these men were not Baptists, it was believed that they considered "themselves pledged, to continue the effective control of the Institution, if redeemed, to that denomination which has honored them with their confidence." Samuel H. Smith, President of the Bank of Washington, was the leader of these new trustees. The Smith group was soon joined by at least one Baptist trustee in a campaign to reduce or eliminate the power of Luther Rice in university affairs.[10]

The ensuing struggle, which lasted from mid-1826 until early 1827, involved much more than just antipathy toward

E.B. Pollard, "Luther Rice and His Place in American Baptist History," Review and Expositor, X (October 1913), 527; William Ruggles to Ira Chase, September 27, 1826, Office of the University Historian, George Washington University; "Columbian College, D.C." Christian Index and Baptist Miscellany, January 28, 1834; U.S., Congress, House, Financial Condition of the George Washington University, 61st Cong., 3rd Sess., 1910, House Doc. 1060, p. 9; "Columbian College," Biblical Recorder, December 8, 1849.

[10]Galusha, Crisis, p. 1; "Columbian College," Christian Watchman, May 26, 1826; "Extract of a Circular Letter from Mr. Rice of the 26th March, 1827," New York Baptist Register, May 26, 1827; Galusha, Crisis, p. 2.

and distrust of Rice. At stake was the nature and control
of the school. By August, 1826, Rice was convinced that
Smith would "not be easy till he gets the College out of
the hands of the Baptists." Their previous writings on
education suggest a deep and irreconcilable conflict between Smith and Rice. "The two great objects of a correct
education," Smith wrote in the late 1790's, "are to make
men virtuous and wise." Virtue as defined by Smith was
"that active exertion of our faculties which in the highest
degree promotes our own happiness and that of our fellow
men." Rice, on the other hand, wrote in 1822 that George
Washington University should not only promote learning of
the type which would develop the faculties, but also serve
as a "nursery of...evangelical piety." Smith thought a
university serving the national interest should exist for
the most intellectually talented and be administered by
trustees chosen on the basis of their scholarly qualifications. Rice was deeply concerned about the education of
Baptist ministers and, as the controversy revealed, was an
advocate of strict denominational control. Part of the
struggle seems to have involved the reappointment of a
young non-Baptist as Professor of Mathematics and Natural
Philosophy, but Rice's basic fear was that the Smith group
would persuade Congress to alter the charter so as to

change the nature and control of the institution.[11]

Failing to dislodge Luther Rice, a step necessary to effecting significant changes at George Washington, the Smith trustees resigned in a body barely nine months after assuming office. Rice immediately initiated a campaign to prevent any future "policy of bringing in infidels, unitarians, etc. to manage the Baptist interest," and the college began assuming a more denominationál cast. Soon after his defeat of "the Infidel, Smith," Rice reported a strong surge of Baptist support for the college. To "save the College to the Baptist denomination" and "ensure Baptist support," he urged constant vigilance to "keep... true Baptists in control of the Board of Trustees at all times." George Washington began to be promoted as a college "mainly designed for the Baptists" and "strictly...

---

[11]Luther Rice to O.B. Brown, August 21, 1826, Rice Letters; Samuel H. Smith, Remarks on Education: Illustrating the Close Connection Between Virtue and Wisdom. To Which Is Annexed A System of Liberal Education, Which Having Received the Premium Awarded By the American Philosophical Society, December 15th, 1797, Is Now Published By Their Order (Philadelphia, 1798), reprinted in Essays on Education in the Early Republic, ed. Frederick Rudolph (Cambridge, Mass., 1965), pp. 170, 212-13; "Columbian College," Latter Day Luminary, III (February 1822), 47; Luther Rice to O.B. Brown, October 10, 1831, Rice Letters; "Columbian College," Christian Index and Baptist Miscellany, February 4, 1834; Luther Rice to O.B. Brown, May 12, 1828, Rice Letters; William Cathcart, The Baptist Encyclopaedia (Rev. ed.; Philadelphia, 1883), p. 1014; Luther Rice to O.B. Brown, August 21, 1826, Rice Letters.

Baptist" in terms of control.[12]   The denomination was told

in 1827:

> By surrendering the Institution, we shall
> depress ourselves, comparatively, in a two-
> fold proportion. First by resigning a most
> efficient means of increasing our own in-
> fluence. Second by putting those who are
> opposed to us (as a denomination) in full
> possession of the same advantages to re-
> tard our progress...Either Episcopalians,
> Unitarians, or Infidels will soon build
> on our ruins, and profit by our misfortunes.[13]

Taking this denominational stance and presenting itself as

"peculiarly advantageous to our Southern friends," George

Washington University in the late 1830's strenuously opposed

use of the Smithsonian bequest to establish a national uni-

versity in Washington.[14]

II

Sectional and local interests, which by the 1850's

were provoking a greatly increased denominational consciousness

---

[12]Circular of the Columbian; Luther Rice to O.B. Brown,
April 25, September 22, May 1, July 14, June 26, and July 12,
1827, Rice Letters; "Baptist College," Columbian Star, December 27, 1828.

[13]Galusha, Crisis, p. 1.

[14]"Baptist College," Columbian Star, December 27, 1828;
Knowles, "History," p. 135; Memoirs of John Quincy Adams,
Comprising Portions of His Diary From 1795 to 1848, ed.
Charles Francis Adams, X (Philadelphia, 1876), 23, 89-90.

within Baptist higher education, developed rapidly after
their appearance at George Washington. They stimulated a
rapid multiplication of Baptist-affiliated institutions.
Cooperation in promoting Baptist colleges in the late 1820's
and the 1830's was limited to agreements among neighboring
and nearby states. Vermont and Connecticut were important
sources of funds and students for Colgate University throughout most of the 1820's. The Ohio Baptist Convention in 1828
recommended George Washington to the brethren in Ohio. Plans
for educational cooperation were formulated by Baptists in
Georgia and South Carolina during the mid-1830's. Yet the
trend which soon developed was toward interstate rivalry
rather than joint efforts. In the early 1830's some Virginia Baptists who had been strong supporters of George
Washington founded the University of Richmond to serve their
own state. The establishment of Wake Forest College a few
years later further reduced southern Baptist support for
George Washington. Despite pleas in 1837 that "brethren of
sister states" disregard "all personal, local, and selfish
considerations" to support a southern Baptist school in
Georgia, neither its predecessor at Washington, Georgia,
nor Mercer University became "an institution for the South."
President Howard Malcom of Georgetown College contended
that "the Baptists in the Mississippi Valley are in fact
and should regard themselves as one vast whole" and should

be deterred by financial considerations, if nothing else,
from "bringing a college to every man's door." He believed
that at least the Baptists of Tennessee should consider
Georgetown as their college. The Tennessee response to
this proposal was foreshadowed by the statement of an agent
for a proposed college in western Tennessee almost a decade
earlier. "We must not think of Colleges and Academies in
other parts of our country," said P.S. Gayle, " and deem
those sufficient; we must possess those self-redeeming principles among ourselves." Union University in Murfreesboro,
Tennessee, not only formed college classes less than five
years after President Malcom's overture but also attempted
to lure Georgetown's students to their institution in 1849
when the Kentucky college was weakened by his resignation.[15]

Rivalry began to develop on even an intrastate level
in the 1830's. Ignoring pleas from Richmond that they "prefer
the public good to local interests," some Baptists in Williamsburg, Virginia, vigorously promoted the establishment of their

---

[15]Howard D. Williams, "The History of Colgate University
to 1869," unpublished Ph.D. dissertation, Harvard University,
1949, pp. 46-47; Ohio Baptist Convention, Minutes, 1828,
p. 16; B.D. Ragsdale, Story of Georgia Baptists, I (Atlanta,
1932), 50; Robert Ryland, The Virginia Baptist Education Society, The Society, the Seminary, the College (Richmond, Va.,
1891), p. 10; Luther Rice to Stephen Chapin, November 10,
1834, Rice Letters; "Mercer University," Christian Index,
November 9, 1837; "Southern Baptist College," ibid., February 9, 1837; "Georgetown College," Baptist Banner and Western Pioneer, September 7, 1843; "Address," Baptist, II (October 1836), 343; "Georgetown College," Tennessee Baptist,
September 13, 1849.

own Baptist theological school. Baptists in Northern Ohio
had already obtained a charter for a college in their region
before President Jonathan Going of Denison finally persuaded
them to abandon their project. By the 1850's several states
had more than one Baptist college. Declaring in 1854 that
"the Green River country has too long succumbed to upper
Kentucky, politically and religiously," and that "there
ought to be and will be a College in this section of the
State," a group of Baptists and local citizens founded
Bethel College in Russellville, about 170 miles from Georgetown College. Ambitious Baptists in the fast-growing region
of northern Georgia opened Cherokee College at Cassville in
1856. With Marshall College in Griffin already in operation,
this gave Mercer two Baptist competitors. Between 1849 and
1859 six Baptist colleges were established in Missouri.[16]

A series of events concerning Shurtleff College during
the years from 1845 through 1855 form an interesting case
study of the decline in public service considerations as

---

[16]S. Jones, Arguments For and Against a Baptist Theological School at Williamsburg, Virginia (Richmond, Va.,
1837), p. 15 et passim; Ohio, Session Laws, 1836-37, pp. 347-
48; Willis A. Chamberlin, "Dr. Jonathan Going's Impress Upon
the Midwest," Chronicle, VIII (July 1945), 112; J.M. Pendleton, Education (Nashville, Tenn., 1854), p. 19; "Georgia Baptist Convention," Christian Index, May 6, 1857; Sandford
Fleming, "American Baptists and Higher Education," six-
volume typescript, ca. 1963, American Baptist Historical
Society, Rochester, New York, I, 138.

sectional and local competition began to raise certain denominational questions. Despite the statewide union of Baptist interests in 1844 through formation of the Baptist General Association of Illinois, deep-seated tensions between northern and southern portions of the state continued to be reflected in denominational affairs. A Shurtleff supporter found it necessary in 1845 to defend the College against accusations that it had become a "Southern institution." Even the question of "whether or not there is to be a college at Alton" was raised at about the same time.[17]

Attacks on Shurtleff intensified during the early 1850's under the direction of what John Mason Peck called "the Chicago clique." This group included Justin A. Smith and LeRoy Church, editors of the Christian Times, and J.C. Burroughs, pastor of the First Baptist Church of Chicago. Having guided Stephen A. Douglas's gift for a University of Chicago into Baptist channels, Burroughs became the first president of the institution, which opened in 1858. The key weapon of the Chicago group was their denominational newspaper. From 1853 through 1856 the Christian Times stirred sectional feelings over Shurtleff and campaigned

---

[17]Charles Chaney, "Diversity: A Study in Illinois Baptist History to 1907," Foundations, VII (January 1964), 46; "Shurtleff College," Western Star, October 7, 1845; "Alton College," Watchman of the Prairies, September 21, 1847.

for a more centrally located and prosperous institution
which would better serve the Baptists of Illinois. Peck
found the "Chicago and Northern folks" to be "cunning and
adroit" in their tactics and determined to control the
organizational, journalistic, and educational interests
of the denomination, "all to answer their sectional purposes."[18]

Two major controversies which weakened Shurtleff's
standing within the denomination were promoted by the
Chicago group. In 1853 Justin Smith led a movement to
force the resignation of most faculty members at Shurtleff
because they supported a current project to revise the King
James Bible. Since Peck was an opponent of revision, even
he was compelled to aid the Chicago group on this point.
Running concurrently with the revision controversy was a
debate over the origins of Shurtleff. A series of articles
from the Alton Weekly Currier by Hubbel Loomis in which he
claimed to be the founder of Shurtleff were reprinted in the
Christian Times during February, 1854. Loomis contended that
the school he opened in Alton in 1832 was not a continuation

18Austin K. deBlois, The Pioneer School: A History of
Shurtleff College, Oldest Educational Institution in the
West (New York, 1900), pp. 130, 128; Thomas W. Goodspeed, A
History of the University of Chicago (Chicago, 1916), pp. 13-
14; "Shall Anything Be Done?" Christian Times, September 15,
1853; letter from J. Teasdale, ibid., October 5, 1853;
deBlois, Pioneer, p. 130.

of Peck's seminary at Rock Spring, but rather the independent foundation for Shurtleff. Loomis placed Peck "in
the background" of Shurtleff's history prior to 1836. Peck
was permitted to reply to Loomis's attack and did so by arguing that "Shurtleff College (formerly Alton) originated
by a suspension and removal of Rock Spring Seminary."
The debate continued for several months, ending in a stale-
mate, and probably creating substantial doubt within the
denomination concerning Shurtleff's claim to being the
oldest college in the West and to being founded by the
pioneer missionary and Baptist hero, John Mason Peck.[19]

19/Erastus Adkins/, A Narrative of Facts and Proceedings
Connected With the Recent Changes in the Faculty of Shurt-
leff College (St. Louis, 1855), pp. 9-10, 13, et passim;
"Popish Persecutions in Shurtleff College, Illinois! The
Inquisition Organized!! The Professors Attainted of Heresy,
etc.!!!" New York Chronicle, August 11, 1855; Austin K. de-
Blois, "Denominational Education Fifty Years Ago," Standard,
March 14, 1903; "Documentary History of Shurtleff College,"
Christian Times, February 2, 1854; "Shurtleff College," ibid.,
July 13, 1854; "Origin of Shurtleff College," ibid., June 8,
1854; "Replication to the Claims of the Fathership of Shurt-
leff College," ibid., July 20, 1854. The debate over Shurt-
leff's origins continued for many decades. Data relevant to
this question and subsequent claims and counterclaims can be
found in the following sources: John Mason Peck to Trustees
of the Baptist Missionary Society of Massachusetts, August
29, 1831, John Mason Peck Correspondence, Andover Newton
Theological School Library; "Operations of the Baptists in
Illinois," Zion's Advocate, December 26, 1832; John Mason
Peck, A Gazetteer of Illinois (Jacksonville, 1834), p. 86;
J. M. Peck, Alton Seminary and College (n.p., ca. 1835),
p. 2; "Illinois," Baptist Advocate, II (June 1836), 142;
Shurtleff College, Catalogue, 1840/41, p. 6; J.M. Peck,
"Historical Sketches--No. II, Illinois," Baptist Banner and
Western Pioneer, August 11, 1842; Justus Bulkley, Historical
Sketch of Shurtleff College, Upper Alton, Illinois (Upper

If Shurtleff was too Southern, unsound on Bible revision, unable to give Baptists clear claim to an educational first in the West, and lacking the prestigious paternity of Peck, the removal or abandonment of this enterprise was that much easier to propose. Such a solution to
the college's financial and other problems was suggested in
a Chicago newspaper as early as 1849. Reporting on a college
removal controversy in New York, the editor asserted:

> The lesson which the history of this...
> ought to teach us...is that a college or
> theological institution is too important
> in promoting the cause of Christ to be
> troubled by prejudice against its removal
> to a more advantageous point.... Military
> men bury their dead wherever they happen

Alton, Ill., 1865), pp. 1-4; Hubbel Loomis, A Documentary
History of Alton Seminary to March 7, 1835, When Its Departments Took the Distinctive Names Alton Theological Seminary,
and Alton College, Which January 12, 1836, Took the Name
Shurtleff College; The School, Called Alton Seminary, or,
Alton Literary and Theological Seminary, Founded by Rev. H.
Loomis, September, 1832, and the Charge Resigned, June 13,
1836 (Alton, Ill., 1854); Jubilee Memorial of Shurtleff College, Upper Alton, Ill. (Alton, Ill., 1877), p. 3; Frank
Adkins, "Baptist History in the Central West," Denison Quarterly, IV (December 1896), 277-78; Justus Bulkley, "Historical Sketch of Shurtleff Prepared for the Seventieth Annual
Commencement of Shurtleff College, June, 1897," Semi-Centennial History of the Alpha Zeta Society of Shurtleff College (Alton, Ill., 1898), pp. xiv-xix; deBlois, Pioneer,
pp. 42-46; John W. Cook, Educational History of Illinois
(Chicago, 1912), p. 300; Memorial Volume of Denison University, 1831-1906 (Columbus, Ohio, 1907), pp. 14, 42; Francis
W. Shepardson, Denison University, 1831-1931, A Centennial
History (Granville, Ohio, 1931), p. 6; G. Wallace Chessman,
Denison: The Story of an Ohio College (Granville, Ohio, 1957),
p. 3; Matthew Lawrence, John Mason Peck, The Pioneer Missionary: A Biographical Sketch (New York, 1940), pp. 59, 63-64,
67; Helene L. Jennings, "John Mason Peck and the Impact of
New England on the Old Northwest," unpublished Ph.D. dissertation, University of Southern California, 1961, pp. 95, 146.

> to fall and move on to meet the enemy
> in the thickest battle; and should the
> soldiers of the cross do less?... A
> few thousand dollars worth of church or
> college buildings, are often a very
> small consideration in comparison with
> the advantages to be gained by a more
> favorable point.[20]

The more "advantageous point" openly promoted a few years

later was Chicago. Since Shurtleff's charter explicitly

prohibited removal, the abandonment of at least college in-

struction in Alton was being urged by the mid-1850's. The

Chicago Baptists, according to Peck, wanted "to bring the

main body of the denomination through the state to work on

their Great University project."[21]

In the eyes of some Baptists this episode might be

viewed as another example of "our local, selfish, divided,

scattering policy" in education.[22] Yet the Chicago enter-

prise was promoted as a more effective instrument of denomina-

tional purpose than Shurtleff and one which could better en-

list the support of Baptists throughout the state. Although

they were often inspired by local sentiments, advocates of

new facilities and improvements in Baptist higher education

---

[20]"Baptist Educational Convention," Watchman of the
Prairies, November 6, 1849.

[21]Shurtleff College, Catalogue, 1840/41, p. 12; deBlois,
Pioneer, pp. 132, 130.

[22]"Education Amongst the Baptists," Christian Index,
April 28, 1843.

during the 1850's usually followed an approach similar to
that of the "Chicago clique." Rather than promoting their
colleges largely in terms of service to public educational
needs, especially on the local level, these men justified
new enterprises on the grounds of improved service to statewide denominational interests. Most communities where new
colleges were to be founded or older institutions relocated
already had a sufficient number of educational and other
cultural agencies and a large enough variety of economic
interests to render widespread local support a less likely
prospect than it had been in previous decades. Establishment of a college in the 1850's required a large measure
of denominational support, and in most states Baptists did
not have the numbers, wealth or desire to support more than
one college of high quality. Intrastate competition among
Baptists from different sections or communities for these
limited resources stimulated greatly increased emphasis on
denominational considerations.

III

Increasing denominationalism not directly connected
with sectional competition appeared at about the same time
in relationships between established colleges and the Baptists of particular states. The emphasis on public service

remained strong well into the 1850's, but during the previous decade a greater denominational consciousness began to emerge in pleas for funds. By the 1850's this trend was reflected in concerns over campus piety, faculty resignations, and shifting attitudes toward state universities. Denominational support to colleges was noticeably increased, and enrollments assumed a less local and probably more Baptist character. Along with these gradual shifts, Baptists began to worry about the extent to which they controlled their colleges.

Baptist colleges presented themselves primarily as contributors to the public good until well into the 1840's, and this theme persisted in the denominational press throughout the antebellum years. President Thomas Malcom of Georgetown argued at great length in 1840 that his college was far from being exclusively Baptist in terms of faculty, students, and educational aims. A similar disclaimer was issued by Wake Forest the year before, and this institution during the 1840's continued to view itself as "gotten up with a view to promote the cause of education in general" and to meet community needs. Shurtleff in the early 1850's was still aiming its appeals at "the great public" and even receiving patronage from Catholics. Howard in the 1850's considered itself "greatly needed by the public for the purposes of general education" as well as "needed by the Baptist denomination to

fill their many empty pulpits." Union thought in 1856
that it still merited the support of the friends of "popular" as well as "ministerial" education. Appeals for non-
Baptist support and students were also issued by Richmond
and Furman in the late 1850's.[23]

After a decade or two of operations supported largely
by local contributions, most colleges found their financial
outlook no better or even worse than when they had started.
Colgate's promoters pointed out in 1838 that "the Institution at Hamilton was established in 1820 and its burden has
been borne upon the shoulders of a comparative few until it
has increased beyond their means." These few could no
longer "sustain it unless the denomination should come forward to their aid." Heavily in debt and with sharply declining enrollments, Colby College came close to extinction
in 1839. First the college turned to the town of Waterville
and quickly raised more than $10,000. But this left three
or four times that amount still to be obtained before the

[23]"Georgetown College," Baptist Banner and Western Pio-
neer, November 19, 1840; "Circular," Biblical Recorder and
Southern Watchman, January 5, 1839; "Wake Forest College,"
Biblical Recorder, August 15, 1846; "Wake Forest College,"
ibid., April 8, 1848; "Shurtleff College Endowment.--Good
Tidings," Watchman of the Prairies, April 22, 1851; deBlois,
Pioneer, p. 119; "Howard College," South Western Baptist,
November 18, 1853; "Plan for Raising Endowment Funds of
Union University--Some Motives for Adopting It," Tennessee
Baptist, July 5, 1856; "Richmond College," Religious Herald,
August 5, 1858; "Furman University," Southern Baptist,
January 25, 1859.

survival of the college could be assured. An agent for
Franklin College reported that of all the money received
by his school up to 1841, "one half or more has been paid
by the citizens in its vicinity." He felt it was now time
"to call the attention of the whole denomination to this
subject," and asked them to join in. Georgetown's local
patronage was greatly diminished by nearby institutions
during the 1840's. Finding other denominations giving almost exclusive support to their own schools, supporters of
Georgetown asked "why should not the Baptists do the same?
They concluded that if the denomination did not come to the
rescue, no one else would. Ohio Baptists were told in 1850
that Denison "in its strength, growth, and merits has outgrown its patronage." The college's success now depended
on "denominational love and pride." Calling in 1854 for a
more "intimate connection between the institution and the
churches," the editor of Maine's denominational newspaper
urged Colby's new president to travel widely and solicit
the Baptist churches, because without help from this source
the college could not prosper.[24]

---

[24]"Hamilton Institution," New York Baptist Register,
January 12, 1838; Ernest C. Marriner, The History of Colby
College (Waterville, Me., 1963), pp. 94-96; "To the Board
of Trustees of the I.B.M.L. Institute," Baptist Banner and
Western Pioneer, August 5, 1841; "Extracts from the Semi-
Annual Report of the President of Georgetown College, Made
to the Trustees, Dec. 22, 1847," Baptist Banner, January 13,

During the 1840's Baptist educators made an increasing number of complaints about denominational neglect. Less than one per cent of Baptist laymen in Kentucky and less than twenty per cent of their clergy were contributors to Georgetown in 1842. By the end of the decade the number actively supporting the college was still only "a mere fraction of the denomination," and it was urged that "all now take hold and finish it." The claims of Mercer were found in 1842 to be "by no means appreciated" by the Baptists of Georgia. An "appalling apathy pervading the churches" on the subject of ministerial education was lamented by the agent for Colgate in the mid-1840's. Ohio Baptists were called upon in 1847 "to wake up to their work" in regard to Denison. Baptists in Virginia were also found to be sleeping when it came to support of Richmond. "From the length of time it has been founded" observed a promoter of Howard, "and taking into consideration the numerical strength and wealth of our denomination in Alabama, it must be evident, to the thoughtful, that the heart and purse of our people are not in the Institution."

1848; "The Claims of Georgetown College on the Baptists of Kentucky," ibid., October 31, 1849; Shepardson, Denison, p. 74; "Waterville College," Zion's Advocate, February 17, 1854.

At the end of the 1850's denominational neglect was still found at Wake Forest.[25]

To bolster their pleas for denominational support, Baptist colleges began claiming a purely denominational paternity and ownership. The variety of arguments used to prove denominational obligations sometimes ignored but usually implied the nondenominational origins and early characteristics of the colleges. Appeals to "the love of your offspring" had been tried as early as 1829 by George Washington, but it was not until the 1840's that other institutions pursued this strategy. Denison was portrayed in 1841 as being "originated by the Baptists of Ohio, and by them it has been...sustained. It is the property not of the Baptist church in Granville, nor of the Trustees, but of the entire denomination." Yet the remainder of this plea suggested that the entire denomination should begin supporting Denison. A more candid and consistent historical stance was taken at Georgetown, where it was asserted that "the denomination

---

25"To the Baptists of Kentucky," Baptist Banner and Western Pioneer, June 16, 1842; "The Claims of Georgetown College on the Baptists of Kentucky," Baptist Banner, October 31, 1849; "Mercer University," Christian Index, August 5, 1842; "To the Churches and Contributors to the Institution at Hamilton," New York Baptist Recorder, August 1, 1845; Shepardson, Denison, p. 65; "Richmond College," Religious Herald, April 15, 1852; "Kent's Communication--Howard College," South Western Baptist, August 14, 1856; William T. Brooks, An Address Delivered Before the Alumni of Wake Forest College, On the Afternoon of June 18th, 1859 (Raleigh, N.C., 1861), p. 14.

must take hold of" the college, and "ought to feel that
it is their institution." South Carolina Baptists were
asked "to take some interest" in Furman "that it may be
our college, the college of the Baptists of South Carolina."
Colby was pictured as "a sacred trust," bequeathed to the
Baptists of Maine "from the fathers who laid its foundations and tenderly guarded its infancy."[26]

Some Baptists disputed, however, whether the fathers
of their colleges had actually founded denominational
schools. Union felt the need to assure the Tennessee Baptists that it was not a "local interest." Despite assertions that Howard was "the creature of and property of the
Baptist State Convention of Alabama," many Baptists in that
state still "looked upon it as the Marion College." Not
until the late 1850's was the denomination found "regarding
it as 'our College'" and a "State Institution." In 1856
Bucknell's promoters still had to argue in seeking denominational support that "the University was designed, not simply

[26]Welling, Brief Chronicles, p. 15; "Commencement at
Granville," Cross and Journal, July 23, 1841; letter from
D.R. Campbell, Baptist Banner and Western Pioneer, Septem-
ber 9, 1847; "Georgetown College," Baptist Banner, April
26, 1848; letter from H.W. Pasley, Southern Baptist,
October 22, 1851; "Are You Ready?" Zion's Advocate,
September 4, 1857.

for the immediate neighborhood, but for THE BAPTISTS OF
PENNSYLVANIA AS A DENOMINATION."[27]

Promoting greater denominational support might be
rather difficult from a historical point of view, but
several less ambiguous means were also available. Where
scholarships had once been sold to anyone, and primarily
to create immediate revenue, longer term considerations
appeared in the 1850's. Sale of scholarships to Baptist
congregations was found "especially beneficial" because it
created "a bond of union...between the churches of our
state, and the College made thus peculiarly their own."
Shifts in emphasis also appeared in articles promoting
annual days of prayer for colleges. In contrast to an
earlier stress on the Christian influence exerted by colleges of all denominations and the saving of individual
souls, a particular concern for the prosperity of Baptist
colleges and "the duty of the churches...to link themselves
more closely to their colleges" was voiced during the 1840's
and 1850's.[28]

27"Baptist Female College at Greenville," Southern Bap-
tist, May 3, 1854; "Female College at Greenville," ibid.,
May 24, 1854; "Georgetown College.--Union University," Tennes-
see Baptist, April 26, 1856; "Howard College," South Western
Baptist, November 4, 1853 and November 19, 1857; letter from
O.N. Worden et al., Christian Chronicle, August 13, 1856.

28"Scholarships for Wake Forest College," Biblical Re-
corder, April 1, 1853; "Prayer for Colleges," Zion's Advocate,
February 10, 1831; "Prayer for Literary Institutions," Zion's
Advocate and Eastern Baptist, February 26, 1840; "Prayer for
Colleges," New York Recorder and Register, February 7, 1855.

A few changes in college faculties suggest that they
too were being shaped to more denominational purposes.
Considerable catholicity characterized some faculties
during this period. At Georgetown in 1840 two professors
belonged to no church, the principal of the preparatory
department was a Methodist, and the principal of the affiliated female academy was a Presbyterian. One of the teachers
in Shurtleff's preparatory department in the late 1840's was
a lay elder in the Presbyterian Church, and the acting president of the college in the mid-1850's was an Episcopalian.
Yet Baptist support was important enough to Colby by the
mid-1840's to force the resignation of a President leaning
toward Unitarianism. Howard's nonclerical president resigned in 1852 to make way for a man with the proper ministerial qualifications. A professor of ancient languages at
Wake Forest was dismissed in 1859 largely because he was not
a Baptist.[29]

Denials of state aid to some Baptist colleges in the
1840's and 1850's suggested that "we must rely upon our own
resources." This impasse probably inspired some contemporary
aggrandizements of the "voluntary principle" in American

[29]"Georgetown College," Baptist Banner and Western Pioneer, November 19, 1840; deBlois, Pioneer, pp. 106, 333, 128-
29; Marriner, History, pp. 103-04; Benjamin F. Riley, History
of the Baptists of Alabama, 1808-1894 (Birmingham, Ala.,
1895), p. 205; George W. Paschal, History of Wake Forest
College, I (Wake Forest, N.C., 1935), 396.

religious and educational life. It more directly encouraged
attacks on state universities such as that launched in North
Carolina in 1855. Where these institutions had once been regarded as fellow contributors to the public good, they now
were denounced as religiously weak if not infidel refuges
for idle and dissipated sons of the rich. Baptists were
warned that there "has not been for years a Baptist Professor" at Chapel Hill. When Basil Manly, a prominent Baptist, resigned the presidency of the University of Alabama
in 1855, promoters of Howard were quick to urge that the
Baptists of the state patronize their college exclusively.
While denouncing state universities, proponents of the denominational college developed a heightened sense of their
own uniqueness. In earlier days they viewed themselves as
just one of many contributors to the cause of general education. Now they began to argue that they had done a much
better job of cultivating interest in education than that
of other agencies such as state universities. By the mid-
1850's denominationalism in education was regarded as an un-
questioned virtue.[30]

---

[30]Keyser, "A History," p. 93; Howard Malcom, "Baccalaureate Address: Delivered by the President to the Graduating
Class in Georgetown College, June 29, 1848," Georgetown Herald, July 19, 1848, clipping in "Howard Malcom Memorial Scrapbook," American Baptist Historical Society, Rochester, New
York, p. 73; "The Comparative Advantages of Denominational
and State Colleges Reviewed," Biblical Recorder, July 12-
August 9, 1855; "Denominational Colleges," ibid., October 6,
1859; Riley, History, p. 256; "Baptist Female College at
Greenville," Southern Baptist, March 15, 1854.

An increased sense of denominational identity among
Baptists in general prepared them to respond to the college
appeals being aimed more directly at them as a group. The
founding of the American Baptist Historical Society in 1853
and the Landmark movement among Southern Baptists in the
same decade were important parts of this growing denominational consciousness. Its educational dimension appeared
in convention and association resolutions expressing an aug-
mented interest in Baptist-affiliated colleges as denominational institutions. Prior to the mid-1840's little mention
of colleges appeared in these records, but by the 1850's
most denominational organizations issued annual endorsements
of Baptist institutions within their geographical sphere.
Although this support was largely verbal, some conventions
instructed their agents to collect funds for colleges as
well as missions, and educational contributions were frequently solicited among those attending denominational
meetings.[31]

Beginnings of an educational awakening within the
denomination in the 1840's were noted in the Baptist press.
The University of Richmond was found to be "gaining a
firmer hold on the regard and confidence of the denomination."

[31]For a discussion of the general resurgence of denominationalism within American Protestanism beginning in the late
1830's, see Lefferts A. Loetscher, "The Problem of Christian
Unity in Early Nineteenth-Century America," Church History,
XXXII (March 1963), 3-16.

It was reported concerning Mercer that "the denomination
in our State are beginning to estimate aright the advantages
afforded for the education of their sons in their own institution." Other sources suggest that this trend intensified
during the 1850's. After a disastrous fire at Howard in
1854 it was reported that "Baptists now begin to feel that
it is their College, and that it is their duty to sustain
it." By the end of the decade former students of Baptist
colleges were sufficiently numerous and prominent to exert
great influence on denominational attitudes toward higher
education. In 1858 nearly half the major Baptist pulpits
in Georgia were occupied by men educated at Mercer. Between fifty and sixty delegates to the North Carolina Baptist Convention that same year had attended Wake Forest.[32]

In contrast to earlier decades, enrollments of Baptist colleges by the 1850's were acquiring a less local
and probably more denominational character. Fewer than
half of the nonministerial college students at Georgetown
in the early 1840's were from Baptist families, and none of
the six recipients of academic scholarships in 1840 were
Baptists. Pleas for more Baptist students which began to

---

[32] "Annual Report," Religious Herald, July 1, 1841; "Mercer University," Christian Index, January 16, 1846; Cahaba
Baptist Association, Minutes, 1855, p. 13; Samuel S. Sherman,
Autobiography of Samuel Sterling Sherman (Chicago, 1910),
p. 69; "Mercer University," Christian Index, December 8,
1858; Brooks, Address, p. 19.

appear in the denominational press in the mid-1840's suggest
that convenience and economy rather than denominational considerations were determining the institutions patronized by
Baptist students. "In too many cases," complained an editorial of 1843, "our brethren, wealthy brethren too, for the
sake of saving a few dollars, will send their children to a
school confessedly inferior, and conducted by another denomination." Baptists were urged to concentrate their patronage
on colleges of their own religious persuasion not only for
denominational reasons but also for the purpose of obtaining
the best quality education for the money expended. Similar
pleas of the late 1840's and the 1850's indicate that lack
of Baptist students was a persistent problem and that many
Baptists did not recognize "the duty of patronizing their
own Literary Institution."[33] Analysis of the geographical
origins of students from fourteen institutions at random
intervals during the years between 1840 and 1860, however,
reveals a gradually increasing percentage of college students

    33"To the Baptists of Kentucky," Baptist Banner and
Western Pioneer, June 23, 1842; report on Georgetown College
enrollment, ibid., July 20, 1843; "Georgetown College," ibid.,
November 19, 1840; "Opening of Our Schools," Alabama Bap-
tist, October 7, 1843; "Mercer University," Christian Index,
September 7, 1848; "It Is the Duty of Baptists to Patronize
Their Own Literary Institutions," ibid., March 10, 1853;
"Mercer University," ibid., September 4, 1856; "Baptists
Should Patronize Baptist Schools," Western Recorder, June
14, 1859; letter from Samuel Wait, Biblical Recorder, July
7, 1859.

drawn from outside a sixty-mile radius of the college but within the confines of the state. It seems highly probable that students coming from this considerable distance were more likely to be of Baptist backgrounds than those from the immediate vicinity of a Baptist college. This trend suggests that the denomination was beginning to respond to college pleas and helping to initiate the shift from generally religious community colleges to state denominational institutions.

As denominational sentiments increased and the nature of Baptist-affiliated colleges began to change, questions were raised concerning the control of these institutions. Such questions often focused on the board of trustees. Most Baptist colleges were controlled by self-perpetuating, incorporated boards of trustees having no formal connection with official denominational bodies. Only Mercer and Furman had trustees chosen directly by a Baptist state convention. Education societies played a role in the election of trustees during the early years of Franklin and Denison. Colgate was governed by the Baptist Education Society of the State of New York until 1846. Even when denominational organizations were involved in trustee elections, however, the difficulties of travel, the natural interest bred by proximity, and the general expediency of control by a small group of well-acquainted men tended to give a local character

to the boards. Almost all of Colgate's trustees prior to
1840 lived within a sixty-mile radius of Hamilton. During
the next two decades trustees from this area usually comprised more than half of the board. Well over sixty per
cent of Shurtleff's trustees in the 1850's resided less
than sixty miles from the college and an even higher percentage of local trustees were elected at Mercer for most
of the antebellum years. Wake Forest attempted a brief
experiment in broader geographical representation but
quickly found that local trustees were more efficient.[34]

[34]For the charters of the institutions in this study,
see: Marriner, History, pp. 609-11, 620-21; U.S. Statutes at
Large, VI, pp. 254-58; William J. Black, "The History of
Georgetown College, Georgetown, Ky.," History of Higher Education in Kentucky, ed. Alvin F. Lewis (Washington, 1899),
pp. 141-42; Ohio, Session Laws, 1831-32, pp. 88-89; Illinois,
Session Laws, 1834-35, pp. 177-80; Indiana, Session Laws,
1835-36, pp. 108-09; Georgia, Session Laws, 1837-38, pp. 152-
53; Paschal, History, I, 62-64, 172-73; Virginia, Session
Laws, 1839-40, pp. 92-95; Mitchell B. Garrett, Sixty Years
of Howard College, 1842-1902, Howard College Bulletin, LXXXV,
No. 4 (Birmingham, Ala., 1927), pp. 166-67; Tennessee, Session
Laws, 1841-42, pp. 108-12; Pennsylvania, Session Laws, 1845-
46, pp. 32-35; First Half Century of Madison University, (1819-
1869) or the Jubilee Volume (New York, 1872), pp. 375-76;
Colgate University: General Catalogue Number, ed. Elmer W.
Smith, Colgate University Publication, XXXVII, No. 2 (Hamilton,
N.Y., 1937), pp. 16-17; Michigan, Session Laws, 1845, pp. 36-
37, 1850, pp. 105-06, 1855, pp. 51-55; John C. Patterson,
"History of Hillsdale College," Collections and Researches
Made by the Michigan Pioneer and Historical Society, VI (1883),
pp. 155-56; South Carolina, Session Laws, 1850, pp. 37-38;
Charter and By-Laws of the University of Rochester (Rochester,
N.Y., 1936). For data on trustee residences, see: Williams,
"History," p. 38; trustee lists in catalogues of Colgate,
Shurtleff, and Mercer; Ragsdale, Story, I, 62, 236; E.W. Sikes,
"The First Board of Trustees of Wake Forest College," Wake
Forest Student, XXVI (September 1906), 1-25; Paschal, History,
I, 102-03.

Local boards, however, were not always dependable from a statewide denominational point of view. Soon after the opening of Georgetown, some Baptists discovered certain dangers in an essentially local board. A group of local Reformers on the board began to accuse the college of being too sectarian to meet community needs. Defenders of the Baptist interests replied that although "citizens of Georgetown, and Scott county, of all religious persuasions, have laudably and liberally contributed to the...institution," this did not mean they should control it or "transform it into a county institution." One Baptist leader went so far as to obtain an injunction against use of certain endowment money for purposes other than the education of ministers. Reformers opposed Regular Baptists on religious grounds but were willing to have a Baptist president. They wanted the college to concentrate on courses in civil engineering and desired an institution operated on more "liberal, highminded and honorable principles."[35]

By the mid-1830's the Baptists were struggling to assert control over the college. When the denomination

35"Georgetown College," Baptist Chronicle and Literary Register, II (August 1831), 23-24; J./onathan/ E. F./arnham/, "Georgetown College--No. 4: Its First Decade," Western Recorder, September 11, 1875; J.T. Johnson, "Baptist Education Society," Christian Messenger, VIII (October 1834), 287; Leland W. Meyer, Georgetown College: Its Background and a Chapter in Its Early History (Louisville, Ky., 1929), pp. 49, 55-56; J.T. Johnson, "Georgetown College," Christian Messenger, VII (April 1833), 110.

sought a charter amendment which would give them power to
elect the trustees and permit a removal of endowment funds
to support a school in another location, non-Baptist citizens of Georgetown and other portions of Scott county complained even more loudly to the state legislature than did
the local Baptists. Local trustees charged that the denomination wanted to remove the entire school to Covington. Denominational leaders replied that they merely were dissatisfied with the board being "a self-perpetuated body of individuals over whom they can have no control." Although a
majority of the board was Baptist, there was no guarantee
that this would always be the case. The denomination emerged
from this struggle with a more thoroughly Baptist board and
college but still without the power of selecting the trustees. And community support was alienated to the extent
that Reformers were able to open another college in town
which initially attracted far more students than that of
the Baptists.[36]

Without the immediate stimuli of community and religious opposition, local control of Baptist colleges was not
extensively questioned until the 1850's. The issue reappeared

[36]"Kentucky Baptist Education Society," Baptist Banner,
March 21, 1835; "Kentucky Baptist Education Society--Infor-
mation Wanted," ibid., October 17, 1835; "Georgetown College,"
ibid., November 21, 1835; "The Georgetown College," ibid.,
July 23, 1836; "Georgetown College," ibid., December 19,
1837; F./arnham7, "Georgetown,"; Meyer, Georgetown, pp. 56-
58.

at Georgetown in 1849 when it was charged that "the college
had passed out of the hands of the community in general, and
become identified with a particular religious denomination
who control it with a view to the accomplishment of a specific object and not for the public good." A reply stressed
the economic advantages of the college to the entire community and asserted that the college had always been controlled
by the Baptists. But apparently neither control nor support
was of a statewide nature, because two years later denominational leaders obtained an amendment to the college charter
which was designed to create these conditions. This amendment incorporated the Kentucky Baptist Education Society and
gave its members the exclusive power to elect Georgetown's
trustees. It was hoped this society would "arouse" Kentucky's Baptists from their "state of apathy" and place the
college "under the direct supervision of the denomination
at large."[37]

In 1850 Illinois Baptists were also worried about the
relationship of college to denomination. Committees were
appointed by denominational organizations to confer with
Shurtleff's trustees on such questions as:

[37]Letter from "A Citizen," Georgetown Herald, August 15,
1849; "To the Baptists of Kentucky," Western Recorder, August
27, 1851; James Moreland, Georgetown College: A History
(Providence, R.I., ca. 1927), pp. 7-8; "Baptist Educational
Convention--Georgetown College," Western Recorder, June 2,
1852.

> Is the charter of Shurtleff College in
> such a form as to secure to the Baptist
> denomination the property belonging to
> the corporation? Do the members of the
> Board of Trustees regard the College as
> a Baptist institution and feel them-
> selves to be the agents of the denomin-
> ation and willing to carry out its wishes,
> both literary and religious?[38]

The trustees admitted that the charter did not bind them or
the school property to the denomination. Their reply emphasized, however, that tradition and current trustee regard for
Shurtleff as a Baptist institution created strong ties between college and denomination. Finding these assurances insufficient, the General Association of Illinois Baptists
asked the trustees to permit the Illinois Baptist Education
Society to nominate the school's trustees in return for official denominational assistance in raising a larger endowment
for Shurtleff. The trustees accepted this plan, which insured that "all the officers of the Institution will receive
their appointment through the voice of our denomination." To
secure greater denominational control, a Baptist Educational
Convention in 1856 directed the trustees to ask the legislature for a charter amendment stipulating that "two-thirds
of the trustees must be members of regular Baptist churches"
and that "the President of the College shall always be a

---

[38]deBlois, _Pioneer_, p. 109.

member in good standing of some Baptist church."[39]

Endowment fund drives of the late 1840's and the 1850's were also related to the question of denominational control. Growing endowments probably loosened local ties by reducing a college's dependence on regular contributions from the immediate vicinity. With denominational interest awakening and financial support increasing, Baptist participation in these fund drives might correspondingly increase denominational ties. Some New York Baptists, however, reached just the opposite conclusion. William Colgate opposed an endowment for the school that later assumed his family name because he felt this would lessen the important "sympathy called forth from the churches by its ever-recurring needs." A compromise proposal in 1847 was more explicit about these concerns. It was suggested that the school obtain "a partial endowment," one which would be large enough so that the institution "cannot live without constant patronage, which would be withdrawn by Baptists on the appearance of the slightest dereliction from the faith."[40]

---

[39]Ibid., pp. 110, 122-23; "Shurtleff College," Christian Times, February 2, 1854; "Educational Convention," ibid., November 12, 1856.

[40]William W. Everts, William Colgate: The Christian Layman (Philadelphia, 1881), p. 187; "The Endowment of Madison University," New York Recorder, May 26, 1847.

IV

Whatever the immediate stimuli, strategic considerations or degree of actual control achieved, Baptists by the 1850's were becoming concerned about the extent to which Baptist-affiliated colleges were denominational institutions. Most of a college's local supporters and a large majority of its local trustees might be Baptists. But could they be depended on to subordinate their local interests to their responsibilities as members of a denomination? The supreme test of these loyalties came when proposals were made to remove certain colleges from the communities where they originated and place them in locations better suited to serving statewide denominational interests.

Removal controversies occurred during the late 1840's and the 1850's at Colgate, Denison, Hillsdale, Bucknell, Mercer, and Franklin. In each case denominational leaders urged that the college be moved to a more populous and wealthier community where it could better serve the interests and cultivate the support of all Baptists in the state. College communities forcefully and, except in the case of Hillsdale, successfully opposed these proposals. Caught in the middle of removal controversies, local Baptists tended to uphold community interests.

Institutional mobility was not a new idea to either American higher education or Baptist colleges in particular.

Yale operated at three different sites before settling permanently in New Haven. Princeton was located at Elizabeth
and then Newark before reaching its present campus. Warren
was the home of Brown until this Baptist-controlled college
moved to Providence in 1770. Were it not for legislative
disapproval, Williams would probably have moved to Northamp-
ton around 1820. In the 1830's it was suggested that George
Washington University move to Richmond, Virginia. The University of Richmond itself moved several miles to a site
nearer the city line in the mid-1830's and soon encountered
a suggestion to move once more, this time to Williamsburg.
Probably sometime during the 1840's a proposal was made to
remove Shurtleff from Alton, but the charter specifically
designated this community as the permanent college site.
Three moves preceded Furman's arrival in Greenville. Some
Nashville citizens attempted in 1854 to obtain President
Joseph Eaton and his talented wife from Union, but the people
of Murfreesboro quickly thwarted this type of removal by
raising a $10,000 endowment for the president's chair.[41]

[41]Edwin Oviatt, The Beginnings of Yale (1701-1726) (New
Haven, Conn., 1916), pp. 231, 250, 307, 320; Thomas J. Werten-
baker, Princeton, 1746-1896 (Princeton, N.J., 1946), pp. 24-25,
36-40; Walter C. Bronson, The History of Brown University,
1764-1914 (Providence, R.I., 1914), pp. 36-37, 48-49, 53;
Leverett W. Spring, A History of Williams College (New York,
1917), pp. 103, 110-12; Memoirs of John Quincy Adams, X, 90;
Robert Ryland, "Richmond College--No. 5," Religious Herald,
December 28, 1843; "Virginia Baptist Seminary," Christian Index, July 7, 1832; H.H. Harris, "Richmond College," in Herbert

288

None of these accomplished or proposed removals, however, evoked a serious confrontation between local and denominational interests.

A variety of immediate stimuli can be identified in the six full-scale removal controversies at antebellum Baptist colleges. After strong initial contributions to the founding and earliest operations of a college, communities sometimes relaxed their efforts. Supporters of Bucknell found in the mid-1850's that many Lewisburg residents were indifferent to the college and the affiliated female academy and "consider it a favor to allow us to locate the schools there." President Malcom even noted a "sustained local hostility." Tensions between college and community appeared at the same time in Penfield, where Mercer supporters were disturbed by a group of residents "continually snarling at the college." These tensions were increased just prior to the removal controversies at both institutions by an increase in the price which townspeople charged students for board. At Colgate

B. Adams, Thomas Jefferson and the University of Virginia (Washington, 1888), p. 271; S. Jones, An Appeal to the Virginia Baptists, Proposing the Establishment of a Theological and Manual Labor School at Williamsburg (Richmond, Va., 1837), p. 18; "Penfield.--The Baptists of Georgia Interested in Its Prosperity," Christian Index, September 25, 1856; Illinois, Session Laws, 1834-35, p. 177; Robert N. Daniel, Furman University: A History (Greenville, S.C., 1951), pp. 21-22, 25-26, 44-47; W.G. Inman, "The History of Union University, Continued in the Southwestern Baptist University," Baptist and Reflector, August 27, 1891; "Union University," Parlor Visitor, I (March 1854), 91; "Commencement at Union University," Tennessee Baptist, July 29, 1854.

and Franklin removal controversies were preceded by a split
of the local Baptist church along town-gown lines and the
temporary establishment of a separate college church.
Growing sectarianism among Granville churches was reported
to be impeding community support for Denison in the early
1850's. Faculty discord was also related to proposals for
removal of Denison, and Mercer was without a president during
its major removal controversy. Communities desiring a college were usually ready to capitalize on such difficulties
and sometimes precipitated removal controversies by making
an offer to troubled institutions. The city of Rochester
prepared a $100,000 inducement for Colgate, Lebanon opened
the debate at Denison with an offer of $30,000, and the
"brethren of Cherokee, Georgia," made several overtures to
Mercer during the mid-1850's.[42]

---

[42]W.G. Inman, "The History of Union University, Continued
in the Southwestern Baptist University," Baptist and Reflector, July 30, 1891; "Removal of the University," Christian
Chronicle, July 23, 1856; "Lewisburg University," ibid., July
30, 1856; University at Lewisburg, "Minutes of Board of Trustees," typescript in the Bucknell University Archives, entry
for July 29, 1856; "Our College and Our Town," Temperance Crusader (Penfield, Ga.), December 6, 1856; "Baptist Convention,"
ibid., April 30, 1857; University at Lewisburg, "Minutes,"
July 29, 1856; "Mercer University," Christian Index, April
15, 1857; Williams, "History," p. 136; John F. Cady, The Cen-
tennial History of Franklin College (n.p., 1934), pp. 72-74;
"The College Meeting in Columbus," Journal and Messenger,
April 2, 1852; Chessman, Denison, p. 46; "Autobiography of
Rev. Jeremiah Hall, D.D., From Notes of Conversations Taken
By His Son, Frank M. Hall," manuscript, ca. 1864, Denison
University Archives, p. 84; "Mercer University--Errors,"
Christian Index, April 15, 1857; Williams, "History," p. 229;

The most common immediate problems concerned enrollments and finances. Collegiate departments were usually not the source of these difficulties. Except at Bucknell, there was no significant drop in college enrollments during the years immediately preceding a removal controversy. All six institutions, however, were suffering from a loss of tuition revenue due to steadily declining enrollments in their preparatory departments. This loss seriously affected the precarious financial condition existing at most of these colleges. Colgate, Denison, and Bucknell were having difficulty meeting current expenses and reducing their budgets at every possible point. Franklin was drawing on permanent funds in order to stay in operation. Hillsdale College needed buildings but was unable to finance them. Yet financial problems cannot provide a sufficient explanation for the series of removal proposals at Baptist colleges beginning in the late 1840's. Such crises were hardly new to these colleges, and Mercer, troubled by three different removal controversies during the 1850's, had endowment funds and real estate totalling over $145,000 in 1855.[43]

Chessman, Denison, p. 48; "Autobiography of Rev. Jeremiah Hall," p. 83; "Georgia Baptist Convention," Christian Index, May 3, 1855; "Baptist Convention," Temperance Crusader, April 30, 1857.

[43]"Institution at Hamilton," New York Baptist Register, May 14, 1847; Chessman, Denison, p. 44; J. Orin Oliphant, The Rise of Bucknell University (New York, 1965), pp. 70-72; Cady, Centennial History, p. 81; Patterson, "History," p. 147; Ragsdale, Story, I, 280.

The frequently made charge that these colleges needed to relocate in larger communities in order to flourish also does not seem to be the common decisive factor in generating removal controversies. "The tree has outgrown the little pot in which it was planted," claimed those advocating removal of Colgate from Hamilton to Rochester. "Granville has got its growth" and "so small a village" cannot adequately support a college, wrote a Baptist from Cincinnati. A newspaper editor in Athens, Georgia, argued that Penfield had failed to meet the expectations of Mercer's founders and could no longer be considered a favorable college site. Such charges were hard to refute when applied to Hamilton or to Hillsdale's original hometown, Spring Arbor. Both were distant from major routes of transportation in the 1850's and located in counties where farm real estate values were below the state average. Penfield could claim the advantage of being located near two major railroad lines but had little to show in terms of local agricultural prosperity. Granville, Lewisburg, and Franklin, however, were quite easily accessible by the mid-1850's and resided in counties where farm real estate values were doubling or tripling.[44]

---

[44]"Our Agents," Annunciator, June 20, 1850; "Why Should Granville College Be Removed?" Journal and Messenger, October 8, 1852; remarks copied from Richards' Gazette (Athens, Ga.), July 23, 1849, Christian Index, August 2, 1849; Farm Real Estate Values in the United States by Counties, 1850-1959, ed. Thomas J. Pressly and William Scofield (Seattle, Wash., 1965), pp. 13, 26-28, 48.

The common stimulus and the basic issue in all six
controversies was more denominational than economic. Distress over enrollments, finances, and college locations reflected not so much the financial difficulties of each situation as a new denominational perspective on these institutions. Baptist educators and other leaders within the denomination did not advocate removals merely as strategies
for survival. Nor were the removalists merely pursuing their
own local interests. Denison's president and Hillsdale's
faculty were largely responsible for initiating removal campaigns at these two institutions. An Albany resident was
one of the leading advocates of removing Colgate to Rochester.
Bucknell's controversy transcended local interests to the
point where a Philadelphia Baptist opposed removal of the
college to a suburb of his own city. Local interests played
a prominent role in removal debate at Mercer, but some leaders
on both sides of the question resided neither in Penfield nor
any of the new sites proposed. The basic concern of most removalists was that neither the rate of progress nor the very
nature of these community colleges measured up to the denominational aspirations they now held for these institutions.
Each removal controversy produced a direct confrontation between new denominational interests and well-established community interests.

The first such confrontation occurred at Colgate in the late 1840's. John N. Wilder, an Albany merchant, spoke for many denominational leaders in the fall of 1847 when he be-gan advocating the removal of the school so that it might be-come "a noble institution worthy of our state and our denom-ination." Wilder found Colgate handicapped in its current location by poor travel facilities, insufficient denomina-tional patronage, and incompetent local trustees.[45] His views were soon supported by some of Colgate's faculty, one of the state's Baptist newspapers, and Baptists in Rochester hoping to obtain the college for their city. Rochester resi-dents from other denominations also joined the removalists, and Syracuse and Utica citizens became interested parties, but the controversy was essentially conducted among Baptists.

Removalists argued that "local interests" should not be allowed "to take precedence over those which pertain to our denomination" and that "Baptists throughout the State own the property and have power to dispose of it as they please." "Shall the pecuniary interests of any small section of the State," they asked, "wrest from...the denomination at large the privilege of determining the future location of their University?" Hamilton Baptists and other citizens replied

[45]John N. Wilder to Asahel Kendrick, October 2, 1847, Asahel Kendrick Papers, Special Collections, University of Rochester Library.

that since their college drew most of its students from outside the vicinity of the town it could not be termed a local
institution. Colgate was effectively serving the Baptists
of New York, they argued, and "public sentiment in the denomination at large," if consulted, "would show a great pre-
ponderance against removal."[46]

Hamilton's appeal to opinion of the denomination at
large resulted from several events in 1848 and 1849 which
clearly demonstrated that most of the denominational leadership favored removal. In August, 1848, the University trustees and trustees of the Baptist Education Society of the
State of New York both voted in favor of removal. To counter
these actions, anti-removalists from Hamilton attempted to
assemble a majority at the annual meeting of the Education
Society. The Society, until 1846 the sole governing body of
the school, still held certain powers in this area and continued to control the institution's property. Anyone who
annually contributed one dollar to the Society became a
voting member. Approximately forty new members, including

---

[46]"To the Friends of Madison University," Supplement to
the Rochester Daily Democrat, November 9, 1847. This and all
newspaper articles cited below regarding Colgate's removal
controversy were found in the "Spear Scrapbook," Colgate University Archives. "Wyoming Address," Supplement to the Rochester Daily Democrat, January, 1848; "Madison University,"
New York Baptist Register, July 6, 1848; "A Candid Appeal,"
Democratic Reflector (Hamilton, N.Y.), December 23, 1847;
"Fraternal Address," New York Baptist Register, August 9,
1849.

a substantial number of non-Baptists, were quickly recruited
from the Hamilton area. They were arbitrarily prevented by
removalists from casting their ballots, however, and a large
majority of the other Society members voted in favor of removal. Two unofficial votes taken by large numbers of denominational leaders in 1849 produced the same result.[47]

As denominational sentiments on the question of removal became increasingly clear, Hamilton's anti-removalists
developed historical, moral, and legal arguments which clearly
revealed the basic issue at stake. Replying to the removalist
argument that Colgate was "the creature and handiwork of the
churches throughout the state," an editorial in Hamilton's
newspaper asserted that the school was "in fact the creature
and handiwork of a few individual Baptists and others in
Hamilton and the surrounding country." Only after the "self-
sacrificing efforts of individuals resident in Hamilton" did

---

[47]Williams, "History," pp. 232-34; George W. Eaton, "Historical Discourse Delivered at the Semi-Centenary of Madison
University, Wednesday, August 5th 1869," The First Half Century of Madison University, (1819 - 1869) or the Jubilee Volume (New York, 1872), pp. 63-64; "Appendix," Democratic Reflector, October 26, 1848; Hezekiah Harvey to Lucy Harvey,
August 21, 1848, Hezekiah Harvey Papers, Colgate University
Archives; Friend Humphrey, et al., Remonstrance Against the
Repeal of an Act Relating to Madison University, Passed April
3, 1848, New York, State Senate, Document No. 52, March 3,
1849, p. 15; "Madison University," New York Recorder, September 20, 1848; "The Meetings at Albany," ibid., June 20,
1849; "Madison University," Democratic Reflector, July 12,
1849; "Baptist Educational Convention," New York Recorder,
October 17, 1849.

"the denomination come forward" to help sustain the institution.[48] This position was soon expanded into a very perceptive general commentary on institutional origins:

> It is local feeling, religious and secular, that has given birth to all the institutions in our land.... They are **first** **known** **at** **home** and then abroad. It is seldom that even a denominational Institution receives aid first from the denomination as such; by it the beginnings of such institutions are frequently regarded with indifference. A few far-sighted men lay the foundation, frequently amid obloquy and derision. They first look well to the 'local interests'-- create a nucleus, deeply imbedded in the 'local feeling'--in congenial soil, where the plant can take deep root. This is true of most institutions, but particularly so in regard to the Baptist Institution in Hamilton.[49]

Since Colgate's founders had been sustained both by "individual Baptists and citizens **not** Baptists" and these Hamilton residents had successfully bid for the school in competition with other towns, it would be morally and legally wrong for the denomination to break this "solemn contract" and these "sacred obligations" between college and community. With the institution's roots so deeply planted in Hamilton, "**interlaced** as intended by its founders with **every** **interest** both **religious** **and** **secular**," the denomination "cannot

---

[48]"Baptist Education Society," Democratic Reflector, June 28, 1848; "Madison University--Forced Issue," ibid., August 31, 1848.

[49]"Provided There Are No Legal Obstacles," ibid., May 24, 1849.

legally or morally be a party to such a controversy."[50]

A similar confrontation of local and denominational interests occurred at Denison in 1852. The college president, nonlocal trustees, and many other denominational leaders believed that removal of the college to a more favorable location would allow an expansion of its functions and increase Baptist support within Ohio. The dwindling proportion of pious students applying for admission strongly suggested that Denison was not adequately serving the denominational interest. One removalist argued that "the denomination placed the college in Granville /and/ have the right to remove /it/." The "right to remove," he contended, "was a democratic doctrine ...illustrated...by the change of state capitols and county seats." Another removalist warned that "denominational schools must be guarded against too much local patronage."[51] J.L. Batchelder, editor of the state denominational newspaper, placed the basic issue suggested by these sentiments into a historical context very similar to that expressed at Colgate:

> We are aware that the history of all our
> denominational institutions will show that
> they have been originated, conducted, and

[50]Ibid.; "A Fraternal Address," New York Baptist Register, August 9, 1849.

[51]"Autobiography of Rev. Jeremiah Hall," pp. 83-85; Shepardson, Denison, p. 85; Henry Bushnell, The History of Granville, Licking County, Ohio (Columbus, Ohio, 1889), p. 239; Chessman, Denison, p. 45; "The College Meeting in Columbus," Journal and Messenger, April 2, 1852.

> sustained by an intelligent few.... But
> ultimately all such institutions have to
> depend on the material support of the
> people--and what is more, the prayers,
> sympathies, and patronage in students of
> the denomination at large. Then surely,
> as a matter of policy, if not of right,
> the control should be ultimately, at the
> proper time, surrendered to the denomina-
> tion which sustains them.[52]

It was soon proposed that the charter be amended so as to
give the Ohio Baptist Education Society the exclusive power
of electing trustees, and several informal denominational
conventions went on record as favoring removal. Yet local
trustees continued to "claim on behalf of the citizens of
Granville the right of its location which they have purchased by their liberal donations."[53]

Tensions between denomination and college community
also characterized removal controversies at Hillsdale in
1853, Bucknell in 1856, Mercer in 1857, and Franklin in 1859.
When Hillsdale was unable to raise a building fund among the
citizens of Spring Arbor, it became clear that the college
"could not meet the expectations of the denomination...in
that locality." Removal of Bucknell to the Philadelphia

---

[52]"The Relations of Boards to Denominations," ibid.,
August 20, 1852.

[53]"Meetings in Cleveland," ibid., October 29, 1852;
"The College-Removal Meeting in Columbus," ibid., June 25,
1852; "College Convention at Columbus, O.," ibid., July 16,
1852; "Granville College," ibid., October 15, 1852.

area was urged on the grounds that "a stronger Baptist
interest could be concentrated" on the school in that location. Removalists found the college too inaccessible
and too much of a community institution. They wanted it
closer to the center of present and potential Baptist patrons. Anti-removalists replied that since "a large portion of the young men studying for the ministry are from
parts of the State remote from the city," Lewisburg was the
best site for a college to serve denominational interests.
Removal of Mercer to a location that would better meet "the
wants of the denomination" was proposed and debated at
meetings of the Georgia Baptist Convention in 1850 and
again in 1855. Baptist leaders were dissatisfied with Penfield and the small number of theological students enrolled.
These concerns reappeared in the larger removal controversy
of 1857 when it was suggested that a new site might be found
which would help the institution "elicit the support of the
mass of Georgia Baptists." Penfield Baptists agreed that
Mercer should be "the State University of the Denomination;"
yet attributed its shortcomings in this respect not to its
location but simply to "the almost uniform neglect" of the
denomination. Franklin's removal controversy involved a
proposal to consolidate the educational interests of Indiana Baptists by removing the college and an even more rural
female seminary to Indianapolis where they could be joined

into a single institution. Removal was supported by the
state denominational newspaper and Baptist leaders dissatisfied with the college's program of ministerial training.
Complaints were also voiced over Franklin's meager local
support.[54]

Most of the new sites proposed during these removal
controversies were in or near major cities. In addition
to Rochester being the chief contender for Colgate, a Philadelphia suburb for Bucknell, and Indianapolis for Franklin,
Cincinnati was the destination supported by many Denison
removalists, and Atlanta was advocated by a leader of the
removal forces at Mercer in 1857. Hillsdale considered
moving to Jackson, one of the three or four largest settlements in Michigan.[55] Baptist leaders promoting such removals were forced to weigh denominational educational

---

[54]Patterson, "History," pp. 146-48; J. Wheaton Smith,
Life of John P. Crozer (Philadelphia, 1868), p. 164; Oliphant, Rise, p. 69; "Lewisburg University," Christian Chronicle, June 25, 1856; "The Removal Question--No. 2," ibid.,
July 30, 1856; "Georgia Baptist Convention," Christian Index,
May 30, 1850; "Georgia Baptist Convention," ibid., April 26,
1855; "Theological Schools," ibid., February 4, 1857; "Georgia
Baptist Convention," Weekly Constitutionalist (Augusta, Ga.),
April 29, 1857; "Our College and Our Town," Temperance Cru-
sader, December 6, 1856; "Mercer University," ibid., February 12, 1857; letter to M.G. Clarke, Witness, November 24,
1858; Cady, Centennial History, p. 82; "Franklin College,"
Locomotive (Indianapolis, Ind.), August 27, 1859, copied from
Witness.

[55]"University Meeting in Cincinnati," Journal and Messenger, March 12, 1852; "Georgia Baptist Convention," Weekly Constitutionalist, April 29, 1857; Patterson, "History," p. 149;
Seventh Census of the United States: 1850, pp. 887-96.

aspirations against the widely held belief that an urban
environment was inappropriate and even dangerous for a college.

Anti-removalist objections to urban sites were vigorous
and persistent. Seeming to assume as a self-evident truth
that a village was the "proper place for a University," defenders of Hamilton advanced the standard argument that cities
were less healthy and less moral than rural settlements. An
opponent of removing Denison to Cincinnati added that even if
urban vices were somewhat exaggerated, "it will be a long,
long while before a notion so universal, and so strongly
fixed, can be eradicated, or even partially removed." To
put an "inexperienced country boy" in contact with worldly
city students, it was argued, "would be like shoving his
frail bark into the wild Niagara without an oar." Gazing
"through the dark smoky atmosphere" of Philadelphia toward
Lewisburg, one Pennsylvania Baptist viewed Bucknell as a
place where his sons could be educated without "the contaminating influence of the city...wrecking their chance of
future usefulness, and periling their souls' salvation."56

Removalists sometimes constructed replies based on
similar assumptions. It was argued that since "the dens of

56"A Candid Appeal," Democratic Reflector, December 23,
1847; "The College Question," Journal and Messenger, March 12,
1852; "Removal of Granville College," ibid., March 19, 1852;
"Removal of Lewisburg University," Christian Chronicle, July
30, 1856.

dissipation in a city are mostly open in the night," students could be quite easily protected by being "strictly required to be in their rooms" after supper. New York removalists made a distinction between "a great Babel like New York" and relatively uncontaminated cities like Rochester, Syracuse, and Utica. Those advocating Chester as the new site for Bucknell contended that this town was fifteen miles from Philadelphia and that such suburbs were protected from urban vices by a Quaker morality.[57]

Less defensive removalist arguments included assertions that "avenues to dissipation are more numerous, more open, and exist in greater variety in a city, but the fewer temptations of a village are fully as destructive in proportion to the population." Since even Eden had been invaded by Satan, it was suggested that "the seeds of sin" might also be found "on that noble lofty hill" in rural Lewisburg. Despite their dangers, cities offered students the anonymity and privacy conducive to "deep and profitable meditations," valuable contact with the ways of the world, and superior educational resources such as large libraries. In reply to arguments that Williams, Dartmouth, Dickinson, and Hamilton were "accomplishing a vast deal more for the cause of general

---

[57]"Shall We Have a University?" Journal and Messenger, March 5, 1852; "Removal of Madison University," New York Recorder, November 24, 1847; "Lewisburg University," Christian Chronicle, July 23, 1856.

education...than those located in cities," removalists noted that "all the great Universities of Europe are in the heart of crowded cities." "Rhode Island College at Warren could never have become what Brown is at Providence," it was claimed, and experiences such as this demonstrated "that a great literary institution flourishes best in the neighborhood of a large city."[58]

Aspirations for a great denominational university suggested by many of the removalist arguments were sometimes more explicitly stated. One major question debated during Denison's removal crisis was: "Shall the institution when removed be restricted to a college in the form in which it now exists, or shall it be so enlarged as to embrace professional as well as literary courses of study?" Removalists advocated "a first-rate institution," and "a school for the times where all may be educated, in every necessary branch of varied learning, either for the Church or the world." A united Baptist effort might produce "a University of un-

[58]"The Removal Question," Journal and Messenger, March 26, 1852; "Removal of Lewisburg University," Christian Chronicle, July 23, 1856; "Removal Question," Journal and Messenger, April 30, 1852; "Removal of Madison University," New York Recorder, November 24, 1847; "The Granville College and Our Educational Affairs in the West," Journal and Messenger, March 5, 1858; "Reply to J.E.," New York Baptist Register, March 16, 1848; "The Removal Question--No. 1," Christian Chronicle, July 23, 1856; "Wyoming Address," Supplement to the Rochester Daily Democrat, January, 1848; "Removal of Madison University," New York Recorder, November 24, 1847; Lewisburg University," Christian Chronicle, June 25, 1856.

rivalled influence and magnitude, in any portion of the
West." In terms of such a "noble enterprise," it was concluded, "a removal does seem to be very desirable for the
Baptist denomination." A similar "proposed enlargement on
a liberal basis" of Colgate when moved to Rochester prompted
anti-removalists to warn that "the denominational character
of the Institution would suffer." Removalists denied this
charge and appeared to consider such risks well worth the
opportunity to create an institution which the Baptist denomination in New York would respect and support.[59]

Community resistance to the elevated educational aims
of denominational leaders and to the removals proposed to
effect these aims took many forms. Important financial and
cultural interests were at stake. Granville stood to lose
tens of thousands of dollars annually injected into the local
economy by students and faculty. Local leaders "clearly
understood that the college was the chief factor of the prosperity in Granville," and local Baptists knew that without

[59]Denison University, Trustee Minutes, March 24, 1852;
"Shall We Have a University?" Journal and Messenger, March 5,
1852; "The Removal Question," ibid., February 13, 1852; "Shall
the College Be Removed?" ibid., March 12, 1852; "The Colleges
--No. III," ibid., April 2, 1852; "The Colleges," ibid., March
12, 1852; "To the Friends of Madison University," Supplement
to the Rochester Daily Democrat, November 9, 1847; "Madison
University and the Rochester Brethren," New York Baptist Register, July 20, 1848; "A Candid Appeal," Democratic Reflector,
December 23, 1847; "Madison University," New York Baptist Register, July 13, 1848.

the college they would have only a third- or fourth-rate
church. Realizing that removal would "deeply and permanently" injure the "intellectual, moral, social, and pecuniary interests" of their "flourishing village," Hamilton
residents estimated that "from thirty to forty thousand
dollars are annually expended in our vicinity by the officers and students of the University," and that its removal
would cause local property to "depreciate a fourth in value."
In addition, "our elegant Bookstore will hardly remain a
month." Local "investments" in the colleges also would be
lost. Hamilton citizens had contributed more than $30,000
to their college, and Granville's contributions to Denison
exceeded $15,000. With these interests threatened, the
initial reaction was sometimes a mass meeting at which the
citizens organized to "fight...nobly, Baptist and non-Baptist
alike, as a community." The committee appointed at such a
meeting in Hamilton to defend community interests consisted
of three lawyers, two businessmen, a physician, and the editor of the local newspaper. None of them belonged to the
Baptist church. In Hamilton and Spring Arbor money was
raised in an immediate effort to retain the college. After
the meeting of 1848 Hamilton also consolidated its control
of the Education Society to the point where only twenty-
eight of the eighty-six members attending the next annual
meeting were nonresidents. Lewisburg's interests were well-

represented by the near majority of Bucknell's trustees

drawn from within a twenty-mile radius of the college.

Unable to control a majority of the board, Spring Arbor

attempted to seize the college records and install a new

slate of trustees. When this manouver failed, citizens even

confiscated books and apparatus and threatened to tar and

feather one of the professors.[60]

The most effective tactic employed by threatened college

communities was a questioning of the legality of removal.

[60]"Removal of Granville College to Lebanon," Journal and Messenger, February 20, 1852; Nathan S. Burton, "Granville's Indebtedness to Jeremiah Hall," Old Northwest Genealogical Quarterly, VIII (October 1905), 381; John Pratt to John Stevens, March 16, 1852, John Stevens Papers, American Baptist Historical Society, Rochester, New York; Kate S. Hines, "The Story of the Granville Baptist Church, Commemorating Its First Century, 1819-1919," typescript, ca. 1919, Denison University Archives, p. 98; Daniel Hascall, et al., Memorial in Relation to the Madison University, New York, State Senate, Document No. 37, February 16, 1849, p. 13; "Madison University," Democratic Reflector, December 2, 1847; "Removal of Madison University. No. II," ibid., July 27, 1848; "Removal of Madison University. A Last Appeal," ibid., August 3, 1848; Oliphant, Rise, p. 70; Hascall, Memorial, p. 13; "Granville College," Journal and Messenger, December 19, 1851; "The College Meeting at Columbus," ibid., April 2, 1852; "Franklin College," Indiana Daily Sentinel (Indianapolis), August 24, 1859; Cady, Centennial History, p. 83; "Madison University," Democratic Reflector, December 2, 1847; Ransom Dunn, "The Story of the Planting: A Reminiscence of the Founding and Early History of Hillsdale College," Reunion, May 13, 1885; Eaton, "Historical Discourse," p. 67; Williams, "History," pp. 216, 218; "Madison University," New York Recorder, September 5, 1849; Letter from Mrs. Barbara C. Winslow, Assistant in Archives, Bucknell University, May 30, 1966; Vivian L. Moore, The First Hundred Years of Hillsdale College (Ann Arbor, Mich., 1944), p. 30; Crisfield Johnson, "History of Hillsdale County," History of Hillsdale County, Michigan, With Illustrations and Biographical Sketches of Some of Its Prominent Men and Pioneers (Philadelphia, 1879), p. 90; Compendium of History and Biography of Hillsdale County, Michigan, ed. Elon G. Reynolds (Chicago, 1903), p. 71.

They constructed a legal argument which rested largely on
the way in which Baptist colleges originated. It was generally contended that contributions to colleges, especially
those made at an early date and by local residents, were given
with the understanding that the school would always remain at
its current site. Removal of an institution thus founded to
a different location would constitute a breach of trust in
terms of contributors no longer living and a breach of contract unless consented to by the living donors. In the case
of Colgate an actual written contract bound six citizens
representing the town of Hamilton to pay $6,000 to the Bap-
tist Education Society in return for the permanent location
of the school in their community. Implied contracts between
denominational groups and local residents who successfully
bid for a school can be identified at four of the other five
colleges. These local contractual arrangements were strengthened by subsequent community contributions, and in Mercer's
case were initiated by sale of land near the campus to
create a college community.[61]

---

[61]"A Candid Appeal," Democratic Reflector, December 23,
1847; Hascall, Memorial, pp. 1-2; "Georgia Baptist Convention,"
Weekly Constitutionalist, April 29, 1857; "The College Meeting
at Columbus," Journal and Messenger, April 2, 1852; Paschal
Carter to John Stevens, June 7, June 28, and October 1, 1852,
Stevens Papers; "Granville College," Journal and Messenger,
October 15, 1852; "Removal of the University," Christian
Chronicle, July 23, 1856; University at Lewisburg, "Minutes
of the Board of Curators," typescript in the Bucknell University Archives, entry for July 29, 1856; Patterson, "His-
tory," p. 152.

In varying forms and with divergent emphases, this basic legal argument played a major role in at least four out of six removal controversies. The legal question appeared several times in the course of Bucknell's controversy but probably did not exert a decisive influence. No mention of legal considerations can be found in the very small amount of information available concerning the dispute at Franklin. Hamilton took its case to the courts in early 1849 and on April 23, 1850, obtained a permanent injunction from a State Supreme Court judge preventing removal of Colgate. The decision in this case was based on certain technicalities, but also contained the judge's observation that "the plaintiffs have a right to prevent the removal." Removalists abandoned the possibility of further legal action at this point and proceeded to found and charter a new institution, the University of Rochester. The one removal effected during this period occurred after a Michigan circuit court judge in late 1854 dissolved an injunction preventing removal of the college at Spring Arbor to Hillsdale. Claiming that they were stockholders in the college corporation, probably by virtue of their contributions, Spring Arbor citizens obtained a preliminary injunction in mid-1853. This injunction was dissolved by a decision that "there were no stockholders of the corporation to be protected by a court of equity." Of all six college communities, Spring Arbor had the least claim on its college, and this decision, unlike that concerning

Colgate, did not become widely known. Participants in the

Denison controversy were well-acquainted with the Colgate

case, and the legal question pervaded this debate from start

to finish. Failure of removalists to agree on a new location

and the pledge of anti-removalists to conduct an ambitious

fund drive which would begin in the immediate vicinity of

the college helped to prevent removal. But the clinching

argument offered by anti-removalists just prior to the de-

nomination's final decision not to remove the college fea-

tured the legal opinion that "Granville College could not be

removed." Similar legal opinion also occupied a prominent

place in the debate at the Georgia Baptist Convention of

1857 and the decision not to attempt a removal of Mercer.[62]

Except for Spring Arbor, college communities were re-

markably successful in retaining Baptist schools. These in-

stitutions were deeply rooted in their respective communities,

---

[62]"The Removal Question. No. 2," *Christian Chronicle*,
July 30, 1856; Lewis E. Theiss, *Centennial History of Bucknell University, 1846-1946* (Williamsport, Pa., 1946), pp. 11-
12; Williams, "History," pp. 239-40, 251-53; *Hascall v. Madison University*, 8 Barbour (N.Y.), 174, 186 (1850); Patterson,
"History," pp. 152, 154; "Autobiography of Rev. Jeremiah Hall,
p. 92; Shepardson, *Denison*, p. 81; "Our Educational Affairs
in Ohio," *Journal and Messenger*, August 27, 1852; "Why Should
Granville College Be Removed?" *ibid.*, October 8, 1852; "Granville College," *ibid.*, October 15, 1852; Chessman, *Denison*,
pp. 44, 52-53; "College Convention at Cleveland," *Journal
and Messenger*, November 5, 1852; "Meetings at Cleveland,"
ibid., October 29, 1852; "Georgia Baptist Convention," *Weekly
Constitutionalist*, April 29, 1857.

and the prospect of prolonged and institutionally damaging legal controversies ultimately discouraged most removalists. Even Hillsdale's removal was far from complete. To avoid further legal difficulties the college trustees obtained a new charter in 1855. The few thousand dollars' worth of college property and equipment in Spring Arbor was abandoned. Little more was removed than the faculty, students, records, and reputation of the college.[63]

The success of anti-removalists, however, did not mean that Baptist colleges would continue as primarily local institutions. Legal opinion in the 1850's confirmed the essentially nondenominational origins and functions of Baptist colleges up to that time, but soon shifted in recognition of the changing nature of the institutions. In 1871 the United States Supreme Court ruled that since state legislatures usually had the right to "amend, alter, or modify" corporate charters, this was a valid procedure for effecting college removals. Anyone making a contract with a private corporation, such as a college, through donations, purchase of scholarships, or other means generally did so with tacit assent to this legislative authority being a part of the

[63]Patterson, "History," p. 153; Ransom Dunn, "The Story of the Planting: A Reminiscence of the Founding and Early History of Hillsdale College," Reunion, May 20, 1885; Patterson, "History," p. 156; Johnson, "History," p. 90; Moore, First Hundred, p. 30.

contract. Citing Hascall v. Madison University, 8 Barbour
(N.Y.), 174 (1850), the court held that there might be some
exceptional cases requiring "judicial discretion," but subsequent court decisions tended to acknowledge legislative
powers regarding charters and were characterized by increasing leniency toward college removals. A favorable
county court decision and certain compensations to Penfield
enabled Mercer to move to Macon in 1871. Howard encountered
no local legal resistance in the mid-1880's when the college
relocated on the outskirts of Birmingham.[64]

Most removal controversies resulted in Baptists deciding to transform the struggling local colleges into
strong state denominational schools without further efforts
at a change in location. The accumulation of buildings and
other facilities quickly strengthened commitments to the
original site. Once the removal issue was settled and denominational interest awakened by the controversies directed
toward institutional improvement, the financial relationship
between college and community became less important. Of the
more than $130,000 subscribed to Colgate's semi-centennial

[64]Pennsylvania College Cases, 13 Wallace (U.S.), 190,
218-19 (1871); Edward C. Elliott and M.M. Chambers, The Colleges and the Courts: Judicial Decisions Regarding Institutions of Higher Education in the United States (New York,
1936), pp. 60-62, 186-89; Spright Dowell, A History of Mercer University, 1833-1953 (Macon, Ga., 1958), pp. 123, 134-
35; Garrett, Sixty Years, pp. 106-19.

fund in the late 1860's, only about $6,000 came from Hamilton
residents. Lewisburg citizens provided slightly more than
ten per cent of the $100,000 subscribed to Bucknell's endow-
ment fund a few years earlier. A contemporary campaign at
Denison raised over $100,000, with $5,000 of this coming
from Granville.[65]

In addition to reflecting the growth of denominationalism within Baptist higher education, removal controversies
raised some interesting questions about the geography of
American higher education and suggest certain conclusions
about the role of denominational colleges in the development
of American society. Hamilton citizens contended in 1849
that "the friends and patrons of all the great Institutions
of Learning in our country have a common interest with us in
the question of the removal of Madison University." Colleges,
they continued, were institutions "which of all others should
be permanent fixtures in a community" and not "thrown upon
the restless sea of the varying sentiments and wishes of the

[65]"Dr. Spear's Report on the Semi-Centennial Fund," The
First Half Century of Madison University, (1819-1869) or the
Jubilee Volume (New York, 1872), pp. 177-79; Justin R. Loomis,
An Address Delivered June 9, 1865, in Commencement Hall, of
the University at Lewisburg, Pa., Before the Students of the
Several Departments, On the Occasion of Their Celebrating the
Completion of the Endowment Fund (Lewisburg, Pa., 1865),
p. 14; Chessman, Denison, p. 95.

successive generations of their patrons and guardians." A
Mercer removalist, on the other hand, thought that colleges
had no more claim to geographical permanency than factories,
courthouses, or statehouses in antebellum America. One par-
ticipant in Denison's controversy asserted that "corporations
can go anywhere;" another argued that a college should not
be like "a traveling menagerie which might be moved on wheels
from one place to another."[66]

If colleges prior to the Civil War had been less firmly
entrenched local institutions, many would probably have mi-
grated to large cities. An Ohio Baptist concluded in 1852
that "it is no less true, educationally, than commercially,
that wares to be profitably disposed of must be brought to
the market."[67] Instead of being centralized in urban areas,
however, American higher education established a pattern of
diffusion in the early nineteenth century which has endured
to the present. Rather than just seeking the small existing
market for higher education, local colleges slowly enlarged
it. And the demand for education which institutions and

[66]"Public Meeting of the Citizens of Hamilton," Democratic Reflector, January 18, 1849; "Georgia Baptist Convention," Christian Index, May 30, 1850; "The College Meeting
in Columbus," Journal and Messenger, April 2, 1852; "Granville College," ibid., October 15, 1852.

[67]"Granville College and Our Educational Affairs in
the West," ibid., March 5, 1852.

their agents helped to create was not limited to urban populations but was quite evenly dispersed throughout the country.
From this point of view, the great number of colleges founded
during the antebellum period created a "collegiate system"
especially well-adapted "to reach, to a very considerable
extent, the masses. of the country."[68] Migration to compete
for the existing market would have seriously reduced the
cultural and economic resources of rural America.

The peculiar mixture of local and denominational forces
assembled in permanently located rural colleges created a
significant anomaly in American cultural development. An
apologist for denominational colleges identified this anomaly
in 1855. "It seems clear," he noted, "that sectarian colleges by the very terms of their existence, enlarge the area
of education." Contrasting sectarian or denominational colleges with state universities, this apologist described the
effects of local collegiate enterprises such as those affiliated with the Baptists:

> Denominational colleges...derive their
> existence in the first instance from
> efforts made among the people: and their
> endowments are raised, and their patron-
> age secured and continued, by employment
> of just such means as must necessarily in-
> crease the number of educated men. Agents
> are sent out from time to time to secure

[68]J.R. Loomis, An Inaugural Address Delivered July 27,
1859 (Philadelphia, 1860), p. 17.

> students, who talk at the public gatherings
> and around the firesides of the masses of
> people. They enlist by their explanations
> and persuasions men who not appreciating
> education themselves would never have sent
> /sons/ to any College, but for these ef-
> forts. They raise their endowments by
> free will offerings, which when made, se-
> cures their interest, and to obtain which
> requires a discussion on the subject of
> education in all its bearings. Many addi-
> tional minds are thus enlisted by appeals
> to their patriotism, their benevolence, and
> their interests--those perhaps who never
> dreamed of educating their sons before such
> efforts were made.[69]

Given the political, religious, and demographic character-

istics of America in the early nineteenth century, it is

doubtful that a more efficient tool for creating a wide-

spread faith in general education could have been devised.

---

[69]"The Comparative Advantages of Denominational and
State Colleges Reviewed," Biblical Recorder, July 12, 1855.

CONCLUSION

FRANCIS WAYLAND AND ANTEBELLUM BAPTIST COLLEGES

When applied to the schools of his own denomination,
particularly on a local level, Francis Wayland's critical
portrait of antebellum colleges is inadequate and misleading.
His observations probably contain more validity for the post-
Civil War collegiate scene than for his own times. Although
there are signs that Baptist colleges in the 1850's were beginning to reduce ties with their local publics and to respond more exclusively to denominational needs, these institutions cannot be accurately characterized as isolated from
and unresponsive to the development of American society prior
to 1861. Wayland may be considered a prophet of late-
nineteenth-century demands, but he should not be used to
read these or a twentieth-century context back into the antebellum years.

The broadly functional nature of Baptist colleges before the Civil War is especially apparent on the local level.
Perhaps the industrializing and urbanizing economy of the
Northeast which Wayland saw in Providence required new types
of nonprofessional and practical higher education. But antebellum Franklin, Indiana, Marion, Alabama, and even Waterville, Maine, had more primitive educational and cultural

316

needs. Elementary schools lacked competent teachers. Secondary and higher education was not readily available to the more ambitious and able local boys. Curricular concerns were secondary to awakening and meeting a general interest in education itself. Public response to rural Baptist colleges, most dramatically demonstrated at commencement celebrations, indicates that these schools filled a cultural vacuum.

The close relationship between Baptist colleges and the communities and regions they served can be seen in the same elements which Wayland used to illustrate collegiate isolation. Trustees, as observed in their response to removal proposals and indirectly through the comprehensive nature of their schools, were more likely to represent community interests than those of a particular sect or class. Professors came into direct contact with the public through their frequent additional tasks as college agents. Students usually ate and often roomed with local families rather than in commons and dormitories. Lack of endowments at almost all Baptist colleges prior to 1861 tied them closely to dependable local support. In their origins and functions these colleges were as much community as denominational enterprises.

Reactions in the Baptist press to Wayland's critique and reform proposals suggest that he did not adequately articulate the concerns or identify the problems of higher education

within his own denomination. Despite his prominent position
as the author of widely used moral philosophy textbooks, men-
tor of many Brown University graduates occupying important
positions within the denomination, and leader in Baptist missionary enterprises, Wayland did not inspire a reform movement in Baptist higher education based on his views of collegiate defects and the remedies required to correct them.
His Thoughts on the Present Collegiate System received little
notice in Baptist periodicals of the 1840's. One of the few
articles offering more than a brief summary of the book agreed
that there were some specific weaknesses in the areas of
government, instruction, and curriculum, but did not mention
Wayland's basic ideas about supply and demand and the relationship between colleges and the general public. This reviewer
suggested that the best way to improve colleges was to raise
admissions standards. The only Baptist journal which gave
enthusiastic support to Wayland's major criticisms was the
Christian Review of Boston. This support was restricted,
however, to endorsing his analysis of the collegiate scene
in New England. Reservations were also expressed as to
whether the public even knew what it wanted, let alone demanded certain educational reforms.[1]

---

[1]"Review of Wayland's Thoughts on the Present Collegiate
System in the United States," Baptist Memorial and Monthly
Chronicle, II (January 1843), 21-23; S.F. Smith, "Present
Collegiate System in the United States," Christian Review,
VII (September 1842), 466-79; "The Public and the Colleges

Wayland's Report of 1850 was more widely noticed and favorably received, but with certain crucial reservations. Immediate support for a more "practical" higher education which "will open our halls of science to a much larger proportion of our youth" came from Baptist editors in Philadelphia and Louisville. Subsequent endorsements of Wayland's proposals were expressed in North Carolina and Ohio. Reactions in Maine ranged from the opinion that "utilitarian studies" would make colleges mere servants of "a money-making age" to a skeptical wait-and-see position on the Brown experiment. Although admitting that Baptist colleges needed some reforms, reviews in two Massachusetts periodicals expressed doubts concerning Wayland's basic tool of analysis. The law of supply and demand formulated by classical economists "is generally acknowledged to be correct in its application to commercial, manufacturing, and agricultural pursuits," one reviewer observed, but "admits of no such wide generalization as to include the various forms of human culture....When applied to education in general,...and especially to higher forms of intellectual and spiritual culture, the

---

of New England," ibid., X (March 1845), 54-71. The major concern of this journal was that the rapid multiplication of colleges in the United States had resulted in "an enormous draught upon the ministry" to staff their faculties. Colleges "absorbed quite a disproportionate share of the clerical talent of the country." This was regarded as a serious "injury...to the moral interests of the country." See "Remarks on Colleges," ibid., XIII (March 1848), 108-12.

principle signally fails, and ever must fail, till men become as greedy for learning as they now are for lucre."
While conceding that "our plans of education require some
modification to suit them to the altered circumstances of the
times," the second reviewer contended that "the limited number of students in College is not so much owing to anything
in the course of study or in the internal arrangements of
these institutions" as to the lack of effort by colleges to
"increase the demand for liberal learning among our people
at large." Rather than having a simple relationship to the
nature of the product supplied, demand in the sphere of education must be created by intermediary means.[2]

In terms of New England these mild and brief points of
dissent may be considered conservative responses to a threat-
eningly accurate critique and a radical but painfully real-
istic reform program. New Englanders had been well-exposed
to arguments for general education. Colleges in this region
might have relaxed their efforts in recent years to augment
enrollments, but it was doubtful that new attempts to sell
classical education would substantially increase demand. As

[2] "Brown University," Christian Chronicle, January 30,
1850; "Reform in Colleges," Baptist Banner, February 13, 1850;
"Wake Forest College," Biblical Recorder, December 17, 1852;
"Removal of Our College," Journal and Messenger, February 27,
1852; "Brown University," Zion's Advocate, May 10, 1850;
"Changes in Colleges," ibid., March 22, 1850; "President Wayland's Report," Christian Review, XV (July 1850), 449-50; "Baptist Institutions of Learning," Watchman and Reflector, June
15, 1850.

Wayland's documents suggest, the economy and professions had reached a stage of development where liberal education was no longer particularly important to individual mobility and success. Only gradually and at a few colleges such as Williams was higher education before the Civil War becoming a consumer item for new urban wealth.[3]

Outside of the urban Northeast, however, Baptist educators saw one of their primary tasks to be the creation of a demand for education per se in a largely uncultivated market. In justifying the rapid multiplication of American colleges "within a certain limit," Robert Ryland found the "analogy between education and mercantile affairs" making the "fallacious" assumption that demand in education, as in commerce, was fairly stationary. The "maxim in political economy that the increase of a commodity tends to diminish its value," Ryland asserted, "does not hold good in regard to education. The more it abounds, the more it is valued," and "its very diffusion creates for it an increased demand." Inspired by this faith and struggling with the task of enlarging a very limited demand for education beyond the elementary level, it is doubtful that Ryland and other Baptist college agents would agree with Wayland's assertion in 1842 that "the

---

[3]On the shift in student origins, see Frederick Rudolph, Mark Hopkins and the Log: Williams College, 1836-1872 (New Haven, Conn., 1956), pp. 68-72.

importance of liberal education is fully admitted by every
American citizen."[4]

Rather than waiting for an educational demand to develop
and then serving it, men like Ryland took initiatives to
stimulate an educational awakening. By the 1850's Baptist
educators increasingly capitalized on denominational interests
and achieved many of their gains within this sphere. But it
was also observed that each antebellum Baptist college "creates
a larger demand for education than it supplies, and thus helps
the general interest while it sustains itself." Contributions
to American cultural development through "improvement of our
academies and common schools" and "influence in awakening a
desire of education" might not become apparent until the present generation had matured. The increased demand for higher
education which resulted from bringing "the means of education to our very door," however, could be partially measured
in terms of enrollments. The total number of students in
classical college courses at the sixteen Baptist colleges in
this study doubled between 1845 and 1850, and it doubled again

---

[4]"Treasurer's Report from 1844 to 1856," Tennessee Baptist, May 10, 1856; An Historical Sketch of Madison University
(Utica, N.Y., 1852), p. 12; "Richmond College--No. 5," Religious Herald, December 28, 1843; Francis Wayland, Thoughts on
the Present Collegiate System in the United States (Boston,
1842), p. 8.

in the 1850's.[5] Considering the way they defined their educational mission and the results they were able to claim even
by 1850, it is not difficult to see why Baptist educators outside New England might find much of Wayland's critique irrel-
evant.

Curricular reforms proposed at Brown were equally un-
suited to the realities of baptist higher education in most
other locations. In the 1840's all but a few colleges were
already giving students the option of a three-year nonclassical course. Designed for "those who intend to devote a part
or all of their time to teaching, or to engage in mercantile
pursuits, or in any department of business," these scientific
or English courses usually led to a B.S. degree.[6] By 1850
almost a third of the total collegiate enrollment at Baptist
institutions in this study was engaged in nonclassical programs. The number of students in these parallel courses increased during the 1850's at about the same rate as classical
enrollments. With the limited existing demand for practical
education being met in this fashion, Wayland's more radical

---

[5]J.R. Loomis, An Inaugural Address, Delivered July 27,
1859 (Philadelphia, 1860), p. 35; "Madison University," New
York Recorder, March 8, 1848; "Our University--No. 1," Christian Index, April 10, 1851. Data from catalogues indicate
that annual enrollments for the 16 colleges totaled more than
1,000 in classical and about 350 in scientific or English collegiate courses by 1860.

[6]Granville College, Catalogue, 1846/47, p. 11; Georgetown College, Catalogue, 1848/49.

reform proposals caused little excitement within his denomination.

To Wayland's assertion that "there has existed for the
last twenty years a great demand for civil engineers," most
Baptist educators would probably have replied that public
pressure for colleges to train such men was not apparent in
their regions. And the creation of demand for this type of
education, even though it might soon be required by the
national economy, would have to wait while more basic local
cultural needs were served. Departments of agriculture were
planned at a few colleges, and one even went into operation
for a term at Denison. But these new programs were apparently
confronted by a rural indifference to agricultural education
similar to that encountered after the Civil War by land-
grant colleges. At Georgetown College, chemistry was taught
"with special reference to agriculture," and the Professor of
Mathematics offered a course in civil engineering, but there
is no evidence of public demand to expand these informal services to limited local needs.[7]

---

[7]Francis Wayland, Report to the Corporation of Brown University on Changes in the System of Collegiate Education, Read
March 28, 1850 (Providence, R.I., 1850), p. 18; J.M. Peck,
"Department of Agriculture in Shurtleff College," Baptist Banner and Western Pioneer, April 9, 1840; G. Wallace Chessman,
Denison: The Story of an Ohio College (Granville, Ohio, 1957),
p. 116; John F. Cady, The Centennial History of Franklin College (n.p., 1934), p. 70; Earle D. Ross, Democracy's College:
The Land-Grant Movement in the Formative Stages (Ames, Iowa,
1942), chaps. v-vi; "Annual Report of the President of Georgetown College to the Board of Trustees," Baptist Banner and
Western Pioneer, July 15, 1847; Georgetown College, Catalogue,
1854/55, p. 15.

Baptist colleges in the 1850's were neither resolutely committed to the status quo nor suddenly awakening to new responsibilities. Many schools did make formal reviews of their curricula in this decade and recommended some "modifications and enlargements." These accommodations to "those whose pursuits in life are to be active rather than literary or professional," however, had been "the tendency of college education for years" previous to Wayland's Report.[8]

Only a few Baptist colleges attempted to accelerate this tendency in order to keep pace with Brown. Union University's curricular reorganization in the mid-1850's closely resembled that devised by Wayland. Although the school did not offer a broad range of technological subjects, only one ancient language was needed for a B.A. degree, and students meeting "a certain standard of scholarship" could complete their studies in less than the usual four years. Furman University opened at Greenville in 1852 with a curriculum divided into six "schools" and allowed a student to plan his own

---

[8] Published reports on curriculum reform include: Plan for the Endowment of Granville College (Columbus, Ohio, 1853); Report to the Board of Trustees of Franklin College on Changes in the Course of Study, Read April 6, 1853 (Indianapolis, 1853); Circular of the Columbian College, Washington, District of Columbia, 1853 (Washington, 1853); Report of the Faculty of Waterville College, On the Condition and Wants of the Institution, With the Action of the Trustees on the Same. At a Special Meeting of the Board, Dec. 18, 1855 (Waterville, Me., 1856). "Report to the Board of Trustees of the University of Rochester," New York Recorder, October 23, 1850.

schedule for achieving proficiency in each division. Unlike the reform program at Brown and Union, both Greek and Latin studies were required for a B.A. degree. The experience of most Baptist educators, however, probably supported a New York Baptist newspaper's estimate in 1850 that "there is far less radical dissatisfaction with the studies pursued under the old system than has been supposed."[9]

The reserved reaction of most Baptist colleges to Wayland's reform proposals was most fully and forcefully expressed at the University of Rochester. Founders of this new urban university received support from Wayland during the late 1840's when they were attempting to remove Colgate University from Hamilton, New York, to Rochester. After failing to effect a removal and deciding to establish their own school, they followed his advice concerning the evils of dormitories. Yet when it came to planning a curriculum, the University dissented from Wayland's Report of 1850. Only a few required courses in modern history and science were added to the traditional plan of study through the junior year. Senior electives in science, mathematics, modern languages,

---

[9]Union University, Catalogue, 1853/54, p. 14, 1854/55, pp. 18-23; Robert N. Daniel, Furman University: A History (Greenville, S.C., 1951), pp. 58-62. For a description of the new curriculum at Brown, see Walter C. Bronson, The History of Brown University, 1764-1914 (Providence, R.I., 1914), pp. 279-83. "Report to the Board of Trustees of the University of Rochester," New York Recorder, October 23, 1850.

and civil engineering were limited to one course per term.
A four-year program with at least two years of Greek and
Latin was required for the B.A. degree. Four years of non-
classical study were needed in order to obtain a B.S.[10]

A rationale for the University of Rochester's curriculum was formulated by a faculty-trustee committee appointed
soon after the publication of Wayland's reform proposals.
The University of Rochester Report, presented September 16,
1850, was printed as a pamphlet similar in form and size to
that issued by Brown earlier in the year. In its analysis of
collegiate problems and objectives, however, the Rochester
Report differed sharply from its more famous predecessor.
Within the context of curricular appraisals and reform efforts at other Baptist colleges, the Rochester Report is a
much more representative document than that written by Wayland.[11]

---

[10]Item copied from the Rochester Daily Democrat of October 28, 1847, Supplement to the Rochester Daily Democrat,
November 9, 1847; Jesse L. Rosenberger, Rochester and Colgate: Historical Backgrounds of the Two Universities (Chicago,
1925), pp. 74, 122-23; University of Rochester, Catalogue,
1850/51, pp. 17-18.

[11]Authorship of the Rochester Report is attributed to
Robert Kelly, a New York merchant. See "Report to the Board
of Trustees of the University of Rochester," New York Recorder, October 23, 1850. Other members of the committee
formulating this plan of study were: a prominent minister
from New York, a lawyer and an educator from Rochester, and
three former professors at Colgate. The Rochester educator
and two of the three college teachers were soon appointed to
the first faculty of the University of Rochester; the third
former Colgate professor assumed a teaching position at the
new Rochester Theological Seminary. See Rosenberger, Rochester and Colgate, pp. 116, 158, 118, 41.

Acknowledging current controversy over the degree to
which colleges were and should be popular and practical institutions, the Rochester Report outlined a middle ground
between radical reform and unyielding conservatism. Criticisms of American colleges based on enrollment figures and
financial reports which recommended greatly increased vocational emphasis to satisfy popular demands and make colleges
self-supporting were found to be faulty in terms of both
diagnosis and prescription. Enrollment and tuition problems,
the Report argued, were caused not so much by the nature of
the curriculum as by "that impatience to rush into business
which characterizes our people. It is to be apprehended that,
no matter what improvements may be made in our systems of
instruction, this spirit of world-seeking enterprise will
long continue to be the main obstacle in the way of inducing
our youth to persevere to the end in the laborious work of a
complete education." With the market for higher education
limited by this trend, the value of education not precisely
determined by demand, and the institutional costs of a first-
rate college prohibiting financial solvency based on tuition
income, "it is entirely fallacious to apply to this subject
the laws which regulate the operations of trade."[12]

---

[12]Report to the Board of Trustees of the University of
Rochester on the Plan of Instruction to be Pursued in the Col-
legiate Department, Presented, September 16, 1850 (Rochester,
N.Y., 1850), pp. 5-10.

The charge of contemporary critics that collegiate education was becoming unpopular because it was impractical led the _Report_ to an affirmation of the still very respectable tenents of faculty psychology. Mental discipline, because of its universal applicability, was the most practical goal which could be achieved in four years of collegiate study. Reformers who called for more technological education in American colleges were making unreasonable demands upon these institutions and reflected the prevailing "looseness in the popular conception of a practical education." A college could teach, however, the "scientific principles and elements, on which some of the more necessary useful arts rest." If it was "accurate and thorough," instruction of this kind would be "of great value to the student, and exceedingly useful to society."[13]

By emphasizing scientific principles rather than vocational skills, the _Report_ concluded, the University of Rochester could "meet the demands of the community, without sacrificing the essential elements and characteristics of sound education, and without injury to the cause of learning." Judicious reforms of the traditional curriculum might enable the University to "take a high position in the scale of reformation and progress." Finding that Latin and Greek still

---

[13]_Ibid._, pp. 15-21, 49.

"have a strong hold on the popular mind, notwithstanding the
prejudices with which they have been assailed on the one hand,
and the extravagant idolatry they have received on the other,"
the Report upheld the values of a classical course. Concerned
with "enlisting the sympathy of all classes in the community"
for their University and with "inducing /students/ to enter
upon a thorough course of instruction," the Report also recommended the option of a rigorous, four-year, nonclassical
course leading to a B.S. degree.[14]

The University of Rochester's Report was much more in
touch with the subtleties and realities of educational supply
and demand in antebellum America than that written by Francis
Wayland. Perhaps the Rochester Report laid the foundation
for late-nineteenth-century educational conservatism as exemplified by the University's first president, Martin B.
Anderson. Attempts to balance quality and popularity in
American colleges might soon be abandoned in favor of emphasis on gentlemanly culture or religious orthodoxy. Yet
contemporary opinion and the experiences of Baptist educators during the antebellum years affirmed the wisdom of the
Rochester Report's analysis and limited reform proposals.
"A collegiate system," remarked President Justin Loomis of
Bucknell, "to be the most useful, must be only so far in

---

[14]Ibid., pp. 10-11, 29-34, 46, 49.

advance of the general public opinion as to lead it, and not so far in advance as to be out of sight."[15]

Francis Wayland's ideas on collegiate reform, especially his basic analogy between laws of supply and demand in commerce and in education, encourage a misplaced emphasis on curriculum and enrollments. Baptist colleges were founded and sustained prior to the Civil War by a delicate balance of community, denominational, and individual interests. Questions of curriculum and of intellectual quality did not figure prominently in the minds of these patrons and supporters. Removal controversies, which raised elementary cultural and economic issues, excited far more discussion among Baptists and the interested public in the 1850's than modifications in the course of study. There is little evidence of student or public desire for greater vocational practicality in higher education. The many factors affecting enrollments render simple theories of supply and demand highly inadequate. The number of students at a college in any given period was more likely to be dependent upon national and local economic conditions, transient institutional difficulties, skills of the current college agent, or a local religious revival than upon the appeal of a particular curriculum.

---

[15]"Report to the Trustees of the University of Rochester," Christian Review, XVI (January 1851), 130-34; Loomis, Inaugural Address, p. 30.

Wayland's critique of early-nineteenth-century colleges
also tends to obscure their role in American cultural development. Despite their seeming isolation from national economic trends, Baptist colleges served numerous cultural and
economic functions on the local level. Needing to cultivate
public as well as denominational support, Baptist colleges
were constantly concerned with their relationship to society
in general and made significant contributions to the growth
of American culture. They helped to disseminate a strong
faith in education, provided secondary and higher education
for thousands who otherwise might not have sought or obtained it, upgraded local culture in many areas, and established a pattern of institutional distribution which gave
rural as well as urban areas a substantial share of American
cultural resources.

SELECTED BIBLIOGRAPHY

The standard reference on antebellum colleges is
Donald G. Tewksbury, The Founding of American Colleges and
Universities Before the Civil War, With Particular Reference
to the Religious Influences Bearing Upon the College Movement
(New York, 1932). Tewksbury examines the origins of denominational colleges within the context of Frederick Jackson
Turner's frontier thesis and the early-nineteenth-century
evangelical movement. Wilson Smith's Professors & Public
Ethics: Studies of Northern Moral Philosophers Before the
Civil War (Ithaca, N.Y., 1956) identifies a subtle shift in
the content of college courses in moral philosophy which is
very useful in understanding the development of American
society in this period. Smith's book also suggests that
through at least one important part of their traditional
curriculum denominational colleges were very much in contact
with the political and social issues of their times. Two
regional studies based on extensive research in primary
sources are: Albea Godbold, The Church College of the Old
South (Durham, N.C., 1944), and Vernon F. Schwalm, "The Historical Development of the Denominational Colleges in the
Old Northwest," unpublished Ph.D. dissertation, University

333

of Chicago, 1926. Godbold emphasizes the denominational
nature of pre-Civil War colleges in Virginia, North Carolina,
South Carolina, and Georgia. Schwalm, who like Godbold made
extensive use of college archives, finds little change during
the years between 1820 and 1870 at the fifteen Baptist,
Methodist, and Presbyterian institutions he describes. Two
interesting denominational histories are: Sylvanus M. Duvall,
The Methodist Episcopal Church and Education Up to 1869 (New
York, 1928), and C. Harve Geiger, The Program of Higher Education of the Presbyterian Church in the United States of
America: An Historical Analysis of Its Growth in the United
States (Cedar Rapids, Iowa, 1940). Although both studies
are based primarily on denominational sources, the authors
find little evidence of official support and control, prior
to 1860, even within these tightly organized denominations.
The major chronicles of Baptist higher education, cited below
in the denominational history section, are by Moehlman, Padelford, Johnson, Keyser, and Fleming. None of these authors
explores the relations between early-nineteenth-century Baptist colleges and their nondenominational environments.

Although this study draws on the resources of more than
forty libraries, college archives, and historical societies,
a large majority of the materials cited below can be found
in one of the three major Baptist collections: American Baptist Historical Society, Rochester, N.Y.; Southern Baptist

Theological Seminary, Louisville, Ky.; Dargan-Carver Library, Nashville, Tenn. Almost all the local histories can be consulted at the American Antiquarian Society, Worcester, Mass., or the Library of Congress. All maps referred to in the footnotes are in the Windsor Memorial Map Room of the Harvard University Library.

The list of denominational periodicals excludes more than thirty antebellum Baptist serials searched and found not to have any data of relevance for this study. Among the titles included are several affiliated with the Disciples of Christ. Except in a few cases where less extensive files were the only ones available, ninety per cent or more of all issues between the dates given have been examined. Volume numbers are listed only for periodicals published at intervals of one month or longer. All but a few of those issued more frequently are weekly newspapers.

Institutional and Local History

Bucknell University

Alumni Catalogue of Bucknell University, Lewisburg, Pennsylvania, 1851-1910. Bucknell University Bulletin, X, No. 3. Lewisburg, Pa., 1910.

/Bell, Adie K./. _Report of the Board of Trustees of the University of Lewisburg to the Patrons and Friends of the University_. Philadelphia, 1858.

Bliss, George R. "Incidents in the Early History of Bucknell University," University Mirror, XII (January 1893), 45-47.

Harris, John H. Thirty Years as President of Bucknell, With Baccalaureate and Other Addresses, compiled and arranged by Mary B. Harris. Washington, 1926.

Jubilee Anniversary of the First Baptist Church of Lewisburg, Pa., 1844-1894. Lewisburg, Pa., 1894.

King, Howard F. "Adie Kyle Bell," L'Agenda. n.p. 1899. pp. 6-9.

Lewisburg Chronicle and West Branch Farmer. Lewisburg, Pa. July, 1847-December, 1857.

Mauser, I.H. Centennial History of Lewisburg, Containing Also a Chronological History of Union County. Lewisburg, Pa., 1886.

Meginness, John F. Otzinachson, Or a History of the West Branch Valley of the Susquehanna. Philadelphia, 1857.

Moore, James. "The Original Manuscript Concerning the Founding of the University at Lewisburg by One of the Founders," Bucknell Mirror, December 10, 1896.

Oliphant, J. Orin. The Beginnings of Bucknell University: A Sampling of the Documents. Lewisburg, Pa., 1954.

_____. "How Lewisburg Became a Canal Port," Northumberland County Historical Society Proceedings and Addresses, XXI (August 1957), 37-66.

_____. The Rise of Bucknell University. New York, 1965.

Oliphant, J. Orin, and Merrill W. Linn. "The Lewisburg and Mifflinburg Turnpike Company," Pennsylvania History, XV (April 1948), 86-119.

Smith, J. Wheaton. Life of John P. Crozer. Philadelphia, 1868.

"Stephen William Taylor," Bucknell Mirror, XXV (May 1906), 1-10.

Stewart, Eric G. "Living in Lewisburg in the 1840's and Early 1850's." Term paper written for History 221, May 17, 1934, Bucknell University Archives.

Taylor, Stephen W. "A Brief History of the Origin of the University at Lewisburg." Manuscript dated April 18, 1850, Bucknell University Archives.

Theiss, Lewis E. "The Beginnings of Bucknell University and Early Lewisburg," Northumberland County Historical Society Proceedings and Addresses, XIV (1944), 136-59.

_____. Centennial History of Bucknell University, 1846-1946. Williamsport, Pa., 1946.

University at Lewisburg. Catalogues. 1850-1861.

_____. "Minutes of the Board of Curators." Typescript in the Bucknell University Archives. October 19, 1847-July 31, 1861.

_____. "Minutes of the Board of Trustees." Typescript in the Bucknell University Archives. February 14, 1846-July 30, 1861.

University Female Institute. Catalogues. 1855-1863.

Colby College

Burrage, Henry S. "The Beginnings of Waterville College, Now Colby University," Collections and Proceedings of the Maine Historical Society, IV (N.S.) (April 1893), 124-145.

The Centennial History of Waterville, Kennebec County, Maine, ed. Edwin C. Whittemore. Waterville, Me., 1902.

Champlin, J.T. A Historical Discourse Delivered at the Fiftieth Anniversary of Colby University, August 20, 1870. Waterville, Me., 1870.

Chaplin, Jeremiah. "To the Trustees of Waterville College." Manuscript dated 1833, Jeremiah Chaplin Papers, Colby College Archives.

Chipman, Charles P. The Formative Period in Colby's History. Waterville, Me., 1912.

Constitution of the Manual Labor Association Connected With Waterville College; With an Address to the Public. Augusta, Me., 1832.

Finley, Raymond S. The History of Secondary Education in Kennebec in Maine. University of Maine Studies, 2nd series, No. 54. Orono, Me., 1941.

General Catalogue of the Officers, Graduates and Former Students of Colby College: Centennial Edition, 1820-1920. Waterville, Me., 1920.

Giveen, Clement M. A Chronology of Municipal History and Election Statistics, Waterville, Maine, 1771-1908. Augusta, Me., 1908.

Hall, Edward W. History of Higher Education in Maine. Washington, 1903.

Hamlin, Charles E. Untitled sketch of Colby College's Department of Manual Labor, Twelfth Annual Report of the Secretary of the Maine Board of Agriculture. Augusta, Me., 1867. pp. 188-92.

Jeremiah Chaplin Papers. Colby College Archives.

Kendrick, Nathaniel. A Discourse Delivered in the Chapel of the Hamilton Literary and Theological Institution, On the Death of Rev. Jeremiah Chaplin, D.D., June 6, 1841. Utica, N.Y., 1841.

Kingsbury, Henry D. "City of Waterville," Illustrated History of Kennebec County, Maine, eds. Henry D. Kingsbury and Simeon L. Deyo. New York, 1892. I, 567-600.

Manuscripts Concerning the Early History of Colby College. Colby College Archives.

Marriner, Ernest C. The History of Colby College. Waterville, Me., 1963.

_____. Kennebec Yesterdays. Waterville, Me., 1954.

Merrill, Samuel P. "Rev. Daniel Merrill, A.M. - An Appreciation," Centennial of the First Baptist Church, Sedgwick, Maine, n.p., ca. 1905.

Pattison, Robert E. Eulogy on Rev. Jeremiah Chaplin, D.D., First President of Waterville College, Me., Delivered in the Baptist Meeting House, Waterville, on the Evening Preceding Commencement, August 8, 1843. Boston, 1843.

Philbrick, Minnie S. Centennial History of the First Baptist Church of Waterville, Maine. Waterville, Me., 1925.

Report of the Faculty of Waterville College, On the Condition and Wants of the Institution, With the Action of the Trustees on the Same. At a Special Meeting of the Board, Dec. 18, 1855. Waterville, Me., 1856.

Ricker, Joseph. Personal Recollections: A Contribution to Baptist History and Biography. Augusta, Me., 1894.

Watchman. Waterville, Me. December 11, 1828-December 30, 1829.

Waterville College: Origin, Progress, and Present State of the College. Portland, Me., 1822.

Waterville College. Catalogues. 1825/26, 1826/27, 1830/31, 1832/33-1836/37, 1838/39, 1841/42, 1843/44-1860/61.

Waterville, Fairfield and Winslow. Souvenir. Past and Present, Progress and Prosperity, ed. J.H. Burgess. Waterville, Me., ca. 1902.

Waterville Intelligencer. Waterville, Me. May 23, 1823-November 6, 1828.

Watervillonian. Waterville, Me. May 29, 1841-May 30, 1842.

Whittemore, Edwin C. Colby College, 1820-1925: An Account of its Beginnings, Progress and Service. Waterville, 1927.

Yankee Blade. Waterville, Me. July 30, 1842-August 5, 1843.

Colgate University

Asahel C. Kendrick Papers. Special Collections, University of Rochester Library.

Baldwin, D.P. "Madison University Thirty Years Ago," Madisonensis, October 10, 1885.

Colgate University, General Catalogue Number, ed. Elmer W. Smith. Colgate University Publication, XXXVII, No. 2. Hamilton, N.Y., 1937.

Democratic Reflector. Hamilton, N.Y. November 1, 1842-November 19, 1845; November 18, 1852-November 8, 1855.

340

Everts, William W. William Colgate: The Christian Layman. Philadelphia, 1881.

The First Half Century of Madison University, (1819-1869) or the Jubilee Volume. New York, 1872.

Hammond, L.M. History of Madison County, State of New York. Syracuse, N.Y., 1872.

Hascall, Daniel, et al. Memorial In Relation to the Madison University. New York, State Senate, Document No. 37, Feb. 16, 1849.

Hascall v. Madison University, 8 Barbour (N.Y.), 174 (1850).

Hezekiah Harvey Papers. Colgate University Archives.

An Historical Sketch of Madison University, Hamilton, N.Y. Utica, N.Y., 1852.

Humphrey, Friend, et al. Remonstrance Against the Repeal of An Act Relating to Madison University, Passed April 3, 1848. New York, State Senate, Document No. 52, March 3, 1849.

Madison University. Catalogues. 1832/33-1860/61.

"Spear Scrapbook." Colgate University Archives.

Statistics of College Aid. n.p., 1851.

Williams, Howard D. First Baptist Church, Hamilton, New York: Historical Sketch, 1796-1961. n.p. n.d.

_____. "The History of Colgate University to 1869." Unpublished Ph.D. dissertation, Harvard University, 1949.

_____. "The Origin of Colgate University," New York History, XIX (July 1938), 239-54.

Woods, Byron A. "In Memoriam, Elder Jabez S. Swan," Special Memorial Service at Hamilton, New York, June 17, 1885. Utica, N.Y., 1885.

Denison University

Annual Meeting of the Ohio Baptist Education Society, and of the Trustees of the Granville Literary and Theological Institution, October 6, 1832. Cincinnati, 1832.

Annual Meeting of the Trustees of the Granville Literary and Theological Institution, and of the Ohio Baptist Education Society, August 14th and 15th, 1833. Cincinnati, 1833.

Annual Meeting of the Trustees of the Granville Literary and Theological Institution and of the Ohio Baptist Education Society, August 13th and 14th, 1834. Cincinnati, 1834.

"Autobiography of Rev. Jeremiah Hall, D.D., From Notes of Conversations Taken By His Son, Frank M. Hall." Manuscript, ca. 1864, Denison University Archives.

Bailey, Silas. Mr. Little's New Year's Sermon: Review of Mr. Little's Twenty-Fifth New Year's Sermon. Columbus, Ohio, 1852.

Booth, Isaiah. "Reminiscences." Undated typescript in the Isaiah Booth folder, Denison University Archives.

Burton, Nathan S. "Granville's Indebtedness to Jeremiah Hall," "Old Northwest" Genealogical Quarterly, VIII (October 1905), 380-81.

Bushnell, Henry. The History of Granville, Licking County, Ohio. Columbus, Ohio, 1889.

Chamberlin, Willis A. "Dr. Jonathan Going's Impress Upon the Midwest," Chronicle, VIII (July 1945), 107-117.

Chessman, G. Wallace. Denison: The Story of an Ohio College. Granville, Ohio, 1957.

Denison University. Catalogues. 1839/40-1841/42, 1843/44-1846/47, 1848/49, 1850/51, 1854/55-1860/61.

Denison University. Trustee Minutes. July 14, 1846-December 5, 1861.

General Information Respecting the Internal Arrangements of the Granville Literary and Theological Institution. Columbus, Ohio, 1836.

Hines, Kate S. "The Story of the Granville Baptist Church, Commemorating Its First Century, 1819-1919." Typescript, ca. 1919, Denison University Archives.

John Stevens Papers. American Baptist Historical Society, Rochester, New York.

Little, Jacob. A New Year's Sermon, Delivered in Granville, Licking County, Ohio, on the First Sabbath of January, 1849. Newark, Ohio, 1849.

———. Twenty-fourth New Year's Sermon. A Discourse Delivered at Granville, Ohio, on the First Sabbath of January, 1851. Granville, Ohio, 1851.

———. Twenty-fifth New Year's Sermon. A Discourse Preached in Granville, Ohio, on the First Sabbath of January, 1852. Granville, Ohio, 1852.

Memorial Volume of Denison University, 1831-1906. Columbus, Ohio, 1907.

Plan for the Endowment of Granville College. Columbus, Ohio, 18

Shepardson, Francis W. Denison University, 1831-1931, A Centennial History. Granville, Ohio, 1931.

/Stevens, John/. "Denison University, Items in Its Character and History." Manuscript, ca. 1868, in the John Stevens folder, Denison University Archives.

Turney, Edmund. The Prospect of Death An Incentive to Christian Consistency and Faithfulness: A Discourse Delivered on the Occasion of the Death of Rev. Jonathan Going, D.D., President of Granville College, With a Sketch of His Life. Hartford, Conn., 1845.

Utter, William F. Granville: The Story of an Ohio Village. Granville, Ohio, 1956.

Franklin College

Alumni Number, 1910. Franklin College Bulletin, I, No. 3. Franklin, Ind., 1910.

Banta, David D. A Historical Sketch of Johnson County, Indiana. Chicago, 1881.

/Banta, David D., et al/. History of Johnson County, Indiana. Chicago, 1888.

Cady, John F. The Centennial History of Franklin College. n.p., 1934.

First Half Century of Franklin College, Jubilee Exercises. Cincinnati, 1884.

Franklin College. Catalogues. 1845/46-1850/51, 1852/53-1858/59, 1860/61.

343

Indianapolis Sentinel. Indianapolis. June-September, 1859.

Locomotive. Indianapolis. June-September, 1859.

Report to the Board of Trustees of Franklin College on Changes
in the Course of Study, Read April 6, 1853. Indianapolis,
1853.

Stott, William F. History of Fifty Years of the First Baptist
Church of Franklin, Indiana. n.p., n.d.

_____. History of Franklin College: A Brief Sketch.
Indianapolis, 1874.

Weekly Democratic Herald. Franklin, Ind. November 24, 1859-
December 20, 1860.

Furman University

The Arts in Greenville, 1800-1960, ed. Alfred S. Reid.
Greenville, S.C., 1960.

Brown, C.C. General Catalog of Furman University...1852-
1899. Sumpter, S.C., n.d.

Crittenden, S.S. The Greenville Century Book. Greenville,
S.C., 1903.

Daniel, Robert N. Furman University: A History. Greenville,
S.C., 1951.

Furman, James C. An Historical Discourse, Delivered Before
the Charleston Baptist Association, At Its Hundredth
Anniversary, Held in Charleston in November, 1851.
Charleston, S.C., 1852.

Furman University. Catalogues. 1851/52-1860/61.

Hewell, Marion M. "Vardry McBee of South Carolina," Proceedings and Papers of the Greenville County Historical Society, 1962-1964. Greenville, S.C., 1965.
pp. 39-48.

McGlothlin, William J. Baptist Beginnings in Education:
A History of Furman University. Nashville, Tenn., 1926.

Reid, Alfred S. "Literary Culture in Mid-Nineteenth Century
Greenville," Proceedings and Papers of the Greenville
County Historical Society, 1962-1964. Greenville, S.C.
1965. pp. 55-74.

William B. Johnson Correspondence. South Carolina Baptist
Historical Collection, Furman University Library.

Georgetown College

Acton, Hul-Cee M. History of the Tau Theta Kappa Society of
Georgetown College. Georgetown, Ky., 1918.

Black, J. William. "The History of Georgetown College, Georgetown, Ky.," History of Higher Education in Kentucky,
ed. Alvin F. Lewis. Washington, 1899.

Bradley, J.N. and Ellis M. Ham. History of the Great Crossings
Baptist Church. Georgetown, Ky., 1945.

Ciceronian Magazine. Georgetown, Ky. I nos. 1-10, March,
1856-February, 1857.

Corey, O.R. "Historical Chronology, General College History:
1775-1954." Typescript in Georgetown College Library.

Dudley, R.M. "The Early History of Georgetown College,"
Georgetown College Magazine, II (January 1887), 125-28.

F./arnham/, J./onathan/ E. "Georgetown College - No. 4: Its
First Decade," Western Recorder, September 11, 1875.

Gaines, B.O. The B.O. Gaines History of Scott County.
2 vols. Reprint of original, 1904 edition. Georgetown,
Ky., 1957-61.

Georgetown College. Catalogues. 1845/46-1860/61.

Georgetown College Magazine. Georgetown, Ky. I no. 1,
March, 1857.

Georgetown Herald. Georgetown, Ky. June 2, 9, 16, July 14,
21, August 8, October 13, 1847; March 8, 22, November 1,
1848; April 11, 25, May 2, June 6, August 1, 15, 1849.

Historical Catalogue of Georgetown College, 1829-1917.
Georgetown College Bulletin, XIV, No. 4. Georgetown, Ky., 1917.

A History of Bourbon, Scott, Harrison and Nicholas Counties, Kentucky, ed. William H. Perrin. Chicago, 1882.

"Howard Malcom Memorial Scrapbook." American Baptist Historical Society, Rochester, New York.

Huddle, Orlando E. "A History of Georgetown College." Unpublished MA thesis, University of Kentucky, 1930.

Meyer, Leland W. *Georgetown College: Its Background and a Chapter in Its Early History.* Louisville, Ky., 1929.

Moreland, James. *Georgetown College: A History.* Providence, R.I., ca. 1927.

Samson, G.W. *Memorial Discourse on the Life and Character of Joel Smith Bacon, D.D., Third President of the Columbian College, in the District of Columbia, Delivered at the E. Street Baptist Church, Washington, D.C., On Sunday, June 27, 1870.* Washington, 1870.

Yager, Arthur. *Historical Sketch of Georgetown College.* Georgetown College Bulletin, I, No. 1. Georgetown, Ky., 1904.

George Washington University

Circular of the Columbian College, D.C. Broadside dated March 26, 1827.

Circular of the Columbian College, Washington, District of Columbia, 1853. Washington, 1853.

The Claims of the Columbian College as Seen in its Past History and Present Condition. Washington, 1857.

Columbian College. *Catalogues.* 1825, 1839/40, 1847/48, 1850/51, 1855/56-1860/61.

Galusha, Elon. *The Crisis Is At Hand.* Whitesborough, N.Y., 1826.

Historical Catalogue of the Officers and Graduates of the Columbian University, Washington, D.C., 1821-1891, comp. H.L. Hodgkins. Washington, 1891.

Iveson L. Brooks Papers. Baptist Historical Collection, Wake
Forest College Library.

Kayser, Elmer L. _The George Washington University, 1821-
1966_. Washington, 1966.

————. _Luther Rice, Founder of Columbian College_. Washington, 1966.

Laws of the Columbian College in the District of Columbia.
Washington, 1856.

Luther Rice Letter Book, January 6-June 2, 1823. Baptist
Historical Collection, Wake Forest College Library.

Luther Rice Letters. Office of the University Historian,
George Washington University.

Pollard, E.B. "Luther Rice and His Place in American Baptist
History," _Review and Expositor_, X (July, October 1913),
335-54, 508-30.

/Rothwell, Andrew/. _History of the Baptist Institutions of
Washington City_. Washington, 1867.

Ryland, Robert. "Reminiscences of My Early College Life,"
Ford's Christian Repository, XLVI (July 1888), 36-39.

Taylor, James B. _Memoir of Rev. Luther Rice, One of the
First American Missionaries to the East_. Baltimore,
1840.

U.S., Congress, House. _Financial Condition of the George
Washington University_. 61st Cong., 3rd Sess., 1910,
House Doc. 1060.

Wait, Samuel. "Journal, December 27, 1826-July 1, 1827." Baptist Historical Collection, Wake Forest College Library.

Welling, James C. _Brief Chronicles of the Columbian College
From 1821 to 1873 and of the Columbian University From
1873 to 1889_. Washington, 1889.

Wilkinson, Lucille W. "Early Baptists in Washington, D.C.,"
Columbia Historical Society _Records_, XXIX-XXX (1928),
211-68.

Hillsdale College

Compendium of History and Biography of Hillsdale County, Michigan, ed. Elon G. Reynolds. Chicago, 1903.

Dunn, Ransom. "The Story of the Planting: A Reminiscence of the Founding and Early History of Hillsdale College," Reunion, 7 weekly installments, May 6-June 17, 1885.

Gates, Helen Dunn. A Consecrated Life: A Sketch of the Life and Labors of Rev. Ransom Dunn, D.D., 1818-1900. Boston, 1901.

Hillsdale College. Catalogues. 1856/57-1860/61.

Johnson, Crisfield. "History of Hillsdale County," History of Hillsdale County, Michigan, With Illustrations and Biographical Sketches of Some of Its Prominent Men and Pioneers. Philadelphia, 1879. pp. 9-93.

"Lives of the Founders and Builders of Hillsdale College," Advance, January 27 and June 23, 1886.

Moore, Vivian L. The First Hundred Years of Hillsdale College. Ann Arbor, Mich., 1944.

Norton, S.W. "Hillsdale College, Hillsdale, Michigan," Collections and Researches Made By the Michigan Pioneer and Historical Society, XXXII (1903), 452-458.

Patterson, John C. "History of Hillsdale College," Collections and Researches Made By the Michigan Pioneer and Historical Society, VI (1883), 137-165.

Roberts, Windsor H. A History of the College Baptist Church, 1855-1955. n.p., n.d.

Howard College

Fiftieth Annual Catalogue and Register of Howard College, East Lake, Alabama, For the Academic Year 1891-92. Birmingham, Ala., 1892.

Garrett, Mitchell B. Sixty Years of Howard College, 1842-1902. Howard College Bulletin, LXXXV, No. 4. Birmingham, Ala., 1927.

Howard College. Catalogues. 1843/44, 1845/46-1860/61.

348

Howard College Magazine. Marion, Ala. I nos. 1, 3-9;
     II nos 2-3, 5-7: October, December, 1858; January-June,
     1859; January, March-May, 1860.

James H. De Votie Letters. Duke University Archives.

Lovelace, Julia M. A History of the Siloam Baptist Church,
     Marion, Alabama. Birmingham, Ala., ca. 1958.

Marion Herald. Marion, Ala. September 21, 1839; October 7,
     1841; December 1, 1841.

Perry Eagle. Marion, Ala. July 31, 1840-October 23, 1840.

Sherman, Samuel S. Autobiography of Samuel Sterling Sherman.
     Chicago, 1910.

Townes, S.A. The History of Marion, Sketches of Life in Perry
     County, Alabama. Marion, Ala, 1844. Reprinted in Ala-
     bama Historical Quarterly, XIV, Nos 3 and 4 (1952), 171-
     229.

Tri-Weekly Commonwealth. Marion, Ala. March 4-December 31,
     1859.

                    Mercer University

Dowell, Spright. A History of Mercer University, 1833-1953.
     Macon, Ga., 1958.

Iveson L. Brookes Papers. Southern Historical Collection,
     University of North Carolina.

Mercer University. Catalogues. 1846/47, 1849/50-1860/61.

Plan, History and Terms of the Mercer Institute, Prepared and
     Published by the Teachers and Trustees of the Executive
     Committee of the Baptist Convention for the State of
     Georgia, Who Have the Supervision of the Institution,
     July, 1834. n.p., n.d.

Ragsdale, B.D. Story of Georgia Baptists. I. Atlanta, 1932.

Sherwood, Adiel. A Gazetteer of the State of Georgia.
     Washington, 1837.

Temperance Banner. Penfield, Ga. February 21, 1852-March
     25, 1859.

<u>Triennial Register and Annual Catalogue, Mercer University,</u>
<u>1897-1898</u>. Macon, Ga., 1898. pp. 16-29.

Weaver, Rufus W. "The Future of Mercer University," <u>Christian</u>
<u>Index</u>, Dec. 20, 1920.

_____. "The Presidents of Mercer During Its First Half
Century," <u>Christian Index</u>, Feb. 18, 1926, 3-5.

University of Richmond

Boatwright, F.W. "The Beginnings of Higher Education Among
Virginia Baptists," <u>Religious Herald</u>, August 13, 1931.

Gaines, R.E. "The Beginnings: The Seminary, the College,
1832-1866," <u>The First Hundred Years: Brief Sketches of</u>
<u>the History of the University of Richmond</u>. Richmond,
<u>Va.</u>, 1932.

Harris, H.H. "Richmond College," in Herbert B. Adams, <u>Thomas</u>
<u>Jefferson and the University of Virginia</u>. Washington,
1888. pp. 271-285.

Jones, S. <u>An Appeal to the Virginia Baptists, Proposing the</u>
<u>Establishment of a Theological and Manual Labor School</u>
<u>at Williamsburg</u>. Richmond, Va., 1837.

_____. <u>Arguments for and Against a Baptist Theological</u>
<u>School at Williamsburg, Virginia</u>. Richmond, Va., 1837.

<u>Proceedings and Annual Report of the Va. Baptist Education</u>
<u>Society, With the Rules and Regulations of the Virginia</u>
<u>Baptist Seminary, etc, etc, etc,</u>. Richmond, Va., 1835.

Richmond College. <u>Catalogues</u>. 1839/40, 1841/42-1844/45,
1846/47-1849/50, 1851/52-1856/57, 1858/59, 1859/60.

<u>Roll of Students of Richmond College, 1865 to 1905, With List</u>
<u>of Graduates, 1849 to 1861</u>. Richmond College Bulletin,
VII, No. 2. Richmond, Va., 1905.

Ryland, Robert. <u>The Virginia Baptist Education Society.</u>
<u>The Society, the Seminary, the College</u>. Richmond, Va.,
1891.

<u>Virginia Baptist Education Society</u>. n.p., 1833.

University of Rochester

Centennial History of Rochester, New York, ed. Edward R.
Foreman. III. Rochester, N.Y., 1933.

General Catalogue of the University of Rochester, 1850-1911.
University Bulletin, VII, No. 2. Rochester, N.Y., 1911.

McKelvey, Blake. *Rochester, the Water-Power City, 1812-1854*.
Cambridge, Mass., 1945.

*Report to the Board of Trustees of the University of Rochester
on the Plan of Instruction to be Pursued in the Collegiate
Department, Presented, September 16, 1850*. Rochester,
N.Y., 1850.

Rosenberger, Jesse L. *Rochester and Colgate: Historical Backgrounds of the Two Universities*. Chicago, 1925.

_____. *Rochester: The Making of a University*. Rochester,
N.Y., 1927.

Strong, Augustus H. "Historical Discourse," *Rochester Theological Seminary General Catalogue, 1850 to 1900*.
Rochester, N.Y., 1900.

University of Rochester. *Catalogues*. 1850/51-1860/61.

Shurtleff College

/Adkins, Erastus/. *A Narrative of Facts and Proceedings
Connected With the Recent Changes in the Faculty of
Shurtleff College*. St. Louis, 1855.

Adkins, Frank. "Baptist History in the Central West,"
Denison Quarterly, IV (December 1896), 256-79.

Babcock, Rufus. *Forty Years of Pioneer Life: Memoir of John
Mason Peck, D.D.* Philadelphia, 1864.

Benjamin Shurtleff Papers. Massachusetts Historical Society.

Brush, Daniel H. *Growing Up With Southern Illinois, 1820-1861*.
Chicago, 1944.

Bulkley, Justus. *Historical Sketch of Shurtleff College,
Upper Alton, Illinois*. Upper Alton, Ill., 1865.

351

Bulkley, Justus. "Historical Sketch of Shurtleff Prepared
   for the Seventieth Annual Commencement of Shurtleff
   College, June, 1897," Semi-Centennial History of the
   Alpha Zeta Society of Shurtleff College. Alton, Ill.,
   1898. pp. xiv-xxix.

Centennial History of Madison County, Illinois, ed. Wilbur T.
   Norton. 2 vols. Chicago, 1912.

"Colleges as a Means of Grace," Baptist Educational Reporter,
   I (June 1867), 25-26.

Cook, John W. Educational History of Illinois. Chicago, 1912.

DeBlois, Austin K. "Denominational Education Fifty Years Ago,"
   Standard, March 14, 1903.

_____. The Pioneer School: A History of Shurtleff College,
   Oldest Educational Institution in the West. New York,
   1900.

Greene, William W. Semi-Centennial History of the Alpha Zeta
   Society of Shurtleff College, Together With Complete
   Rosters of Active and Honorary Members. Alton, Ill.,
   1898.

Jennings, Helene L. "John Mason Peck and the Impact of New
   England on the Old Northwest." Unpublished Ph.D. dissertation, University of Southern California, 1961.

John Mason Peck Correspondence. Andover Newton Theological
   School Library.

Jubilee Memorial of Shurtleff College, Upper Alton, Ill.
   Alton, Ill., 1877.

Lawrence, Matthew. John Mason Peck, The Pioneer Missionary:
   A Biographical Sketch. New York, 1940.

Loomis, Hubbel. A Documentary History of Alton Seminary to
   March 7, 1835, When Its Departments Took the Distinctive
   Names Alton Theological Seminary, and Alton College,
   Which January 12, 1836, Took the Name Shurtleff College:
   The School, Called Alton Seminary, or, Alton Literary
   and Theological Seminary. Founded by Rev. H. Loomis,
   September, 1832, and the Charge Resigned June 13, 1836.
   Alton, Ill., 1854.

Peck, J.M. Alton Seminary and College. n.p., ca. 1835.

Peck, J.M. A Gazetteer of Illinois. Jacksonville, Ill.,
     1834.

_____. A Guide For Emigrants, Containing Sketches of
     Illinois, Missouri, and the Adjacent Parts. Boston, 1831.

_____. A New Guide For Emigrants to the West, Containing
     Sketches of Michigan, Ohio, Indiana, Illinois, Missouri,
     Arkansas, With the Territory of Wisconsin and the Adjacent
     Parts. Boston, 1837.

"Record Book of the Rock Springs Theological and High School,
     Rock Springs, Illinois, 1824-1831." Typescript in the
     Dargan-Carver Library, Nashville, Tennessee.

Shurtleff College. Catalogues. 1839/40, 1841/42, 1844/45-
     1849/50, 1851/52-1860/61.

Shurtleff College: Its Financial Concerns, Condition and Pros-
     pects. Broadside dated August 1, 1845. Upper Alton,
     Ill., 1845.

Shurtleff, Hiram S. "Benjamin Shurtleff, M.D.," Memorial
     Biographies of the New England Historic Genealogical
     Society, I (1880), 32-36.

Strange, A.T. "John Tillson," Journal of the Illinois State
     Historical Society, XVII (January 1925), 715-23.

Waggener, H. Farr. The First Baptist Church of Upper Alton:
     A History of One Hundred Years. Alton, Ill., ca. 1930.

Wright, David. Memoir of Alvan Stone of Goshen, Mass. Boston,
     1837.

Union University

"Alumni Association of Union University," Union University,
     Catalogue, 1910/11, pp. 94-98.

A History of Rutherford County, ed. Carlton C. Sims. n.p.,
     ca. 1947.

/Howell, R.B.C./. "A Memorial of the First Baptist Church,
     Nashville, Tennessee, From 1820 to 1863." Typescript
     in the Dargan-Carver Library, Nashville, Tennessee.

Inman, W.G. "The History of Union University, Continued as
     the Southwestern Baptist University," Baptist and Re-
     flector, nine installments, July 30, 1891-January 7, 1892.

Inman, W.G.   "Planting and Progress of the Baptist Cause in
    Tennessee." Microfilmed typescript, ca. 1920, Dargan-
    Carver Library, Nashville, Tennessee.

Prospectus and Course of Studies of Union University of Ten-
    nessee. Nashville, Tenn., 1848.

Tennessee Telegraph. Murfreesboro, Tenn. March 14, 1838;
    May 2-16, September 12, November 21, 1840; February 6,
    October 23, 1841; November 13, 1845.

Union University. Catalogues.   1851/52, 1853/54, 1854/55,
    1856/57, 1857/58.

                    Wake Forest College

General Catalogue of Wake Forest College, North Carolina,
    1834/35-1891/92, comp. C.E. Taylor. Raleigh, N.C., 1892.

Gorrell, J.H. "A Short Story of Wake Forest, Town and College,"
    Wake Forest Student, XXXIX (January 1920), 162-73.

Paschal, George W. History of Wake Forest College. I. Wake
    Forest, N.C., 1935.

_____. "President Samuel Wait," Wake Forest Student, XLIV
    (January 1927), 187-198.

Samuel Wait Correspondence. Baptist Historical Collection,
    Wake Forest College Library.

Sikes, E.W. "The First Board of Trustees of Wake Forest
    College," Wake Forest Student, XXVI (September 1906),
    1-25.

_____. "The Genesis of Wake Forest College," Publications
    of the North Carolina Historical Commission, I (1907),
    538-557.

Wait, Samuel. "The Origin and Early History of Wake Forest
    College," Wake Forest Student, II (September, October
    1882), 11-17, 49-58.

Wake Forest College. Catalogues. 1836/37, 1838/39, 1839/40,
    1848/49, 1850/51, 1851/52, 1854/55, 1856/57-1859/60.

Wallace, D.R. "Reminiscences of Old Wake Forest," Wake Forest
    Student, XXVIII (January 1909), 320-30.

Denominational History

Secondary Sources

Ashton, Dean. "Isaac Eaton, Neglected Baptist Educator,"
Chronicle, XX (April 1957), 67-79.

Baker, Robert A. "Organizational Differences Between Northern
and Southern Baptists in the Nineteenth Century," Chronicle, XV (April 1952), 68-75.

Baker, Robert A. Relations Between Northern and Southern
Baptists. Fort Worth, Texas, 1948.

Baptist Concepts of the Church, ed. Winthrop S. Hudson.
Philadelphia, 1959.

Barnes, William W. The Southern Baptist Convention, 1845-1953.
Nashville, Tenn., 1954.

Baxter, Norman A. History of the Freewill Baptists: A Study
in New England Separatism. Rochester, N.Y., 1957.

Benedict, David. Fifty Years Among the Baptists. New York,
1860.

_____. A General History of the Baptist Denomination in
America and Other Parts of the World. 2 vols. Boston,
1813.

Boyd, Jesse L. A History of Baptists in America Prior to
1845. New York, 1957.

Burrage, Henry S. History of the Baptists in Maine. Portland,
Me., 1904.

Campbell, Jesse H. Georgia Baptists: Historical and Biographical. Macon, Ga., 1874.

Carroll, B.H., Jr. The Genesis of American Anti-Missionism.
Louisville, Ky., 1902.

Cathcart, William. The Baptist Encyclopaedia. Rev.ed.
Philadelphia, 1883.

The Centennial Record of Freewill Baptists: 1780-1880. Dover,
N.H., 1881.

Chaney, Charles. "Diversity: A Study in Illinois Baptist History to 1907," Foundations, VII (January 1964), 41-54.

Christian Index, History of the Baptist Denomination in Georgia: With Biographical Compendium and Portrait Gallery of Baptist Ministers and Other Georgia Baptists. Atlanta, 1881.

Cook, Harvey T. Education in South Carolina Under Baptist Control. Greenville, S.C., 1912.

Cox, A., and J. Hoby. The Baptists in America: A Narrative of the Deputation From the Baptist Union in England to the United States and Canada. New York, 1836.

Fleming, Sandford. "American Baptists and Higher Education," six-volume typescript, ca. 1963, American Baptist Historical Society, Rochester, New York.

Garrison, Winfred E., and Alfred T. De Groot, The Disciples of Christ: A History. St. Louis, 1948.

Gates, Errett. The Early Relation and Separation of Baptists and Disciples. Chicago, 1904.

Goen, C.C. Revivalism and Separatism in New England, 1740-1800. New Haven, Conn., 1962.

Hague, William. Christian Greatness In a Scholar: A Discourse on the Life and Character of Rev. Irah Chase, D.D. Boston, 1866.

Holcombe, Hosea. A History of the Rise and Progress of the Baptists in Alabama. Philadelphia, 1840.

Hudgins, Ira D. "The Anti-missionary Controversy Among Baptists," Chronicle, XIV (October 1951), 147-63.

Hudson, Winthrop S. "The Associational Principle Among Baptists," Foundations, I (January 1958), 10-23.

_____. "Stumbling into Disorder," Foundations, I (April 1958), 45-71.

Jennings, Walter W. Origin and Early History of the Disciples of Christ. Cincinnati, 1919.

Johnson, Charles D. Higher Education of Southern Baptists: An Institutional History, 1826-1954. Waco, Texas, 1955.

Keyser, Donald. "A History of Baptist Higher Education in the South to 1865," unpublished Th.D. dissertation, Southern Baptist Theological Seminary, 1955.

Lambert, Byron C. "The Rise of the Anti-Mission Baptists: Sources and Leaders, 1800-1840," unpublished Ph.D. dissertation, University of Chicago, 1957.

Lewis, Frank G. A Sketch of the History of Baptist Education in Pennsylvania. Chester, Pa., 1919.

Lumpkin, William L. Baptist Foundations in the South: Tracing Through the Separates the Influence of the Great Awakening, 1754-1787. Nashville, Tenn., 1961.

Millet, Joshua. A History of the Baptists in Maine; Together With Brief Notices of Societies and Institutions, And A Dictionary of the Labors of Each Minister. Portland, Me., 1845.

Moehlman, Conrad H. "American Baptists and Education," Colgate-Rochester Divinity School Bulletin, IV (November 1931) 87-102.

Mcsteller, James D. "The Separate Baptists in the South," Chronicle, XVII (July 1954), 143-54.

Newman, Albert H. "Baptist Ministerial Education Seventy-Five Years Ago," Rochester Theological Seminary Bulletin (June 1925), 345-361.

Padelford, Frank W. "The Story of Baptist Education," Colgate-Rochester Divinity School Bulletin, XI (October 1938), 5-18, 74-86.

Paschal, George W. History of North Carolina Baptists, I. Raleigh, N.C., 1930.

Pendleton, James M. "The Condition of the Baptist Cause in Kentucky in 1837," Memorial Volume...of the General Association of Baptists in Kentucky. Lousville, 1888. pp. 1-16.

Posey, Walter B. The Baptist Church in the Lower Mississippi Valley, 1776-1845. Lexington, Ky., 1957.

Riley, Benjamin F. History of the Baptists of Alabama, 1808-1894. Birmingham, Ala., 1895.

_____. A Memorial History of the Baptists of Alabama. Philadelphia, 1923.

Ryland, Garnett. The Baptists of Virginia, 1699-1926. Richmond, Va., 1955.

Semple, Robert B. A History of the Rise and Progress of the Baptists in Virginia, revised and extended by G.W. Beale. Richmond, Va., 1894.

Spencer, J.H. A History of Kentucky Baptists. From 1769 to 1885, Including More than 800 Biographical Sketches. 2 vols. Cincinnati, 1886.

Sweet, William Warren. Religion on the American Frontier, 1, The Baptists, 1783-1830. New York, 1931.

Teague, E.B. "An Outline Picture of the Baptist Denomination in Alabama in Former Times." Typescript ca. 1880 in Special Collections of the Howard College Library.

Torbet, Robert G. "Bases of Baptist Convention Membership: An Historical Survey," Foundations, VI (January 1963), 26-41.

_____. A History of the Baptists. New rev. ed. Valley Forge, Pa., 1963.

_____. A Social History of the Philadelphia Baptist Association, 1707-1940. Philadelphia, 1944.

Ward, Richard H. "The Development of Baptist Higher Education in Tennessee." Unpublished Ph.D. dissertation, George Peabody College for Teachers, 1953.

Wayland, Francis. Notes on the Principles and Practices of Baptist Churches. New York, 1857.

Weaver, Rufus. "The Invasion of the South by the Sainted Baptist Yankees," Chronicle, VII (October 1944), 164-66.

Wilson, Carl B. The Baptist Manual Labor School Movement in the United States: Its Origin, Development and Significance. Baylor University Bulletin, XL, No. 4. Waco, Texas, 1937.

Annuals

Proceedings of the Triennial Convention, 1814-1846, and Annual Reports of the Board of Managers, 1814-1846, collated on microfilm by Leo T. Crismon. Nashville, Tenn., 1961.

Southern Baptist Convention. _Proceedings_. 1845-1861.

Proceedings of the First Anniversary of the General Convention of Western Baptists at Cincinnati, Commencing on the Fifth of November, 1834. Cincinnati, 1835.

****

American Baptist Almanac. Philadelphia. 1841-1861.

American Baptist Register for 1852, ed. J. Lansing Burrows. Philadelphia, 1853.

Freewill Baptist Register. Dover, N.H. 1824-1861.

Southern Baptist Almanac and Annual Register. Nashville, Tenn., 1848-1852.

****

Annual Report of the Baptist Education Society of the United States, Philadelphia, July 13th and 14th, 1814. Philadelphia, 1814.

First Annual Meeting of the Baptist Education Society of the North-Western States, Held at Beloit, Wisc., Nov. 5th & 6th, 1852. With the Constitution of the Society and Address of the Board. Racine, Wis., 1852.

Freewill Baptist Education Society. _Annual Reports_. 1841-1856.

Northern Baptist Education Society. _Annual Reports_. 1814-1861.

Pennsylvania Baptist Education Society. _Reports and Minutes_. 1840-1861.

Western Baptist Education Society. _Proceedings_. 1835-1837, 1849-1855.

****

Alabama Baptist Convention. _Minutes_. 1835, 1839, 1842-1861.

Cahaba Baptist Association, Alabama. _Minutes_. 1831, 1838, 1853, 1855.

Columbia Baptist Association, Virginia /includes Washington, D.C.7. Minutes. 1820-1855.

Georgia Baptist Convention. Minutes. 1826, 1827, 1830-1861.

Georgia Baptist Association. Minutes. 1830-1861.

Illinois Baptist Convention. Minutes. 1834-1844.

Baptist General Association of Illinois. Minutes. 1845-1861.

Edwardsville Baptist Association, Illinois. Minutes. 1833-1845, 1847-1857, 1859-1861.

Indiana Baptist General Association. Minutes. 1833-1843, 1845-1858, 1860.

Flat Rock Baptist Association, Indiana. Minutes. 1833, 1835-1854.

Mount Zion Baptist Association, Indiana. Minutes. 1855, 1861.

Indianapolis Baptist Association, Indiana. Minutes. 1858-1860.

General Association of Baptists in Kentucky. Minutes. 1849-1861.

Elkhorn Baptist Association, Kentucky. Minutes. 1822-1861.

Maine Baptist Convention. Minutes. 1824, 1825, 1827-1861.

Bowdoinham Baptist Association, Maine. Minutes. 1800-1829.

Kennebec Baptist Association, Maine. Minutes. 1830-1861.

North Carolina Baptist Convention. Minutes. 1830-1861.

Raleigh Baptist Association, North Carolina. Minutes. 1850, 1854.

Tar River Baptist Association, North Carolina. Minutes. 1856-1858, 1860, 1861.

Ohio Baptist Convention. <u>Minutes</u>. 1826-1861.

Columbus Baptist Association, Ohio. <u>Minutes</u>. 1820-1861.

Northumberland Baptist Association, Pennsylvania. <u>Minutes</u>.
    1844, 1845.

Baptist General Association of Virginia. <u>Minutes</u>. 1825-1861.

Dover Baptist Association, Virginia. <u>Minutes</u>. 1830-1861.

Periodicals

<u>American Baptist</u>. Boston; Utica, McGrawville, N.Y. January
    7, 1846-June 25, 1861.

    January 7, 1846-June 27, 1850 as <u>Christian Contributor
    and Free Missionary</u>.

<u>American Baptist Magazine</u>. Boston. I-XV, September, 1803-
    December, 1835.

    September, 1803-December, 1816 as <u>Massachusetts Baptist
    Missionary Magazine</u>; January, 1817-November, 1824 as
    <u>American Baptist Magazine and Missionary Intelligencer</u>.

<u>American Baptist Memorial</u>. New York; Philadelphia; Richmond,
    Va. I-XV, January, 1842-December, 1856.

    January, 1842-September, 1844 as <u>Baptist Memorial and
    Monthly Chronicle</u>; October, 1844-December, 1851 as
    <u>Baptist Memorial and Monthly Record</u>; January-October,
    1852 as <u>Baptist Memorial and Family Book</u>; November-
    December, 1852 as <u>Baptist Memorial and Christian Keep-
    sake</u>; 1853 as <u>Baptist Memorial and Monthly Record</u>.

<u>Annunciator</u>. Rochester, N.Y. April 4, 1850-October 6, 1851.

<u>Baptist Advocate</u>. Cincinnati. I-II, January, 1835-December,
    1836.

Baptist Champion. Macon, Ga. July 15, 1859-April 26, 1860.

Baptist Chronicle and Literary Register. Georgetown, Ky.
I-III, January, 1830-December, 1832.

January, 1830 as Baptist Herald and Georgetown Literary
Register; February-March, 1830 as Baptist Chronicle and
Georgetown Literary Register.

Baptist Correspondent. Marion, Ala. January 18-July 25, 1860.

Baptist Inquirer. Franklin, Ind. I nos. 1-3, May-July, 1843.

Baptist Family Magazine. Philadelphia. I no. 1-V no. 4.
January, 1857-April, 1861.

Baptist Messenger. Elizabeth City, N.C. September 5, 1849-
March 5, 1851.

Baptist Messenger. Memphis, Tenn. September 16, 1859-March
21, 1861.

Baptist Record. Philadelphia. I-11, February, 1836-December,
1837; January 10, 1838-December 24, 1845.

February, 1836-December, 1837 as Monthly Paper of the
Baptist General Tract Society.

Baptist Watchman. Knoxville, Tenn. September 25, 1855-
November 12, 1858.

Biblical Recorder. New Bern, Raleigh, N.C. January 7, 1835-
June 26, 1861.

March 3-December 29, 1838 as Biblical Recorder and Southern
Watchman.

Christian Chronicle. Philadelphia. August 5, 1846-July 25,
1861.

<u>Christian Gazette</u>. Philadelphia. March 15, 1834-January 16, 1835.

<u>Christian Index</u>. Philadelphia; Washington, Penfield, Macon, Ga. July 4, 1829-June 26, 1861.

1829-1830 as <u>Columbian Star and Christian Index</u>; July 6, 1833-January 20, 1835 as <u>Christian Index and Baptist Miscellany</u>.

<u>Christian Messenger</u>. Madison, Indianapolis, Ind. August 30, 1843-December 11, 1849.

<u>Christian Messenger</u>. Georgetown, Ky.; Jacksonville, Ill. I-XIV, November, 1826-April, 1845.

<u>Christian Reflector</u>. Worcester, Mass. July 1, 1838-May 11, 1848.

<u>Christian Register</u>. Zanesville, Ohio. January 1-April 22, 1852.

<u>Christian Repository</u>. Louisville, Ky. I-X no. 8, January, 1852-August, 1861.

<u>Christian Review</u>. Boston; New York; Baltimore; Rochester, N.Y. I-XXVI no. 4, March, 1836-October, 1861.

<u>Christian Secretary</u>. Hartford, Conn. February 2, 1822-March 15, 1839.

<u>Christian Times</u>. Chicago. August 31, 1853-June 26, 1861.

<u>Columbian Star</u>. Washington; Philadelphia. February 2, 1822-December 27, 1828.

<u>Correspondent</u>. Nashville, Murfreesboro, Tenn. I-II, May, 1838-April, 1840.

Cross. Frankfort, Ky. January 9, February 6-20, 1834.

Evangelical Inquirer. Richmond, Va. I, October, 1826-
    September, 1827.

Freewill Baptist Quarterly. Providence, R.I.; Dover, N.H.
    I-IX, January, 1853-October, 1861.

Gospel Advocate. Georgetown, Ky. I-II, January, 1835-
    December, 1836.

Journal and Messenger. Cincinnati, Columbus, Ohio. July 22,
    1831-June 28, 1861.

    July 22, 1831-March 21, 1834 as Baptist Weekly Journal of
    the Mississippi Valley; March 28, 1834 - at least May 31,
    1839 as Cross and Baptist Journal of the Mississippi
    Valley; November 1, 1839-April 16, 1847 as Cross and
    Journal; April 23, 1847-July 27, 1849 as Western Chris-
    tian Journal; August 3, 1849-December 14, 1849 as
    Christian Journal.

Landmark. Hamilton, N.Y. August 1, 1850.

Latter Day Luminary. Philadelphia; Washington. I-VI,
    February, 1818-December, 1825.

Monthly Miscellany. Atlanta, Ga. 1 nos. 1-7, January-July,
    1849.

Morning Star. Dover, N.H. April 16, 1851-April 2, 1856.

New York Baptist Register. Utica, N.Y. February 20, 1824-
    January 16, 1855.

    February 20, 1824-February, 1825 as Baptist Register.

New York Chronicle. New York. I-II, January, 1849-December,
    1850.

364

New York Chronicle. New York. October 5, 1850-October 2,
1852; August 11, 1855.

New York Recorder. New York. July 3, 1845-December 25, 1850.

New York Recorder and Register. New York and Utica. January
23-June 20, 1855.

North Carolina Baptist Interpreter. Edenton, New Bern, N.C.
January 17, 1833-December 6, 1834.

North-Western Baptist. Chicago. September 20, 1842-September
20, 1844.

Parlor Visitor. Nashville, Tenn. I-VII no. 6, January, 1854-
June, 1857.

Primitive Baptist. Tarborough, N.C. January 9-December 18,
1836.

Regular Baptist Miscellany. Zanesville, Ohio. I-II no. 9,
October, 1829-June, 1831.

Religious Herald. Richmond, Va. January 11, 1828-June 27,
1861.

Signs of the Times. New-Vernon, Middleton, N.Y.; Alexandria,
Va. February 13, 1833-December 15, 1837.

Southern Baptist. Charleston, S.C. January 3, 1835-December
15, 1860.

January 3, 1835-December 30, 1836 as Southern Baptist
and General Intelligencer; January 7, 1837-February 8,
1838 as Southern Watchman and General Intelligencer;
September, 1845-August, 1846 as Carolina Baptist.

South Western Baptist. Marion, Montgomery, Tuskegee, Ala.
February 4, 1843-June 27, 1861.

February 4, 1843-at least September 8, 1848 as Alabama
Baptist; February 23, 1849-July 24, 1850 as Alabama Baptist Advocate.

Tennessee Baptist. Nashville, Tenn. I-II, January, 1835-
December, 1836; January 16-December 16, 1837; IV-V no. 2,
January, 1838-February, 1839; June 29, 1844-June 29, 1861.

January, 1835-February, 1839 and June 29, 1844-April 24,
1847 as Baptist.

Watchman of the Prairies. Chicago. August 10, 1847-February
22, 1853.

Western Religious Magazine. Cincinnati, Zanesville, Ohio.
I-II no. 10, June 20, 1827-April, 1829.

Western Baptist Review. Frankfort, Louisville, Ky. I-V no. 5,
September, 1845-October, 1850.

Western Recorder. Shelbyville, Louisville, Ky. March 21,
1835-June 29, 1861.

1834-December 27, 1838 and January 6, 1848-May 28, 1851
as Baptist Banner; January 3, 1839-December 23, 1847 as
Baptist Banner and Western Pioneer.

Western Star. Jacksonville, Ill. January 7, 1845-February
16, 1847.

Witness. Indianapolis. September 25, 1856-December 29, 1858.

Zion's Advocate. Portland, Me. November 11, 1828-June 28,
1861.

May 15, 1839-December 27, 1842 as Zion's Advocate and
Eastern Baptist.

Addresses and Sermons

Anderson, Martin B. The End and Means of a Liberal Education:
An Inaugural Address, Delivered July 11, 1854. Rochester,
N.Y., 1855.

Babcock, Rufus, Jr. The Claims of Education Societies; Especially on the Young Men of Our Country. Boston, 1829.

_____. The Teacher's Office: Inaugural Address of Rev. Rufus Babcock, Jr., President of Waterville College, July 29, 1834. Augusta, Me., 1834.

Bacon, Joel S. An Inaugural Address, Delivered in Georgetown, Ky., July 26, 1830. Georgetown, Ky., 1830.

Baptist, Edward. Address Delivered Before the Trustees, Faculty and Students of Howard College, Marion, Perry County, November 16, 1846. Tuskaloosa, Ala., 1846.

Binney, J.G. The Inaugural Address of the Rev. J.G. Binney, D.D., As President of the Columbian College, D.C., Wednesday, June 17, 1855. Washington, 1857.

Brooks, William F. An Address Delivered Before the Alumni of Wake Forest College, On the Afternoon of June 18th, 1859. Raleigh, N.C., 1861.

Chapin, Stephen. An Inaugural Address Delivered in the City of Washington, March 11, 1829. Washington, 1829.

_____. Triumphs of Intellect. A Lecture Delivered October, 1824, In the Chapel of Waterville College. Waterville, Me., 1824.

Colton, Simeon. An Address, Delivered Before the Philomathesian and Euzelian Societies, in Wake Forest College, June 16, 1842. Fayetteville, N.C., 1842.

Cushman, Robert W. Temptations of City Life: An Address to Young Men on the Temptations of Cities. Boston, 1847.

Eaton, George W. Address, and Poem, Delivered Before the Beta of the Sigma Phi, At Its Anniversary Meeting, Clinton, July 26th, 1842. Utica, N.Y., 1843.

_____. An Inaugural Address, Delivered in the Chapel of the Hamilton Literary and Theological Seminary, June 4, 1834. Utica, N.Y., 1835.

Going, Jonathan. Inaugural Address at the Anniversary of the Granville Literary and Theological Institution, August 8, 1838. Columbus, Ohio, 1839.

Hooper, William. Inaugural Discourse Delivered Before the Board of Trustees of the Furman Institution At Their Meeting, May 20, 1838. Charleston, S.C., 1838.

Jeter, J.B. Importance of an Enlightened Ministry. A Sermon Delivered at the Annual Meeting of the Virginia Baptist Education Society, Saturday, June 7th, 1834. Richmond, Va., 1834.

Keen, T.G. Characteristics of the Times, Strong Incentives to Intellectual Effort: An Address Delivered Before the Franklin and Adelphi Societies of Howard College, At Their Anniversary, Held at Marion, Alabama, July 24, 1850. Tuskaloosa, Ala., 1850.

Knowles, James D. Oration Delivered at the Columbian College in the District of Columbia, July 4, 1823. Washington, 1823.

Landrum, Sylvanus. Sermon on Ministerial Education Preached Before the Georgia Baptist Convention. Penfield, Ga., 1852.

Loomis, Justin R. An Address Delivered June 9, 1865, in Commencement Hall, of the University at Lewisburg, Pa., Before the Students of the Several Departments, On the Occasion of Their Celebrating the Completion of the Endowment Fund. Lewisburg, Pa., 1865.

_____. An Inaugural Address, Delivered July 27, 1859. Philadelphia, 1860.

Lynd, S.W. Address Delivered Before the Ohio Baptist Education Society, At the Annual Meeting Held in Granville, October 6, 1832. Cincinnati, 1832.

Maginnis, John S. An Inaugural Address, Delivered at the Chapel of the Hamilton Literary and Theological Institution, August 21, 1839. Utica, N.Y., 1840.

Manly, Basil, Jr. A Plea for Colleges. Philadelphia, 1854.

Mercer, Jesse. Knowledge Indispensable to a Minister of God. Washington, Ga., 1834.

Meredith, T. Address Delivered Before the Literary Societies of the Wake Forest Institute, North Carolina, Nov. 24th, 1836. Newbern, N.C., 1837.

Orr, J.L. An Address Delivered Before the Philosophian and Adelphian Societies of the Furman University at Their Annual Meeting, Greenville, S.C., July 18, 1855. Greenville, S.C., 1855.

368

Pendleton, J.M. Education. Nashville, Tenn., 1854.

Reynolds, J.L. Inaugural Discourse Delivered Before the Board of Trustees of the Furman Institution at Their Annual Meeting, Dec. 11, 1841. Columbia, S.C., 1842.

Ryland, Robert. A Sermon Delivered Before the Baptist Education Society of Virginia, June 4, 1836. Richmond, Va., 1836.

Sanborn, A. An Oration Delivered on the Anniversary of the Literary Fraternity of Waterville College, in Waterville, July 28th, 1829. Waterville, Me., 1829.

Sanders, B.M. Valedictory Address, Delivered Before the Trustees, Faculty, Students, and Friends of the Mercer University, Greene County, Ga., Dec. 12, 1839. Washington, Ga., 1840.

Staughton, William. Address Delivered at the Opening of the Columbian College in the District of Columbia, January 9, 1822. Washington, 1822.

Stevenson, George S. The Educated Farmer: An Oration Before the Euzelian and Philomathesian Societies of Wake Forest College, North Carolina, Delivered June 13, 1855. Raleigh, N.C., 1855.

Storer, Bellamy. An Address Delivered Before the Literary Society of Granville College, Ohio, At the Annual Commencement, July 17th 1844. Cincinnati, 1844.

Taylor, George B. The Thinker: An Address Delivered in Richmond, Va., Monday, June 30, 1856 Before the Society of Alumni of Richmond College, At Their First Annual Meeting. Richmond, Va., 1856.

Taylor, Stephen W. Inaugural Address Delivered at the Commencement of the University at Lewisburg, Pennsylvania, on Wednesday, August 28, 1850. n.p., n.d.

_____. Motives: An Inaugural Address Delivered in the Chapel of the Hamilton Literary and Theological Seminary, August 19, 1835. Utica, N.Y., 1835.

Williams, William R. The Conservative Principle in Our Literature: An Address Before the Literary Societies of the Hamilton Literary and Theological Institution (Madison County, N.Y.) Delivered in the Chapel of the Institution, on the Evening of Tuesday, June 13, 1843. New York, 1844.

Winkler, E.T. <u>Religious Liberty: An Address Delivered Before
the Philosophian and Adelphian Societies of the Furman
University At Their Annual Meeting, Greenville, June 24th,
1853.</u> Charleston, S.C., 1853.